IFLA International Federation of Library Associations and Institutions

학교도서관 가이드라인

IFLA 학교도서관 가이드라인

1판 1쇄 인쇄 _ 2017년 01월 10일
1판 1쇄 발행 _ 2017년 01월 20일

옮긴이 _ 이종권·정영주
펴낸이 _ 홍정표

펴낸곳 _ 글로벌콘텐츠
등록 _ 제 25100-2008-24호

공급처 _ (주)글로벌콘텐츠출판그룹
대표 _ 홍정표 이사 _ 양정섭 디자인 _ 김미미 기획·마케팅 _ 노경민
주소 _ 서울특별시 강동구 천중로 196 정일빌딩 401호 전화 _ 02-488-3280 팩스 _ 02-488-3281
홈페이지 _ www.gcbook.co.kr

값 23,000원
ISBN 979-11-5852-125-7 93020

·이 도서의 국립중앙도서관 출판예정도서목록(CIP)은 서지정보유통지원시스템 홈페이지(http://seoji.nl.go.kr)와 국가자료공동목록시스템(http://www.nl.go.kr/kolisnet)에서 이용하실 수 있습니다.(CIP제어번호: CIP2016029410)

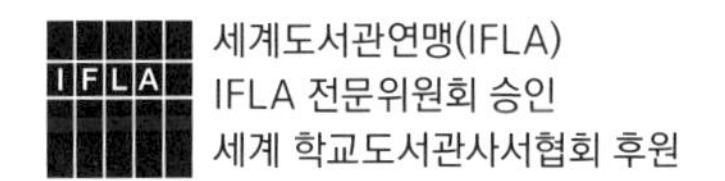

세계도서관연맹(IFLA)
IFLA 전문위원회 승인
세계 학교도서관사서협회 후원

2015. 6 개정

IFLA International Federation of Library Associations and Institutions

학교도서관 가이드라인

IFLA 학교도서관 상임위원회
슐츠 존스(Barbara Schultz-Jones)·오베르그(Dianne Oberg) 편
이종권·정영주 옮김

이 책의 구성

목차

제1장 학교도서관의 사명과 목적

제2장 학교도서관의 법적 재정적 기반

제3장 학교도서관의 인적자원

제4장 학교도서관의 물리적 자원 및 디지털 자원

제5장 학교도서관의 프로그램 및 제반 활동

제6장 학교도서관의 평가 및 홍보

서문

본 가이드라인은 IFLA/UNESCO 학교도서관 가이드라인(IFLA 전문 보고서 77)의 개정판이다. 학교도서관 가이드라인 초판은 2002년 당시 학교도서관 자원센터라고 칭한 학교도서관 분과에서 개발하였다. 본 가이드라인은 학교도서관 전문가 및 교육경영자들의 의사결정을 지원하기 위하여 지속적으로 개발하여 왔다. 본 가이드라인은 모든 학생들과 교사들이 학교도서관이 제공하는 질 좋은, 효과적인 프로그램과 서비스에 접근, 활용할 수 있도록 보장하기 위해 마련한 것이다.

본 개정판은 IFLA 총회 기간 동안의 여러 워크숍, 평소 학교도서관 관계자들 간 온라인을 통한 개별적 서면 의견교류와 평가검토 등 세계 각국 많은 사람들의 토의와 토론 및 조언 끝에 얻어진 결과물이다. 본 가이드라인의 제정은 IFLA 학교도서관 분과의 상임위원회 임원들과 세계 학교도서관 사서협회(IASL: the International Association of School Librarianship) 이사진, 그리고 이 프로젝트를 위하여 전문성과 열정을 가지고 참여해주신 세계 학교도서관 공동체 회원들의 노력으로 이루어진 것이다. 아울러 이 가이드라인을 IFLA 고유의 특성에 맞도록 검토하고 조율해 주신 IFLA 직원들에게 감사를 드린다.

또한 다음에 소개하는 IFLA 학교도서관 상임위원회 임원 및 직원들에게 특별한 감사를 드린다.

Nancy Achebe(Nigeria), Tricia Adams (UK, Information Coordinator/Web Editor), Lisa Astrom (Sweden), Lesley Farmer (USA, Blog/Newsletter Editor), Karen Gavigan (USA), Rei Iwasaki (Japan), Mireille Lamouroux(France), Randi Lundvall(Norway), Danielle Martinod(France), Luisa Marquardt (Italy), Dianne Oberg(Canada, Secretary), Barbara Schultz-Jones (USA, Chair), and Annike Selmer(Norway). Corresponding Members: Lourense Das(Netherlands), Patience Kersha(Nigeria), B. N. Singh(India), Diljit Singh(Malaysia). Officers and directors of IASL: Lourdes T. David(Philippines), Busi Diamini(South Africa), Nancy Everhart(USA), Elizabeth Greef(Australia, Vice-President), Madhu Bhargava(India), Kay Hones(USA,

Vice-President), Geraldine Howell (New Zealand), Katy Manck (USA, Treasurer), Luisa Marquardt(Italy), Dianne Oberg(Canada), Diljit Singh(Malaysia, President), Ingrid Skirrow(Austria), Paulette Stewart(Jamaica), and Ayse Yuksel-Durukan(Turkey).

또한 본 가이드라인의 작성 및 검토의 여러 단계에서 수고를 아끼지 않은 다음의 동료 직원들에게도 감사드린다.

Ingrid Bon (Netherlands), Foo Soo Chin(Singapore), Veronika Kaman(Hungary), Susan Tapulado(Philippines), Ross Todd(USA), and Gloria Trinidad(Philippines).

슐츠 존스(Barbara Schultz-Jones), 회장

오베르그(Dianne Oberg), 사무총장

IFLA 학교도서관 분과위원회

2015년 6월

학교도서관 선언. 1999년에 발표된 IFLA/UNESCO 학교도서관 선언으로 세계 여러 나라 학교도서관들이 공통의 목적을 추구하기 위해 공유하는 문서: 학교도서관, 모두를 위한 교수학습. 학교도서관 직원들이 UN 어린이 권리선언(1959), UN 어린이 권리보장 결의문(1989), UN의 세계 각지 고유민족 권리보장에 대한 선언(2007) 등이 천명한 가치와 IFLA의 핵심 가치를 알리고 보장하기 위한 것이다. 선언문에는 학교도서관의 비전이 제시되어 있다. 이는 학교공동체 전체를 통하여 교사와 학생들의 교수학습을 촉진하기 위한 것이다.

학교도서관 가이드라인. 모든 가이드라인 항목은 우리가 성취하기를 바라는 것과 우리가 합리적으로 달성할 수 있는 것 사이를 적절히 조정하여 표현한 것이다. 작성에 참여한 모든 사람들은 학교도서관에 부여된 사명과 가치를 바탕으로 하여 본 가이드라인을 구상하였다. 그리고 작성자들은 각자 담당 분야에서 학교도서관의 직원들과 학교 교육경영자들을 염두에 두고, 정보 자원이 풍부하고 학교도서관을 원활히 지원하는 지역의 학교에서도 학교공동체의 학습요구 및 변화하는 정보환경에 철저히 대응해 나가야 한다는 점을 유념하여 작성하였다.

학교도서관의 목적. 학교도서관의 목적은 학생들을 책임의식과 윤리의식, 그리고 정보활용능력을 갖춘 능동적 참여시민으로 길러내는 데 있다. 학생들의 정보활용능력이란 학생들이 스스로 정보 필요성을 깨닫고, 아이디어가 넘치는 현대 세계 속에서 정보추구활동을 활발히 전개하며 자기 주도적으로 학습할 수 있는 능력을 의미한다. 학생들은 문제해결 능력, 신뢰성 있는 관련 정보들을 적절히 연결하고 활용하는 능력을 갖출 때 자신감을 얻는다. 학생들은 정보기술 도구(technology tools)를 이용하여 정보에 접근할 수 있고, 그들이 배운 바를 정보기술을 활용하여 서로 연결할 수 있다. 학생들은 상황에 따라 복잡한 답안 또는 답이 없는 문제에 대해서도 정보기술을 자유롭게 활용해 볼 수 있다. 또한 그들은 보다 높은 학습 목표를 설정하여 양질의 학습 결과물을 창안해 낼 수 있다. 정보활용능력이 있는 학생들은 융통성이 있고, 변화에 잘 적응할 수 있으며, 개별학습과 그룹학습 양 측면에서 그들의 기능을 적절히 발휘할 수 있다.

학교도서관의 기본 틀. 학교도서관은 지역, 광역, 국가라는 큰 틀 안에 존재하면서 학생들에게 민주시민으로서 지식정보사회를 살아가는데 필요한 능력을 개발할 수 있는 평등한 기회를 제공한다. 학교도서관이 이러한 교육문화 환경변화에 적응하여 지속적으로 발전하기 위해서는 법적, 재정적으로 끊임없는 뒷받침이 이루어져야 한다.

학교도서관은 또한 학생들 및 학교공동체의 다른 구성원들의 권리와 책임에 따른 윤리적 구조 속에 존재한다. 학교도서관에서 일하는 모든 종사자들(자원봉사자들을 포함)은 학교공동체 구성원들과의 업무수행 과정에서 서로 간에 지켜야 할 고도의 윤리기준을 준수할 책임이 있다. 학교도서관에서 일하는 사람은 도서관 서비스를 제공하는 데 있어 자신의 안락과 편리를 추구하기보다는 도서관 이용자의 권리를 먼저 충족하도록 노력해야 하며, 개인적인 입장이나 신념에 따른 편견을 가져서는 안 된다. 도서관 종사자들은 모든 어린이, 청소년, 성인들에게 그들의 능력, 배경과 관계없이 평등하게 대해야 하며, 이용자들의 프라이버시를 보호하고, 알권리를 충족시켜 주어야 한다.

학교도서관의 인력관리. 학교도서관의 역할은 교수학습을 보다 용이하게 해주는 데 있다. 그러므로 학교도서관의 서비스와 제반 활동은 교과교사와 동등한 수준의 교육자적 능력을 갖춘 전문사서가 주도해야 한다. 학교도서관 사서가 학교 내에서 리더십을 발휘하기 위해서는 학교 내의 다른 지도자들, 즉 교육행정가나 교육전문가와 동등한 정도의 높은 교육수준을 갖추어야 한다. 학교도서관의 운영을 지원하는 행정요원이나 기술요원들은 학교도서관 사서들이 교육, 경영, 협력, 리더십의 역할을 원활하게 수행할 수 있도록 지원할 수 있는 숙련된 능력 있는 직원들을 배치해야 한다. 학교도서관의 인력운영 형태는 지역에 따라 법적, 경제적, 교육적 기반구조에 따라 다양할 수 있다. 그러나 세계 각국에서 지난 50년 이상 수행해온 연구들의 결과에 따르면 학교도서관 사서는 도서관과 관련된 공식교육 및 교실 수업을 담당해야 한다. 학교도서관 사서는 교육, 독서지도, 리터러시 개발, 도서관 경영, 교사들과의 협업, 기타 지역교육사회와의 연계 등과 같은 복잡하고 전문적인 역할을 발전적으로 수행해야 한다.

학교도서관 장서. 학교도서관 사서는 학교도서관의 교육자료 개발 및 유지를 위해 학교 경영자 및 교사들과 함께 일해야 한다. 장서개발정책은 해당 학교의 교육과정 및 교내의 여러 특수한 관심과 요구 및 학교 밖 지역사회의 다양한 상황을 바탕으로 수립되어야 한다. 장서개발정책에서는 장서의 구축이 교과교사들과 협동적 노력으로 이루어져야 한다는 점을 분명히 해 두어야 한다. 교과교사들은 학생들의 필요성을 잘 파악할 수 있는 주제전문가로서 도서관의 장서를 개발하는 데 중요한 역할을 담당해야 한다. 또한 학교도서관은 학교 내 구성원들의 인구학적 특징을 반영하여 국가적, 민족적, 문화적, 언어적으로 고유하고 독특한 자료들을 국내외적으로 활발하게 수집해야 한다.

학교도서관의 교육프로그램: 학교도서관 사서들은 다음과 같은 핵심적인 교육활동에 초점을 두어 프로그램을 수행해야 한다.

- 리터러시 향상 및 독서능력 개발
- 미디어 및 정보 리터러시(예: 정보 리터러시, 정보기술능력, 정보경쟁력, 정보의 홍수, 미디어 리터러시, 트랜스 리터러시)
- 자기주도 학습(예: 문제해결 학습, 비판적 사고능력)
- 정보기술의 통합적 활용 능력
- 교과교사를 위한 전문성 개발
- 문학 및 문화의 감상

학교도서관 사서들은 미디어 및 정보기술 교육의 체계적인 구조와 중요성을 인식하고, 교과교사들과의 협력을 통하여 학생들의 능력향상을 위해 노력해야 한다.

학교도서관의 평가. 평가는 지속적인 경영개선 사이클에서 매우 중요한 요소이다. 평가는 도서관의 프로그램과 서비스를 학교의 목적과 일치시키는 데 도움을 준다. 평가는 학생들과 교사들, 도서관 직원, 그리고 보다 광범위한 지역사회에 대하여 학교도서관의 프로그램과 서비스가 제공하는 편익이 무엇인지를 제시해 준다. 평가는 프로그램과 서비스 개선에 필요한 증거를 제공해 주며, 도서관 직원과 이용자들에게 도서관의 유용성, 프로그램 및 서비스의 가치를 이해하는데 도움을 준다. 평가를 성공적으로 실시함으로써 기존 프로그램과 서비스를 새롭게 개선하고, 새로운 프로그램과 서비스 개발의 방향을 설정할 수 있다.

학교도서관에 대한 지속적인 지원: 평가는 또한 도서관의 권익 옹호와 홍보에도 필수적인 이니셔티브를 제공한다. 교수학습에 있어 학교도서관의 역할이 언제나 잘 이해되는 것은 아니므로, 학교도서관의 이해관계자 그룹 및 자금을 지원하는 서포터스 그룹, 기타 지원 조직들과의 관계 구축을 위해서도 도서관의 평가는 필수적이다.

본 문서에 대하여: 이 문서는 IFLA 학교도서관 분과에서 발간한 학교도서관 가이드라인의 개정판이다. 이 가이드라인은 학교도서관 전문가 및 교육경영자들의 의사결정을 지원하기 위하여 지속적으로 개발되어 왔다. 이 가이드라인은 모든 학생들과 교사들이 학교도서관의 효과적인 프로그램과 서비스에 접근, 활용할 수 있도록 보장하기 위해 마련된 것이다. 본 개정판 초안은 IFLA 총회 기간 동안의 여러 워크숍, 평소 학교도서관 관계자들 간 온라인을 통한 개별적 서면 의견교류와 평가검토 등 세계 각국 많은 사람들의 토의와 논쟁 및 조언 끝에 얻어진 결과물이다. 이 가이드라인의 제정은 IFLA 학교도서관 분과의 상임위원회 임원들과 세계 학교도서관 사서협회(IASL: the International Association of

School Librarianship) 이사진, 그리고 이 프로젝트를 위하여 전문성과 열정을 가지고 참여해 주신 세계 학교도서관 공동체 회원들의 노력으로 이루어진 것이다.

슐츠 존스(Barbara Schultz-Jones), 회장

오베르그(Dianne Oberg), 사무총장

IFLA 학교도서관 분과위원회

2015년 6월

제안사항

다음의 제안사항들은 학생들 및 교사들에게 학교도서관의 전문 직원들이 제공하는 도서관 서비스와 프로그램에 접근, 이용할 수 있도록 보장하기 위하여 학교도서관 전문가와 교육 의사결정자들을 지원할 목적으로 개발한 것이다. 이 제안사항들은 본 가이드라인의 내용과 맥을 같이한다. 가이드라인의 해당 부분은 각 제안사항의 말미에 제시하였다.

이 제안사항들을 개별 학교도서관의 기획, 개발, 이용촉진, 평가 등의 어느 한 부문에 활용하고자 원하는 사서들은 각 해당 학교도서관에 관련되는 제안사항들을 평가할 수 있는 평가척도(예: "그렇다, 보통이다, 그렇지 않다(부록 D: 평가 체크리스트 샘플) 또는 "탐색 단계, 구체화 단계, 확정단계, 미래 실행단계"(주요 검토 지표: 캐나다 학교도서관 공통 운영기준 2014, 9쪽 참조))를 이용할 수 있다.

제안 1. 학교도서관의 사명과 목적은 IFLA/UNESCO 학교도서관 선언에 천명한 원칙과 UN 어린이 권리보장 결의문, UN 세계 각지 고유민족 권리보장에 대한 선언, 그리고 IFLA가 추구하는 핵심 가치에 따라 분명하

게 기술되어야 한다. [개관, 1.7]

제안 2. 학교도서관의 사명과 목적은 국가 교육행정 당국, 광역 및 지역 교육 행정당국의 기대 그리고 각 학교의 교육과정에 부합하도록 정의하여야 한다. [개관, 1.1-1.8]

제안 3. 계획은 학교도서관의 성공적 경영에 필수 불가결한 세 가지 측면, 즉 숙련된 학교도서관 전문사서, 학교의 교육과정을 지원하는 충실한 장서 수집, 학교도서관의 지속적 성장과 발전을 담보하는 명시적 미래계획을 포함하여야 한다. [1.1-1.8]

제안 4. 학교도서관이 해당 학교공동체의 변화하는 요구를 충족하도록 하기 위해서는 사서의 업무와 함께 학교도서관 서비스와 프로그램에 대한 모니터링과 평가를 정기적으로 실시하여야 한다. [1.9, 6.1-6.4]

제안 5. 학교도서관의 법제는 정부 당국이 가장 적정한 수준에서 법의 제정 및 법적 보장에 대한 사항을 명확하게 규정하여 모든 학생들이 이용하는 도서관을 지속적으로 개선할 수 있도록 해야 한다. [2.1-2.2, 2.4-2.7]

제안 6. 학교도서관의 법제는 정부 당국이 가장 적정한 수준에서, 도서관 접근의 평등권, 정보와 프라이버시의 자유, 저작권 및 지적재산권, 그리고 어린이의 알 권리를 포함하여 학교 공동체에 속한 모든 구성원들의 윤리적 책임을 담보할 수 있는 법조항을 명확히 규정해야 한다. [2.3, 3.6-3.8]

제안 7. 학교도서관의 서비스 및 프로그램은 학교도서관의 수업 및 교실수업으로서 공식적 교육과정으로 운영하여야 하며 전문직 학교도서관 사서가 이를 주도하여야 한다. [3.1-3.4]

제안 8. 학교도서관 전문사서의 역할, 즉 교육(예: 리터러시 및 독서능력 증진, 탐구중심 및 자원기반 교육), 학교도서관 경영, 학교 전역에 걸쳐 도서관의 리더십 유지 및 협력, 지역사회 연계, 도서관 서비스의 개선 등을 포함한 제반 역할을 분명하게 규정해야 한다. [3.5, 3.5.4]

제안 9. 학교도서관의 전 직원-전문사서, 준전문사서, 자원봉사자-는 학교도서관의 정책지침에 따른 그들의 역할과 책임, 즉 모든 이용자에 대한 접근의 평등, 프라이버시 보호, 그리고 알권리를 분명하게 이해하여야 한다. [3.1, 3.2, 3.6, 3.7]

제안 10. 학교도서관의 전 직원은 해당 학교의 교육과정, 국가적, 윤리적, 문화적 정체성에 맞는 실물장서 및 디지털자원의 개발에 노력해야 한다. 또한 목록, 보존전시, 자원공유를 통한 자료의 접근성 향상을 위해 노력해야 한다. [4.2.3, 4.3, 4.3.1-4.3.4]

제안 11. 학교도서관의 시설, 장비, 장서 및 서비스는 교사와 학생의 요구에 맞도록 교수학습을 지원할 수 있어야 한다. 이러한 시설, 장비, 장서, 서비스는 교수와 학습의 변화 요구에 따라 개선되어야 한다. [4.1-4.3]

제안 12. 학교도서관과 공공도서관 그리고 대학도서관들은 그들이 속해 있는 전 지역사회 구성원들의 평생학습을 지원하는 각기 부여된 책임을 다하기 위한 책임 분담의 차원에서 정보자원과 서비스를 강화할 수 있도록 연계망을 구축해야 한다. [4.2, 5.4]

제안 13. 학교도서관 사서의 핵심적 교육활동은 리터러시 향상 및 독서능력 향상에 초점을 두어야 한다. 이에는 미디어 및 정보 리터러시 교육, 탐구기반 교육, 정보기술 통합교육, 그리고 교사들의 전문성 개발 등이 있다. [5.2-5.7]

제안 14. 학교도서관을 통하여 제공하는 서비스와 프로그램은 학교도서관의 전문사서가 교장, 교육과정 책임자, 동료교사, 도서관 직원들, 그리고 그 지역의 문화, 언어, 원주민, 기타 학교의 학술적, 교육적, 사회적 목적 달성에 기여하는 모든 사람들과 협력하여 개발해야 한다. [3.5, 3.5.4, 5.1-5.8]

제안 15. 실증적 평가 실행을 염두에 두고 학교도서관 프로그램 및 서비스를 마련해야 하며, 학교도서관의 프로그램 및 서비스의 전문성 향상 및 학교의 교수학습에 긍정적 기여를 할 수 있는 실질적 데이터를 제공해야 한다. [5.1, 5.2]

제안 16. 학교도서관의 현재 이용자 및 잠재 이용자, 그리고 이해관계자 및 의사결정권자 사이의 계획적이고 체계적인 소통을 바탕으로 학교도서관 서비스 및 프로그램의 이용과 지원을 촉진해야 한다. [6.4, 6.5]

개관

세계 여러 나라 학교도서관들은 각기 형태는 다르지만 "모두를 위한 교수 학습" 증진이라는 공통의 목적을 지니고 있다. 이러한 이유로 학교도서관 직원은 모든 사람들에게 평등한 기회를 보장해야 한다. 학교도서관 직원은 UN어린이 권리선언(1959), UN어린이 권리보장 결의문(CRC 1989), UN세계 각지 고유민족 권리보장에 대한 선언(2007), 그리고 국제도서관연맹(IFLA)의 핵심 가치를 준수해야 한다.

- 정보, 아이디어, 영상이미지 저작물에 대한 접근의 자유, 그리고 세계 인권선언 제19조에 명시한 표현의 자유 원칙을 보장
- 개인, 지역공동체, 각종 조직들은 그들의 사회적, 교육적, 문화적, 민주 정치적, 경제적 복지를 위하여 정보, 아이디어, 영상이미지 저작물에 대한 보편적이고 평등한 접근을 필요로 한다는 신념
- 수준 높은 도서관 정보서비스 제공으로 정보 접근을 보장할 수 있다는 확신
- 세계도서관연맹의 모든 회원들이 그들의 시민권, 장애, 출신 종족, 성, 지리적 위치, 언어, 정치이념, 민족, 종교와 관계없이 그들의 활동

으로부터 유익을 얻도록 보장(www.ifla.org/about/more).

이 가이드라인은 IFLA/UNESCO 학교도서관 선언에 나타난 학교도서관 발전을 위한 기본 원칙에 바탕을 두고 있다(부록 A 참조). 1999년에 처음 공표된 이 학교도서관 선언은 세계 여러 나라 언어로 번역되었으며, 학교와 지역사회 그리고 여러 나라에서 학교도서관의 위상을 증진하는 데 일익을 담당해 왔다.

학교도서관 선언은 "정부는 교육담당부서를 통하여 본 선언문의 원칙을 실현하기 위한 전략, 정책, 계획을 개발해야 한다."고 명시하고 있다. 본 가이드라인은 전 세계의 국가 및 지역에서 의사결정자들에게 학교도서관 선언의 취지를 알리고, 전 도서관계에 지원 및 가이드를 제공하기 위해 지속적으로 개발해 온 문서이다. 본 문서는 학교 경영자들에게 학교도서관 선언에 나타난 제반 원칙을 실천하도록 도와주기 위한 것이다. 학교와 학교도서관은 나라에 따라 매우 다양한 모습으로 존재하기 때문에 각 지역에서는 본 가이드라인을 각기 해당 지역의 정서적 맥락 속에서 인식, 해석, 적용할 필요가 있다.

본 문서는 도서관에 대한 영감과 기대를 동시에 추구한다. 이 가이드라인의 작성자들은 학교도서관의 사명과 가치에서 많은 영감을 얻었다. 그리고 학교도서관의 직원과 교육경영 의사결정자들은 아무리 학교도서관의 정보자원이 풍부하고 도서관을 원활히 지원하는 지역의 학교라고 해도 그들이 일하는 학교공동체의 학습요구를 파악하고 변화하는 정보환경에 철저하게 대응하는 전반적 개선 노력을 기울여야 한다는 것을 인식할 필요가 있다.

본 가이드라인은 전체적으로 우리가 성취하기를 바라는 것과 합리적으로 성취할 수 있는 것 사이의 간극을 조정하도록 안내하고 있다. 중요한 것은 학교도서관 사서들이 그들의 실제 업무에서 이 가이드라인을 적용하여 해당 지역사회의 상황에 맞는 학교도서관 서비스와 프로그램을 개선해 나가는 일이다. 표준 및 가이드라인은 현장의 상황을 가장 잘 아는 사람들의 '공감'을 얻어야 한다. 예산 증액 및 인력 증원 또는 시설을 개선할 경우, 그러한 변화가 학생들의 학습 및 교사들의 교육이라는 관점에서 기여한다는 실증적 증거가 있어야 한다. 이는 표준이나 가이드라인의 적용에 따르는 논쟁 그 이상으로 현장의 실질적인 논쟁을 불식시키는 데 필요하다.

예산, 정보기술, 장서, 직원, 시설에 대한 기준을 충족하는 일이 반드시 최선의 교수학습 환경을 보장해 주는 것은 아니다. 더욱 중요한 것은 학교 구성원들이 학교도서관에 대해 생각하는 방식이라 할 수 있다. 즉, 학교도서관 서비스 윤리에 대한 직원들의 태도(예: 청소년 생활의 개인차 고려) 및 학교도서관의 교육적 목적(예: 교수와 학습의 개선 발전) 등을 어떻게 생각하고 인지하느냐가 중요하다. 시설, 장서, 직원, 정보기술은 그러한 목적을 위한 하나의 수단일 뿐이다.

학교장이나 학교 이해관계자 및 학교도서관 직원은 항상 다음과 같은 질문을 던져야 한다. 즉 학생들과 교사들이 학교도서관 서비스와 프로그램에서 얻을 수 있는 가치는 무엇인가? 과거 40여년에 걸친 연구에서는 인력과 정보자원이 적절하게 지원된 학교도서관들은 학생들의 학업 성취도에 중대한 영향을 끼쳤다는 것을 보여주고 있다. 학교도서관의 가장 핵심적인 자원은 교사들과 협업하여 가능한 최선의 지식을 축적하고 학생들에게 의미있는 학습경험을 창의적으로 제공해주는 수준높은 전문사서라 할 수 있다.

IFLA 학교도서관 가이드라인은 각기 다른 지역에서 각기 다른 방식으로 학교도서관의 개발 및 발전을 지원하는 데 활용할 수 있다. 개발도상국이나 신생국들의 학교도서관에 대한 가능성을 평가하는 것은 하나의 도전적인 일일 것이다. 그러나 학교도서관의 윤리적, 교육적 목적은 이러한 개발도상 환경 속에서도 다양하고 창의적인 방법으로 표출되어야 하며, 때로는 학교도서관 개발의 가장 기초가 되는 문맹퇴치라는 벽돌쌓기를 통해서 시작되어야 한다. 혁신적 도서관 프로젝트의 사례들은 몇 년 전 IFLA 후원으로 발간한 책 "학교도서관의 글로벌 전망: 그 프로젝트 및 실행 사례(Global Perspectives on School Libraries: Projects and Practices)(Marquardt & Oberg, 2011)"에서도 찾아 볼 수 있다. 또 학교도서관 가이드라인을 개발, 실행, 개선한 사례들은 최근 IFLA 후원으로 출판한 책 "학교도서관 가이드라인의 글로벌 적용사례(Global Action on School Library Guidelines) (Schultz-Jones & Oberg, 2015)"에서 찾아 볼 수 있다.

IFLA/UNESCO 학교도서관 선언은 학교도서관의 개발에 대한 기본 원칙을 천명하고 있다. 또한 학교도서관 가이드라인은 그 기본 원칙을 실행하는 구체적 방향을 제시하고 있다. 학교도서관 가이드라인은 "모두를 위한 교수 학습"을 지원하는 데 있어 최선의 도서관 서비스를 제공하기 위한 노력을 기울이기 위해서는 세계적인 관점과 지역적인 관점을 아울러 갖추어야 한다고 강조하고 있다.

세계적 관점

이 학교도서관 가이드라인은 전 세계적인 기회균등과 사회정의라는 포괄적이고 원대한 비전을 제시한다. 이러한 비전은 21세기의 맥락 속에서 실현될 것이며, 변화와 역동성, 그리고 다양한 수준 및 영역간의 상호작용을 통해서 특성화 될 것이다. 전 세계적으로, 사람들의 삶은 글로벌화라는 시대적 트렌드의 영향을 받고 있다. 글로벌화란 사회적 경제적 안정 및 변화, 디지털 및 모바일 기술의 진화, "녹색" 환경의 지속 가능성 등이다.

교육은 교육과정의 변화 및 기술발전을 통하여 변화하고 있다(예: 클라우드 컴퓨팅, 게임, 스마트폰, 1대 1 컴퓨팅). 학교와 대학에 소요되는 공공 비용의 감축을 위해 많은 나라들은 법적, 경제적 맥락에서 새로운 교육 재정 모델을 필요로 한다. 세계적으로 고등학교 졸업자 수는 증가하고 있으나, 전문학교 졸업자 수는 여러 나라에서 답보상태에 있다. 사회경제적 변화에 따라 학교와 대학에서 외국인 학생의 수가 늘어나고 제2외국어를 배우는 학생의 수도 증가하고 있다. 유비쿼터스 기술은 학습자들의 정보 접근방법 및 상호작용 방법을 변화시키고 있다(OECD, 2014).

도서관은 디지털 및 "오픈" 엑세스 데이터, 자기주도 학습, 통합적 학습의 영향을 받고 있다. 세계 각국 정부는 유럽연합(European Union)에서 설정한 다음 7가지 디지털 아젠다의 주제를 근간으로 그들의 계획을 개발하고 있다(http://ec.europa.eu/digital-agenda/en).

1) 단일 디지털 시장 - 시장 장벽이 무너지고 온라인 서비스와 콘텐트가 국경을 넘나들며 자유롭게 유통

2) 정보처리의 상호운용 및 표준화 - IT장비의 새로운 표준, 애플리케이션, 데이터의 보존, 그리고 서비스가 인터넷에서처럼 언제 어디서나 자유롭게 유통
3) 신뢰성 및 보안 - 개인의 데이터 보안 및 사이버 테러에 대한 공동대응 규정 강화
4) 고속 및 초고속 인터넷 구현 - 고속 접근과 고속 다운로드 제공을 위한 투자 확대
5) 연구 및 혁신 - 상용화 혁신을 위한 정보통신 기술(ICT) 투자의 확대
6) 디지털 리터러시, 디지털 기술, 디지털 융합 강화 - 특히 취약계층에 대한 정보격차를 해결하기 위한 교육과 훈련
7) 정보통신기술의 편익 - 에너지 소비의 감소, 네트워크 공공 서비스, 그리고 문화유산에 대한 자유로운 접근 제공

이러한 디지털 아젠다에서 보는 것처럼 학교도서관 직원들은 디지털 기술을 개발하고 활용할 필요가 있다. 또한 학생들과 교사들이 디지털 기술과 지식을 개발, 활용할 수 있도록 학교공동체의 다른 구성원들과 협력하여 업무를 추진해야 한다. 세계적으로 학교도서관 서비스와 프로그램은 디지털 기술과 모바일 기술의 변화에 따라 큰 영향을 받아왔으며 앞으로도 그럴 것이다. 이러한 변화는 디지털 시민권의 원리에 대한 교육의 필요성을 높이고 있다.

지역적 관점

이 학교도서관 가이드라인의 의도는 지역적 맥락에서, 특히 교육과정

과 법제도에 알맞게 적용, 실행하도록 하는 것이다. 학교도서관의 개발에 대한 법적인 문제는 교육법 또는 도서관법, 양 법 공히, 또는 한 가지 법에만 규정되어 있을 수 있다. 학교의 교육과정은 국가적 또는 지역적으로 개발되어 있고, 이 교육과정은 특히 학교도서관의 사명, 역할, 목적을 나누어 정의하거나 이들을 전체적으로 포괄하여 정의하는 경우도 있다.

학교도서관 가이드라인의 의도는 학교도서관과 지역사회가 요구하는 교육의 성과를 창출하고, 학교도서관이 학교공동체의 정보요구, 사회적, 윤리적, 문화적, 언어적, 기타 학교 내·외에 거주하는 지역주민들의 사회적 요구에 부합하도록 정부, 도서관협회, 학교, 학교 경영자 그룹 및 지역사회를 안내하고 유도하는 것이다.

학교도서관 가이드라인은 정부 공무원 및 학교 관리자를 포함한 의사결정자들에게 양질의 학교도서관 서비스가 청소년의 교육적 성취에 기여한다는 실증적 연구들을 제시할 것을 주문한다. 학교도서관 가이드라인은 또한 학교도서관 직원들이 변화하는 교육 사회적 환경에 발맞추어 그들의 역량을 개발하고 적용할 수 있게 함으로써 변화에 앞장서는 촉매제로서의 역할을 하도록 유도한다.

참고문헌

Marquardt, L., & Oberg, D. (2011). *Global perspectives on school libraries: Projects and practices.* The Hague, Netherlands: De Gruyter Saur.

Schultz-Jones, B. & Oberg, D. (2015). *Global action on school library guidelines.* The Hague, Netherlands: De Gruyter Saur.

OECD (Organization for Economic Co-operation and Development). (2014). *Education at a glance* 2014: OECD *indicators.* Paris: OECD Publishing. Retrieved from dx.doi.org/10.1787/eag-2014-en

제1장

학교도서관의 사명과 목적

학교도서관은 오늘날 지식정보사회에서 성공적으로 살아가는 데
필요한 기본 정보와 아이디어를 제공해 준다.
학교도서관은 학생들에게 평생학습능력과 상상력을 길러주며
책임 있는 시민으로 살아갈 수 있는 능력을 길러준다.
-학교도서관 선언에서

1.1 개관

본 장에서는 IFLA/UNESCO 학교도서관 선언(1999)이 정의한 학교도서관의 사명과 목적에 대하여 부연 설명한다. 학교도서관 선언에는 학교도서관은 학생들은 물론 교육자들에게 전체 학교공동체를 통하여 교수와 학습을 독려하고 개선하는 강화제로서의 비전을 제시한다. 선언서에 나타난 핵심 이슈들은 후속 장들에서 자세히 논의한다.

1.2 맥락

학교도서관은 전 세계적으로 학생들과 교사들 그리고 학습 공동체를 지원하고 독려하기 위하여 공간(물리적 공간 및 디지털 공간), 정보자원, 도서관 활동과 서비스에의 접근을 제공하는 학습 환경으로서 존재한다. 학교도서관의 성장은 학생들에게 보다 나은 사회에 기여하고 적용할 수 있는 지식을 갖추도록 하는 교육의 성장과 맥을 같이 한다. 학교도서관의 시설과 운용의 정도는 세계적으로 다양하지만, 모든 학교도서관은 학생들의 학습을 지원하고 증진하는데 초점을 맞춘다. 학교도서관은 개인, 소집단, 대중에게 지적 내용, 정보 리터러시, 사회문화 개발 등 광범위한 배움의 기회를 제공한다. 학교도서관의 학습자 지향적 운영은 학교의 교육과정을 지원하고, 확장하며, 개별화 시킨다.

〈사례〉

루부토 도서관 프로젝트(Lubuto Library Project)는 잠비아(Zambia)에서 고아 및 취약계층 어린이 청소년들에게 문화적 자원 및 교육적 경험을 제공한다.

1.3 학교도서관의 정의

학교도서관은 학교의 물리적 학습 공간 및 디지털 학습 공간으로서 독서, 질문, 조사연구, 사고력, 상상력 등 창의성을 발휘하는 장소이며 학생들에게 지식 정보로의 여행 및 개인적, 사회적, 문화적 성장을 돕는 센터이다. 이러한 물리적 공간 및 디지털 공간은 여러 가지 명칭으로 알려져 있다(예: 학교미디어 센터, 정보의 수집검색 센터, 도서관 자원센터, 학습공유를 위한 도서관). 그러나 대체로 학교도서관은 그 시설과 기능적인 측면의 용어로 사용되어 왔다.

50여년 이상 이룩된 세계 도서관 연구들을 종합하면((see, for example, Haycock, 1992, in LRS(2015) School Libraries Impact Studies in the USA www.lrs.org/data-tools/school-libraries/impact-studies/and Williams, Wavell, C.,and Morrison(2013) in the United Kingdomwww.scottishlibraries.org/storage/sectors/schools/SLIC_RGU_Impact_of_School_Libraries_2013.pdf) 학교도서관을 다음과 같이 분명하게 정의할 수 있다.

- 학교도서관에는 교육, 독서지도, 문해력 개발, 도서관 경영, 교사들과의 협업, 교육 공동체와의 협조 등 복합적 역할을 수행할 수 있는 공식적 학교도서관 전문교육을 받은, 교실 수업이 가능한 유능한 사서가 있어야 한다.
- 학교도서관은 이용 대상자에 알맞은 양질의 다양한 정보자료(인쇄자료, 멀티미디어, 디지털 자료)를 구비하고 학교의 공식, 비공식 교육과정을 지원할 뿐 아니라 개별 프로젝트나 개인 능력 개발을 지원해야 한다.

- 학교도서관은 지속적인 성장과 발전을 위한 분명한 정책과 계획을 가지고 있어야 한다.

학교도서관은 다른 교육시스템과 마찬가지로 성장과 발전을 추구한다. 그러나 학교도서관에는 학교도서관의 사명과 목적의 달성을 위해 필수적인 3가지 특성이 있다. 연구에 따르면 학생들의 학습에 미치는 학교도서관의 잠재적 영향력은 학교에서 이러한 3가지 특성을 어느 정도로 수행해 내는가에 달려 있다.

학교도서관은 다음과 같이 운영해야 한다.

- 학교의 물리적 공간 및 디지털 공간은 모두에게 개방되고 접근이 가능해야 한다.
- 정보의 공간, 즉 인쇄자료, 멀티미디어, 디지털 보존자료 등 모든 미디어에 걸쳐 양질의 정보자원에 평등하고 자유롭게 접근할 수 있어야 한다.
- 개인적인 호기심, 창의력, 그리고 학습을 위한 안전한 공간을 제공하고 이용을 독려해야 한다. 학생들이 도서관에서 다양한 주제의 자료, 특히 논쟁의 여지가 있는 자료들도 개인적으로 안전한 상태에서 이용할 수 있어야 한다.
- 교육적 공간, 학생들의 학습공간은 수용능력 및 정보와 지식을 적절히 활용할 수 있는 환경을 갖춰야 한다.

- 다양한 정보기술 도구, 소프트웨어, 전문가들의 창조적 공간, 발표 및 공유를 위한 기술적 공간을 제공해야 한다.
- 학교 공동체는 모든 면에서 독서능력과 리터러시를 기를 수 있는 리터러시 센터를 운영해야 한다.
- 디지털 도구를 적절하고도 윤리적으로, 안전하게 이용하며 배울 수 있는, 그리고 개인의 아이디와 정보를 보호할 수 있는 디지털 시민의식 양성센터를 운영해야 한다.
- 가정에서는 갖추기 어려운 정보자료, 정보기술, 정보능력 개발에 평등하게 접근할 수 있도록 공동체 내의 모든 사람들에게 적절한 정보환경을 제공해야 한다.
- 전체 공동체 구성원들이 문화적, 전문적, 교육적 행사를 개최할 수 있는 열린 사회적 공간(예: 이벤트, 회의, 전시, 자료)을 제공해야 한다.

1.4 학교 내에서의 학교도서관의 역할

학교도서관은 학교 내에서 다음에 강조하는 교육과정의 내용과 통합한 활발한 교육 프로그램을 제공하는 교수학습센터가 되어야 한다.

- 자원 기반 역량 - 다양한 형태의 정보자료에 대한 검색, 접근, 평가와

관련한 수용능력 및 이용 분위기. 여기에는 자원으로서의 사람 및 문화적 소품들이 포함된다. 이러한 역량에는 정보기술 도구를 이용한 자료원의 검색, 접근, 평가와 디지털 및 인쇄자료의 개발도 포함된다.

- 사고 기반 역량 - 조사 및 연구의 과정에서 데이터와 정보를 이용하여 보다 고차적으로 생각하는 과정, 그리고 깊은 지식의 심도 있는 이해를 통한 발표물의 창안, 산출물을 유도하는 중요 연구 분석을 수행할 수 있는 역량과 분위기가 조성되어야 한다.
- 지식 기반 역량 - 지식의 창조, 구축, 그리고 지식에 대한 깊은 이해를 바탕으로 한 새로운 지식의 생산과 공유에 초점을 맞춘 조사연구 역량 및 분위기가 조성되어야 한다.
- 독서 및 리터러시 역량 - 독서에서 즐거움을 찾고, 독서를 즐기는, 복합적 플랫폼, 즉 여러 가지 형식과 방법으로 텍스트를 변환, 소통, 배포함으로써 텍스트에 대한 이해와 의미를 개발할 수 있게 하는 역량 및 분위기가 조성되어야 한다
- 개인 상호작용 역량 - 자료기반 조사연구와 학습에 참여하여 연구자, 정보이용자, 지식생산자, 그리고 책임 있는 시민의 일원으로 사회문화적 교류를 할 수 있는 역량 및 분위기가 조성되어야 한다
- 학습관리역량 - 학생들에게 단위별로 교육과정에 대하여 준비, 계획하고, 성공적으로 과정을 수행할 수 있도록 하는 역량 및 분위기가 조성되어야 한다

학교도서관 사서는 교육과정 내용 및 결과들을 분명하게 연계하여 개별 또는 협업 지도를 통하여 위와 같은 역량을 개발하는 데 주도적인 역할을 해야 한다.

1.5 효과적인 학교도서관 프로그램의 조건

연구에 의하면 학교도서관 프로그램의 가장 중요한 조건은 학교도서관 직원의 전문성이라는 것이 밝혀졌다. 교육프로그램(예: 계획적이고 종합적인 교수학습활동 제공)이 없는 학교도서관은 교수와 학습에 어떤 영향도 미칠 수 없다는 것이다. 이는 양질의 학교도서관 직원이 수행한 역할에 대한 연구에서도 나타나고 있으며, 본 가이드라인의 3.4 부분에 그 내용이 요약되어 있다.

학교도서관은 독서, 탐구, 협력수업의 성과를 창출하는 학교의 중심지라는 인식을 바탕으로 명확하게 구조화 된 정책 틀 안에서 경영되어야 한다. 도서관정책에는 학교 전체에 걸친 요구를 주의 깊게 반영하여야 하며, 학교의 현실, 학풍, 사명, 목적, 목표를 잘 반영하여야 한다. 도서관정책을 통한 행정적 지원 또한 필수적인데, 이는 학교도서관이 그 역할을 다할 수 있게 하며, 학교도서관 프로그램의 효과를 충분히 달성할 수 있도록 하기 때문이다. 도서관의 시설 및 실물자원과 디지털자원, 그리고 인적자원은 효과적인 학교도서관 프로그램의 활성화를 위하여 필수적이며, 이는 후속 장들에서 다시 논의할 것이다.

1.6 학교도서관의 비전

학교도서관은 미래에 대비한 비전을 설정해야 한다. 지역에 따라 비전은 각기 달리 표현할 수 있지만, 비전의 출발점은 언제나 학교도서관에 두어야 한다. 궁극적으로, 교육의 중심 역할을 하는 학교도서관은 그 비전 확립을 통하여 미래에도 복합적 기능을 다하는 교수학습센터로서의 본질적 역할을 할 수 있다.

비전은 2013년 IFLA 트렌드 보고서((trends.ifla.org)에 명시된 5가지 핵심 트렌드를 반영할 수 있다.

1) 정보에 접근할 수 있는 새로운 정보기술을 광범위하게, 그리고 세부적으로 반영한다.
2) 온라인 교육이 널리 보급되어 글로벌 교수학습에 혼란을 줄 수 있다.
3) 개인의 프라이버시와 정보 보호의 범위가 재 정의될 것이다.
4) 고도 연결망 사회가 되고, 새로운 목소리와 새로운 그룹에게 권한

을 부여한다.

5) 글로벌 정보 경제는 새로운 정보기술에 의해 변화될 것이다.

1.7 학교도서관의 사명

학교도서관의 사명은 학교라는 공통의 목적을 공유, 실행하는 학교조직의 일부로서 학교도서관의 성격, 목적, 역할에 대한 정의이다. 세계적인 학교도서관의 사명은 1999년 IFLA/UNESCO 학교도서관 선언(부록 A)에 명시되어 있다. 개별 학교도서관의 사명은 IFLA/UNESCO 학교도서관 선언의 사명과 보조를 맞추면서도, 각 학교와 도서관이 위치한 지역의 교육적 맥락과 일치하도록 정해야 한다. 이는 도서관의 핵심자원에 대한 방향을 제시하고, 구성원들의 요구를 파악하고 이해함으로써 지역사회에 봉사한다는 기본 의도를 명시하는 것이다. 즉 여러 가지 스킬, 자원, 요구 충족을 위한 역량, 그리고 지역사회에 유익한 성과를 낼 수 있도록 정의한다. 즉 학생들이 미래의 시민으로서 생애 직업을 준비하는데 필요한 교육적 목적에 부합하도록 해야 한다.

1.8 학교도서관의 서비스

학습 공동체의 요구를 충족하기 위해서 학교도서관은 다양한 서비스를 제공해야 한다. 이러한 서비스는 학교도서관의 내부 또는 외부에서 제공할 수 있다. 정보통신기술(ICT)을 활용한 서비스 역시 학교와 가정의 모든 영역에 도서관의 서비스가 미칠 수 있도록 한다. 정보기술 기반의 강력한 네트워크를 통하여 장서 및 지역사회 자원, 디지털 자원에 접근할 수 있게 하고, 조사연구 및 지식을 구성, 발표, 공유할 수 있도록 한다.

학교도서관 서비스는 다음을 포함한다.

- 교사들의 전문성 개발(예: 독서 및 리터러시, 테크놀로지, 탐구조사방법)
- 학업 성취를 위한 독서 및 리터러시 프로그램 활성화 및 개인적 감성 충족
- 탐구기반 학습 및 정보 리터러시 개발
- 다른 도서관과의 협업(공공도서관, 정부기관 및 지역사회 정보자원)

학교도서관은 교육공동체에 중요한 가치를 제공한다. 이러한 부가가치는 도서관에 있는 장서를 넘어서 활발한 학교도서관 프로그램과 유능한 학교도서관 사서가 제공하는 수준 높은 서비스로 그 범위가 확장되는 것이다.

1.9 학교도서관 서비스 및 프로그램 평가

학교도서관 서비스 및 프로그램 평가는 학교도서관의 발전을 위해 필수적인 과정이다. 평가는 목적달성 여부를 따져보는 것이다. 즉 평가는 학교도서관의 서비스와 프로그램이 학교 공동체의 요구에 얼마나 충족하는지를 가늠해 보는 것이다. 평가는 또한 학교도서관 이해관계자들의 의견을 반영하고, 학교도서관에 대한 그들의 지원을 이끌어냄으로써 도서관의 서비스와 프로그램을 지속적으로 개선해 나가는 데 도움이 되어야 한다. 어떠한 평가 방법 또는 접근방법을 선택할 것인가는 해당 학교 공동체의 요구 및 도서관의 발전 수준에 달려있다(예: 프로그램의 질, 이해관계자들의 인식, 프로그램의 내용, 프로그램의 영향).

프로그램의 전반적인 질적 수준에 초점을 두는 평가라면 국제적, 국가적, 지역적 표준을 이용하여 도서관의 전체적인 측면을 시험해 볼 수 있다(예: 직원, 시설, 정보기술, 장서, 교육프로그램 등). 학교도서관의 성과 개선에 초점을 둔 평가, 즉 실증적 평가를 위해서는 학생들의 학습 결과물, 교육의 유형(분반, 등급, 또는 주제)과 관련되는 데이터를 활용할 수 있다. 즉, 학생, 교사, 학부형에 대한 설문 조사, 도서관의 대출 및 목록시스템의 기록 데이터를 활용할 수 있다. 평가 및 경영, 홍보에 대해서는 본 가이드라인의 제6장에서 좀 더 자세히 다룬다(이용촉진, 마케팅, 공공관계).

참고문헌

American Association of School Librarians. (2014). *Governing documents*. Retrieved from www.ala.org/aasl/about/governing-docs

American Association of School Librarians. (2011). *Standards for the 21st century learner*. Retrieved from www.ala.org/aasl/standards-guidelines/learning-standards

Hay, L., & Todd, R. J. (2010). *School libraries 21C*. NSW Department of Education and Training. Retrieved from www.curriculumsupport.education.nsw.gov.au/schoollibraries/assets/pdf/21c_report.pdf

Haycock, K. (1992). *What works: Research about teaching and learning through the school's library resource center*. Seattle, WA: Rockland Press.

IFLA/UNESCO School Library Manifesto. (1999). Retrieved from www.ifla.org/publications/iflaunesco-school-library-manifesto-1999

Library Research Service [Colorado State Library, Colorado Department of Education]. *School libraries impact studies*. Retrieved from www.lrs.org/data-tools/school-libraries/impact-studies/

Groupe de Recherche sur la Culture et la Didactique de l'information. (2010). *Parcours de formation à la culture de l'information* [The learning path to an information culture]. Retrieved from http://culturedel.info/grcdi/?page_id=236

Williams, D., Wavell, C., & Morrison, K. (2013). *Impact of school libraries on learning: Critical review of published evidence to inform the Scottish education community.* Aberdeen, Scotland: Robert Gordon University, Institute for Management, Governance & Society (IMaGeS). Retrieved from www.scottishlibraries.org/storage/sectors/schools/SLIC_RGU_Impact_of_School_Libraries_2013.pdf).

제2장

학교도서관의 법적 재정적 기반

지역, 광역, 중앙정부는 법적, 정책적으로 책임을 지고
학교도서관을 지원해야 한다.
학교도서관은 유능한 직원, 자료, 정보기술 및 제반 시설을 위한
적절하고도 지속적인 재정을 확보해야 한다.
학교도서관은 무료로 운영되어야 한다.
-학교도서관 선언에서

2.1 개관

학교도서관은 교육사회의 요구에 부응하여 각기 도서관이 위치한 지역사회에서 전체 구성원들의 편익을 위해 봉사해야 한다. 학교도서관은 지역, 광역, 중앙정부 당국에서 평등한 학습권을 보장해야 하며, 지식정보사회에 필요한 능력발전을 위해 평등한 기회를 제공해야한다는 확고한 기반 위에 성립된다. 학교도서관은 진화하는 교육적, 문화적 환경에 부응하기 위하여 지속적인 법적, 재정적 지원을 받아야 한다.

2.2 법적 기반 및 이슈

세계적으로 볼 때, 학교도서관과 정부당국 사이에는 다양한 관계 모델이 존재한다. 또한 도서관 활동 및 재정에 대한 법률도 다양하고 복잡하다. 예를 들면 학교도서관에 관한 법, 정책, 기준이 교육부 또는 문화부의 소관으로 되어 있기도 하고, 상기 두 부처의 공동책임으로 분산되어 있기도 하다. 몇몇 나라들은 학교도서관에 대한 책임을 각 시·도 또는 지방자치단체에 전체적 또는 부분적으로 분담시키기도 한다.

학교도서관들은 각기 그 지역의 관행에 따라 오랜 기간에 걸쳐 법적, 정치적으로 연계되어 있으며, 지역의 조사연구, 발견, 창조, 비판 및 혁신을 위한 학습센터로서 자리매김해 왔다. 학교시스템의 내부 또는 외부 공히 학교도서관은 학생들의 지적 개발 및 능력 발전에 대한 수요를 지속적으로 충족시켜줄 수 있는 지식정보자원의 개발 및 유지에 대한 체계적인 가이드라인을 갖춰야 한다.

2.3 윤리적 기반 및 이슈

학교도서관은 학습공동체내 학생들 및 구성원들의 권한과 책임을 고려한 윤리적 기본 틀 안에 존재한다. 학교도서관은 지역의 모든 문화적, 언어적 고유성을 지닌 독특한 인구 구성원들을 모두 아우르는 포괄적 접근방법을 취한다. 기록된 지식과 정보에 대한 접근의 평등 및 지적 자유를 보장하는 핵심 가치는 세계인권선언문 제19조 및 세계도서관연맹의 가치에 실려 있다(www.ifla.org/about/more).

기타 고려사항은 다음과 같으나 여기에 한정되는 것은 아니다.

- 도서관 권리장전
- 정보 및 프라이버시의 자유
- 저작권, 지적 재산 및 표절에 관한 문제
- 어린이 권리보호
  (www.un.org/cyberschoolbus/humanrights/resources/child.asp)
- 고유민족의 권리보호
  (http://undesadspd.org/indigenouspeoples/declarationontherightsofindigenouspeoples.aspx)

학교도서관은 교육프로그램을 통하여 학생들에게 책임 있는 시민으로서 요구되는 능력을 개발시켜 주고, 정보의 자유, 지적재산 및 표절에 관련한 문제 등 학습공동체의 윤리적 문제에 대한 능력과 이해력을 갖도록 해 준다.

2.4 학교도서관 발전을 위한 인프라 구축

학교도서관의 개발 및 운영을 체계적으로 지원하기 위해서는 반드시 국가 및 지역 행정단위별로 교육을 책임지는 행정부서가 확립되어 있어야 한다. 당국의 학교도서관 서비스 및 활동운영에 대한 기초적 지원 노력이 있어야만 학생들과 교사들이 학교도서관을 교수 학습의 장으로 이해하고 접근할 수 있게 된다. 그러한 교육 서비스센터의 업무에는 다음과 같은 문제들이 포함된다. 즉 학교도서관 사서의 양성 및 계속교육, 전문인들과의 상담, 조사연구, 학교도서관 사서협회 및 전문단체와의 협력, 그리고 학교도서관의 기준과 가이드라인의 개발 등이다.

학교도서관 서비스 및 활동의 성격과 범위는 나라 또는 학교에 따라 다양하다. 하지만 학생들 및 그 가족들의 인구이동이 증가함에 따라 전 지역의 학교에 공통되는 통일성 및 접근성을 유지함으로써 학교 교육공동체의 요구를 충족할 수 있도록 교육시스템의 역량을 강화해 나가야 한다.

〈사례〉

미국 텍사스주는 1967년 법률에 의거 주내 교육구청을 지원하기 위하여 20군데에 걸친 교육서비스센터를 설립하였다. 이 교육서비스센터의 역할은 교육구청들이 다음과 같은 세 가지 주요 목적을 수행할 수 있도록 조율하는 것이다. 즉 각 교육구청 내 학생들의 학업성취 지원, 각 교육구청의 효율적·경제적 운영지원, 주도적 실행을 위한 법률가 또는 감독관 파견 등이다. 교육서비스센터는 도서관의 전문성 개발, 정보기술 지원, 그리고 학교행정관, 사서 및 교사들을 위한 교육프로그램을 운영한다.

2.5 정책

학교도서관은 독서 및 탐구를 위한 핵심 자원이라는 인식을 기반으로 분명한 정책 구조의 틀 안에서 운영해야 한다. 학교도서관 정책은 학교 전체를 포괄하고 학교의 필요성이라는 정책마인드에 의거하며 학교의 교풍, 사명, 목적, 목표 및 학교의 현실을 반영하여 수립해야 한다.

정책은 학교도서관이 교육 공동체의 모든 구성원을 위한 것이라는 점을 분명히 해야 한다. 학교도서관 정책은 학교도서관의 전문사서가 교사들 및 학교행정가들(예: 학교의 최고위층인 교장, 교육 관련 직원)과 협력하여 함께 개발하여야 한다. 정책의 초안은 학교 공동체에 널리 회람하여 공개토론의 과정을 거쳐야 한다. 최종 합의된 정책은 정책의 개발 및 이행에 따른 철학, 개념, 의도를 주지시키고, 실천을 담보하기 위하여 널리 공유해야 한다. 정책에 근거한 관련정책문서 및 계획들은 다음 사항들과 관련한 학교도서관의 역할을 상세히 밝혀두어야 한다.

- 해당 학교의 공식 비공식 커리큘럼
- 해당 학교의 학습 방법
- 국가 및 지역의 표준 및 기준
- 학생들의 개인학습 및 인성개발
- 교사들의 요구
- 학업 성취 수준 제고
- 탐구 능력 개발
- 독서 동기 및 독서 능력 증진
- 열린 마음 및 시민 정신 확립

이 모든 것이 현실적 정책 틀 속에서 고안되어야 하며 실천을 위한 후속 계획들이 뒤따라야 한다. 실천계획은 목적, 업무, 전략, 모니터링, 평가 등으로 구성되어야 한다. 정책 및 실천계획들은 정기적으로 검토하여 실효성을 유지해야 한다.

2.6 계획 수립

학교도서관의 기획은 사서가 적극적으로 나서서 학교행정담당자 및 교사진, 그리고 학생들과 대화를 통해 학교도서관과 학교공동체 내의 다른 조직과의 관계를 설정해야 한다. 기획과정에서 고려해야 할 중요한 요소들은 다음과 같다.

- 국가적, 세계적, 미래지향적으로 지속가능한 개발 목적 설정
- 국가적 그리고 각 학교 수준에서의 교육적인 사명, 철학, 목적, 목표 설정
- 학교도서관의 학교에 대한 가치 및 교육 과정에서 이해관계자, 교육문화 당사자, 재정 지원자들의 역할을 기술하는 비전의 제시
- 학교도서관에 대한 현재의 요구 평가 및 학습센터로서 존재해야 마땅한 미래의 비전 제시
- 우수한 정보자원, 시설, 물리적 환경, 디지털 환경에 대한 도서관과 학교 공동체와의 상호 연계 및 접근에 대한 계획
- 미래의 기술발전 및 정보서비스 전달의 변화 가능성에 대비한 정보기술 개발계획
- 학생 중심, 학교공동체 중심의 역동적 활동 계획
- 학교도서관 사서 인력의 전문 능력 개발 계획
- 실증적 조사연구를 통해 학생들의 성공에 대한 도서관 서비스의 영향을 보여줄 수 있는 지속적 개선을 위한 평가계획

〈사례〉

인도네시아의 어느 지역에서는 학교의 직원이 학교도서관의 직원, 정부 당국 및 국제개발기구와 협력하여 학교도서관 모델을 개발한 사례가 있음.

2.7 예산

학교도서관은 교육 및 정보의 기반으로서 도서관의 경영활력을 유지하기 위하여 지역 실정을 고려한 적정 예산을 확보해야 한다. 예산 지출은 학교도서관의 정책적인 틀과 밀접하게 연계되어야 하며 학생, 교사, 직원의 인력개발을 위한 투자를 반영해야 한다.

학교도서관의 사서는 학교의 중간 관리자와 협업함으로써 학교공동체에 양질의 정보자원 및 서비스를 제공하기 위한 책임을 지고 예산을 확보해야 한다. 학교도서관에 대한 재정은 다음에서 제시하는 조사결과를 반영해야 한다.

- 학교도서관의 교수학습인력, 보조인력 및 장서가 해당 학교의 교육성취에 최적의 규모와 질을 달성할 수 있는지를 나타내는 예측 지표
- 표준 평가에서 높은 점수를 받는 학생들이 학교도서관의 인력과 서비스에 접근하는 정도와 도서, 정기간행물, 온라인자료, 기타 비매

(무료) 자원 등으로부터 영향을 받는 정도(예: 2013년도에 Kachel & Lance이 수행한 IASL(International Association of School Librarianship) www.iasl-online.org/research/abstracts)연구

예산은 전 회계연도에 걸쳐 면밀한 계획 아래, 정책의 틀과 연계하여 집행되어야 한다. 예산계획의 요소는 부록 B에 제시되어 있다. 연간보고서는 도서관의 예산이 어떻게 사용되었는지, 도서관의 프로그램과 정보자원에 지출된 금액이 그러한 업무의 수행에 충분했으며, 필요한 정책 목적을 달성했는지를 분명히 나타내야 한다. 연간보고서는 학교도서관의 서비스와 프로그램의 질 및 학교에서의 교수학습에 미친 영향에 대한 증거를 포함하여야 한다. 학교도서관 경영에 있어 평가의 유용성과 필요성에 대한 사항은 본 가이드라인의 제6장에서 좀 더 상세히 다룬다.

참고문헌

American Association of School Librarians. (2011). *Standards for the 21st century learner.* Retrieved from www.ala.org/aasl/standards-guidelines/learning-standards

American Library Association. (2010). *Intellectual Freedom Manual* (8th ed.). Retrieved from www.ala.org/advocacy/intfreedom/iftoolkits/ifmanual/intellectual

American Library Association. (1996). *Library Bill of Rights.* Retrieved from www.ala.org/advocacy/intfreedom/librarybill

Australian School Library Association. (2000). *School Library Bill of Rights.* Retrieved from www.asla.org.au/policy/bill-of-rights.aspx

Hay, L. & Todd, R. J. (2010). *School libraries 21C.* NSW Department of Education and Training. Retrieved from www.curriculumsupport.education.nsw.gov.au/schoollibraries/assets/pdf/21c_report.pdf

International Federation of Library Associations. (2015). *Indigenous Matters Special Interest Group.* Retrieved from www.ifla.org/indigenous-matters

International Federation of Library Associations. (2015). *Lesbian, Gay, Bisexual, Transgender and Queer/Questioning Users Special Interest Group*. Retrieved from www.ifla.org/lgbtq

International Federation of Library Associations. (2015). *IFLA/UNESCO Multicultural Library Manifesto*. Retrieved from www.ifla.org/node/8976

Kachel, D. E., & Lance, K. C. (2013). Latest study: A full-time school librarian makes a critical difference in boosting student achievement. *School Library Journal*, 59(3), 28.

제3장

학교도서관의 인적자원

학교도서관 사서는 학교도서관의 계획 및 경영책임자로서
인사관리에서 전문 능력과 자질을 갖춘 적임자를 배치함으로서 전문성을 확보해야 한다.
학교도서관 사서는 학교의 모든 구성원들과 협력하여 일하고,
공공도서관 및 기타 기관과도 유대관계를 가지고 업무를 수행해야 한다.
-학교도서관 선언에서

3.1 개관

학교도서관의 핵심적 기능은 정보와 아이디어에 물리적, 지적으로 접근할 수 있게 하는 것이다. 학교도서관 프로그램의 질적 수준과 풍부성은 기본적으로 학교 내·외에서 활용 가능한 인적자원의 전문성에 달려있다. 학교공동체의 교수학습 수요를 충족하기 위해서는 해당 학교의 규모 및 특성에 맞는 숙련되고 의욕적인 충분한 수의 직원들이 필수적으로 있어야한다. 학교도서관에서 근무하는 모든 직원은 학교도서관의 서비스와 정책, 규정된 의무와 책임을 분명히 숙지하고 각 직무의 역할 기대에 적합한 고용조건 및 보수체계에 따라 일할 수 있어야 한다.

3.2 인적자원의 운용 및 원칙

학교도서관은 교수와 학습을 원활하게 지원하는 조직이므로 도서관 프로그램 역시 교실 수업을 담당하는 교과 교사와 동동한 수준의 교육과 자격을 갖춘 전문가가 이끌어야 한다. 학교도서관 사서가 리더십을 발휘하기 위해서는 학교 내의 다른 리더들, 즉 교육행정가나 교육전문가와 동일한 수준의 교육과 자격을 갖출 필요가 있다. 학교도서관 사서가 교육, 경영, 협업, 리더십의 전문적 역할을 수행할 수 있도록 충분한 시간을 보장하기 위해서는 숙련된 행정직원 및 기술직원들이 학교도서관의 운영을 적절히 지원해야 한다.

3.3 학교도서관 사서의 정의

학교도서관 사서는 독서, 탐구, 연구, 사고력, 상상력, 창의성 등 교수학습의 중심이 되는 물리적 공간 및 디지털 공간의 운영을 책임지고 있다. 이러한 학교도서관 사서의 역할을 반영하는 명칭은 여러 가지로 알려져 있다(예: 학교도서관 사서, 학교도서관 미디어 전문가, 사서교사, 자료전문가). 하지만 학교도서관 사서라는 명칭이 가장 보편적으로 사용되고 있다. 학교도서관 사서의 자격은 사서 교육에 교사 교육 또는 도서관 미디어 전문가 교육을 포함 또는 제외하는 등 나라에 따라 다양하다.

학교도서관을 어떻게 정의하느냐의 문제도 나라에 따라 공공도서관 서비스에 학교도서관을 포함하는 경우도 있어 다양하게 나타난다. 학교도서관의 인력운영 패턴 역시 지역적 맥락, 즉 지역의 법제, 경제개발 정도, 교육 인프라 수준에 따라 다르다. 그러나 지난 50여 년간의 조사 연구(예: Haycock, 1992, in LRS(2015) 학교도서관에 영향을 미치는 요인에 관한 연구 www.lrs.org/data-tools/school-libraries/impact-studies)에서 보면 학교도서관 사서는 교육, 독서 및 리터러시 개발, 학교도서관 경영, 교과교사들과의 협업, 지역사회 교육공동체와의 협력 등 복합적인 역할을 수행할 수 있는 전문가로서의 능력을 갖추고 도서관 및 교실 수업에 필요한 공식 교육을 받아야 하는 것으로 나타났다.

〈사례〉

프랑스의 중학교 및 고등학교도서관 사서(자료전문가)는 일반 교과교사와 동등한 수준의 교육을 받은 인력을 채용하고 연수 훈련을 시킨다.

〈사례〉

이탈리아의 남부 티롤지방에서는 볼차노 주정부가 사서직의 교육 훈련 및 자격기준(볼차노 주정부의 법률 17/1990; 2006. 3. 4 볼차노 노동규약)에 의거 유치원부터 고등학교도서관에 근무할 학교도서관 사서를 채용한다. 학교도서관 보조사서는 중등교육(유치원-고등학교)을 받고 별도로 사서 교육과정(적어도 1년 이상의 이론 및 실습 교육)을 이수해야 한다. 고급의 학교도서관 사서는 고등교육(적어도 3년간의 학사학위)을 반드시 이수해야 한다. 다음을 참조할 것: Berufsbilder "BibliothekarIn" und "DiplombibliothekarIn" (예: 사서 및 고급 사서 직무요건, www.provinz.bz.it/kulturabteilung/bibliotheken/1459.asp)

〈사례〉

포르투갈에서는 2009년부터 학교사서(서지전문가)를 도서관 전문가인 사서교사로 변경하여 임명하고 있다. 다음의 "Formacao"(교육) 사이트를 참조할 것 www.rbe.mec.pt/np4/programa.html

3.4 학교도서관 프로그램 제공에 요구되는 사서의 역량

학교도서관 전문사서의 자질에는 다음과 같은 사항들이 포함된다.

- 교수학습, 커리큘럼, 교수설계 및 수행
- 프로그램 관리 - 기획, 개발 및 디자인, 실행, 평가/개선
- 장서개발, 장서관리, 자료조직, 검색

- 정보 가공 및 정보표현 방법 - 문자리터러시, 정보 리터러시, 디지털 리터러시
- 독서지도
- 어린이와 청소년문학에 대한 지식
- 독서에 영향을 미치는 장애에 대한 지식
- 의사소통 및 협업 능력
- 디지털 및 미디어 운영 능력
- 윤리 및 사회적 책임의식
- 공공 서비스 - 공중 및 사회에 대한 책임의식
- 지속적인 전문성 개발을 통한 평생교육의 실천
- 학교도서관의 역사 및 가치에 대한 사서들 간의 인식 공유

학교도서관 사서의 전문성 및 자질개발은 대학의 학위과정을 통하여 또는 교사자격 및 사서자격 취득 이후 계속교육 프로그램을 통하여 여러 가지 방법으로 성취할 수 있다. 학교도서관 사서의 교육목적은 교수능력과 사서능력을 동시에 갖추게 하는 데 있다.

학교도서관 사서 교육을 위한 특별프로그램이나 교육과정을 운영하는 나라에서는 사서의 핵심역량 개발에 더하여 교육(학습, 교육과정, 교수법)에 대한 이해, 디지털 및 미디어기술, 청소년, 문화, 그리고 리터러

시에 대한 이해 능력을 갖추어야 한다. 또한 이 분야 교육에서는 창의적 사고방식과 문제해결능력, 그리고 정보 리터러시에 대한 깊은 종합적인 이해능력을 갖추어야 한다. 학교도서관 교육은 학교공동체의 일원으로서, 변화에 대한 대응 또는 변화의 촉매자로서 도서관 측면에서 전문적 리더의 역할을 다할 수 있게 해야 한다.

〈사례〉

프랑스에서는 교사를 위한 역량 강화 참고시스템(Referentiel de competences des enseignants)을 운영하면서 학교도서관 사서를 포함하여 어떤 교사라도 본인의 능력을 향상할 수 있도록 교육과정 리스트를 제시하고 있다. 이 리스트에는 학교도서관 사서를 위한 문헌정보학 특별과정이 포함되어 있다. 정보 리터러시 능력은 교육공동체에 속해있는 모든 구성원들이 갖추어야 할 필수 능력으로 인정되어야 한다. 정보 리터러시 능력은 효과적인 협력수업을 위한 전제 조건이기 때문이다.

3.5 학교도서관 전문사서의 역할

학교도서관 전문사서의 핵심적인 역할은 교육, 경영, 리더십, 협업, 그리고 지역사회 협력이다. 아래에 이들 각각에 대하여 자세히 논의한다.

3.5.1 교육

학교도서관 사서의 교육적 역할은 학생들에 대한 개별 교육, 소그룹 교육, 교실 수업 등 다양하며, 동료 교사들을 위한 공식, 비공식 교육안내도 포함된다. 학교도서관 사서의 교육 업무중 핵심적 활동은 제5장에서 논의하며 다음 사항을 포함한다.

- 리터러시 및 독서능력 증진
- 정보 리터러시(정보 일반능력, 정보에 대한 이해력, 숙련된 정보검색, 미디어 리터러시, 트랜스 리터러시)
- 탐구기반 학습(문제기반 학습, 비판적 사고)
- 정보기술의 통합사용능력
- 일반 교사를 위한 전문성 개발

〈사례〉

교사 안내를 위한 여러 가지 교육 모델이 사용되고 있다. 다음은 프랑스의 교사 교육 모델이다.

Benchmarks for the implementation of the learning path to an information culture[Reperes pour la mise en œuvre du Parcours de formation a la culture de l'information]; from Belgium, Media literacy skills: A major educational challenge [Les competences en education aux medias: un enjeu educatif majeur]; and from UNESCO Media and information literacy: A training program for teachers [Education aux medias et a l'information: programme de formation pour les enseignants].

3.5.2 경영

학교도서관 전문사서의 경영 관리적 역할은 학교도서관의 최적 활용을 위한 자료관리 시스템 및 도서관 업무 프로세스의 조직이라 할 수 있다. 이는 도서관의 시설(물리적 및 디지털 환경), 정보자원(실물 및 디지털 자료), 교육 프로그램 및 서비스(물리적 및 디지털서비스) 등을 포함한다. 인적자원의 관리 - 도서관 직원의 모집, 선발, 교육훈련, 감독, 평가 - 역시 전문사서의 중요한 역할이다.

3.5.3 리더십과 협력

학교도서관 사서의 주요 역할은 학교전체의 사명과 목적에 기여하는 것이다. 학교의 행정요원 및 교과 교사들과의 협력에 있어 사서는 교수학습을 지원하는 도서관 서비스와 프로그램을 기반으로 교과과정을 개발, 실행해야 한다. 사서는 정보 자원과 관련되는 지식과 기술을 활용하여 교수학습 활동, 즉 각종 프로젝트 수행, 문제해결 활동, 리터러시 활동, 독서지도 및 문화 활동에 기여해야 한다. 학교도서관 사서는 단독으로 또는 학교 내 다른 전문가와 협력하여 정보기술을 통합적으로 활용함으로써 교과교사 및 행정요원들의 전문성 개발에도 일정부분 역할을 수행해야 한다.

협업은 학교도서관 사서가 필수적으로 수행해야 하는 활동이다. 사서가 학교의 경영 관리자와 협력함으로써 학교도서관이 학교의 사명과 목적에 기여하고 있다는 점을 이해시켜야 한다. 학교도서관 사서는 교장, 교감, 부장교사에게 직접 보고할 수 있어야 하며, 학교의 전반적인 계획 수립 및 기타 팀워크 활동에 주도적으로 참여할 수 있어야 한다. 학교 공동체 내에서 학교도서관 사서는 통합교과적 프로젝트와 학제적 학습이 용이하도록 부서 간 협력 업무를 수행해야 한다. 학교도서관 사서는 다른 학교의 사서들과 협력하여 지속적으로 전문성 향상 및 개발을 위해 노력해야 한다.

〈사례〉

미국의 텍사스 주 북부에서는 많은 학교도서관의 수석 사서들이 매월 회의를 갖고 새로운 프로그램 및 서비스에 대하여 발표하고 아이디어를 교환한다.

〈사례〉

영국에서는 지역별로 잘 조직된 학교도서관 사서 모임이 있어 교육훈련 및 네트워킹 기회를 가짐으로써 각 학교의 목적을 충족시키고 있다.

3.5.4 지역사회 참여

지역사회 참여는 프로그램, 장서개발, 그리고 다양한 문화적, 언어적 특성을 가진 원주민, 기타 특수 인구집단을 도서관으로 안내하는 외부 연계활동을 포함한다. 학교도서관은 어린이 교육에 있어 학생 가족의 중요성 및 지식의 세대 간 전수와 소통의 가치를 인식하지 않으면 안 된다.

어린이들은 가정과 지역사회의 보호를 받으며 자라고 있다. 따라서 학교도서관은 다양한 배경을 가진 사람들이 평등하게 이용하고 참여할 수 있도록 포괄적인 접근방법을 취할 필요가 있고, 그들의 사회적, 교육적, 문화적, 정치적, 경제적 삶을 평등하게 지원할 수 있는, 정보접근 및 창의적 아이디어와 상상력을 촉진해 줄 수 있는 적정 수준의 서비스를 제공할 필요가 있다. 지역사회의 핵심 가치 중 하나는 부와 지식의 세대 간 전수라고 할 수 있다. 어린이들에게 효과적이고도 의미 있는 방법으로 지식을 전수하는 것은 학교도서관이 속해 있는 지역사회의 주류 문화에 따라 다를 수 있다. 모든 어린이들에게 '정체성'과 '소속감'을 심어 주는 일은 리터러시 및 학업성취에 필수적인 요소이다.

학교도서관은 가능한 한 지역 내 공공도서관이나 도서관협회 등 다른 도서관 및 단체와 연계해야 한다. 해당 지역사회에서 어린이 청소년에 대한 도서관 서비스를 개선하기 위해서는 학교도서관과 공공도서관이 협력해야 한다. 협약서는 문서로 작성하고 협력에 관한 일반사항, 협력 분야의 정의 및 특수요건, 재정부담 및 분담에 관한 사항, 협력기간 및 시간 스케줄 등을 포함한다. 협력 분야를 예를 들면 직원의 공동 훈련, 협력적 장서개발 및 프로그램 운영, 디지털 네트워크 서비스 협력, 학급단위 공공도서관 방문, 독서 및 리터러시 프로그램 공동운영, 어린이 청소년 도서관 서비스 마케팅 공동운영 등이다.

〈사례〉

노르웨이 오슬로에서는 교육청과 공공도서관이 협력 협정을 맺고 시내 120개 학교와 정기적으로 여러 관련 문제들을 논의하여 해결한다. 공공도서관의 학교 서비스는 학교에 자문 인력 및 정보 자료를 지원해 주는 것이다. 자문 인력은 독서지도 및 리터러시, 장서개발, 학교도서관 공간 구성 등의 여러 분야를 도와준다. 학교사서 및 교사들은 이 메일이나 전화로 도움을 요청할 수 있다. 공공도서관은 학교에서 구입할 수 없거나 또는 정기적으로 이용할 수 없는 자료를 학교도서관이나 해당 교실로 직접 제공할 수 있다.

3.5.5 도서관 프로그램 및 서비스 개선 촉진

도서관 프로그램 및 서비스 촉진 활동이란 학교도서관이 제공해야 할 자료에 대하여 이용자들과 의사를 소통하고, 이용자가 원하는 필요한 프로그램과 서비스를 제공하는 것이다. 학교도서관이 제공하는 프로그램, 서비스, 시설들을 적극적으로 개선함으로써 학교 구성원들은 학교도서관을 학습 파트너로서의 역할, 프로그램, 서비스, 정보자료 제공자로서의 역할을 하는곳으로 인식하게 된다. 학교도서관 서비스의 대상은 학교장 및 학교행정요원, 부서장, 교사, 학생, 학부모들이다. 중요한 것은 학교의 특성 및 목표 대상별 특성에 맞추어 의사소통을 적절히 조정하는 것이다.

학교도서관은 학교경영자 및 교직원과의 협력에 관한 업무개선 계획을 수립하여야 한다. 그 계획에는 다음의 요소, 즉 활동 목표, 각 목표의 달성을 위한 구체적 활동 계획, 목표 달성 여부를 측정할 수 있는 평가 방법을 포함해야 한다.

3.6 학교도서관 준 전문직의 역량 및 역할

학교도서관의 준 전문직(예: 도서관 보조원, 도서관 기술기능직)은 사무적, 기술적 기능을 수행함으로써 사서의 업무를 보조하고, 사서에게 관련 업무를 보고하는 인력이다. 학교도서관 준 전문직원은 서가정리, 대출, 반납, 자료처리, 온라인 대출 및 목록 서비스, 디지털 자원 접근 서비스 등과 같은 도서관의 일상적 업무를 담당하므로 이러한 업무에 요구되는 교육 훈련을 받아야 한다.

3.7 학교도서관 자원봉사자의 역량 및 역할

자원봉사자를 급여를 받는 도서관 직원을 대체하는 인력으로 여겨서는 안 된다. 자원봉사자는 학교도서관 사서의 감독 아래 일정한 공식적 협약 틀 내에서 학교도서관 활동에 참여하고 업무를 지원하는 역할을 한다. 학생들 역시 사서의 감독아래 명백히 정의된 역할 내에서 학교도서관 자원봉사자로 일할 수 있다. 학생 자원봉사자는 상급 학년을 대상으로 공식적 지원절차를 통하여 선발하고 전시, 서가 정리, 저학년 대상 책 읽어주기, 친구들에게 독서자료 추천 등의 업무를 수행할 수 있도록 훈련을 시켜야 한다.

〈사례〉

미국 미시건주 한 초등학교에서는 도서관 지원팀을 구성하여 도서관을 원활하게 운영할 수 있도록 지원하고 있다. 이 학생들은 주 1회 서가 정리, 유치원 교실 대출 장서 수거, 그리고 신착 자료의 바코드 및 라벨 작업을 돕는다.

〈사례〉

이탈리아 로마에서는 특별활동 프로그램에 등록한 고등학교 학생들이 도서관을 원활하게 운영하도록 지원하며, 동시에 그들의 인성개발에도 도움을 받는다. 학생들은 특히 도서관 수리 및 재단장 기간에 많은 도움을 주며, 이 때 협력 방법, 관심 확대, 자아 존중 의식 증진 등의 긍정적 자극을 받는다.

〈사례〉

헝가리에서는 2012년부터 중학생 대상으로 지역사회에 도움이 되는 봉사활동을 수행하도록 의무화하고 있다. 이러한 봉사활동은 학교 및 공공도서관에서 수행할 수 있다.

3.8 윤리적 기준

자원봉사자를 포함하여 학교도서관에서 일하는 모든 사람은 학교 공동체의 모든 구성원들을 대상으로 또는 각기 서로 간 업무를 수행하는 데 있어 높은 윤리기준을 지켜야 한다. 그들은 자신의 안락과 편리에 앞서 이용자의 권리 보호를 위해 노력해야 하며, 도서관 서비스의 제공에 있어 개인적인 신념이나 태도로 인한 편견을 배제해야 한다. 모든 어린이, 청소년, 그리고 어른들 모두 그들의 능력이나 배경에 관계없이 평등하게 대해야 한다. 모두의 프라이버시와 알 권리를 지속적으로 보장해야 한다.

자원봉사자를 포함하여 학교도서관에서 일하는 모든 사람은 도서관의 핵심 가치, 즉 도서관직의 책무, 서비스, 지적 자유, 합리성, 문맹퇴치와 학습, 지식 정보 접근의 평등, 프라이버시 보호, 민주주의 등을 간직하도록 노력해야 한다. 지식 정보 접근에의 평등 및 지적 자유에 대한 핵심 가치는 세계인권선언 제19조 및 세계도서관연맹(IFLA)의 가치에 포함되어 있다(www.ifla.org/about/more).

참고문헌

American Library Association. (2010). *ALA/AASL Standards for initial preparation of school librarians.* Retrieved from www.ala.org/aasl/education/ncate

CLEMI: Centre de liaison de l'enseignement et des médias d'information. (2013). *Proposition pour un référentiel enseignant en éducation aux médias* [Proposal for a repository in teaching media literacy] [pdf en ligne]. Retrieved from www.clemi.org/fichier/plug_download/29480/download_fichier_fr_referentiel_clemi_version2.pdf

Conseil supérieur de l'éducation aux m?dias. (2013). *Les compétences en éducation aux medias: Un enjeu éducatif majeur* [Media literacy skills: A major educational challenge]. Belgique: CSEM.

Gorman, M. (2000). *Our enduring values: Librarianship in the 21st century.* Chicago: American Library Association.

International Federation of Library Associations. (2012). *Professional Codes of Ethics for Librarians.* Retrieved from www.ifla.org/faife/professional-codes-of-ethics-for-librarians

International Federation of Library Associations. (2015). *Indigenous Matters Special Interest Group.* www.ifla.org/indigenous-matters

International Federation of Library Associations. (2015). *Lesbian, Gay, Bisexual, Transgender and Queer/Questioning Users Special Interest Group.* Retrieved from www.ifla.org/lgbtq

International Federation of Library Associations. (2015). *IFLA/UNESCO Multicultural Library Manifesto.* Retrieved from www.ifla.org/node/8976

Markless, S. (Ed.). (2009). *The innovative school librarian: Thinking outside the box.* London: Facet Publishing. [See Chapters 1 & 2, pp. 1-46.]

Ministère de l'éducation nationale. (2013). Référentiel de compétences des enseignants [Competency framework for teachers]. *Bulletin officiel de l'éducation nationale*, n°30, 25/07/2013.

National Forum on Information Literacy. (2014). *Policy statement on the importance of certified school librarians.* Retrieved from http://infolit.org/nfil-policy-statement-school-librarians

Simpson, C. (2003). *Ethics in school librarianship: A reader.* Worthington, OH: Linworth.

Wilson, C., Grizzle, A., Tuazon, R., Akyempong, K., & Cheung, C.K. (2012). *Education aux médias et à l'information: programme de formation pour les enseignants* [Media education and information: A training program for teachers]. Paris: UNESCO.

제4장

학교도서관의 물리적 자원 및 디지털 자원

학교도서관 직원은 문학작품에서 사실자료에 이르기 까지,
인쇄자료에서 전자자료에 이르기 까지,
현장접근에서 원격접근에 이르기 까지 책과 정보원을 이용할 수 있도록 지원한다.
도서관 자료는 교수용 텍스트 및 교수방법에 있어
교과서를 보충하며 수업 내용을 풍부하게 한다.
–학교도서관 선언에서

4.1 개관

학교도서관의 물리적 자료와 디지털 자료는 시설, 장비, 그리고 교수학습을 위한 장서를 포함한다. 정보기술은 점차 학교와 지역사회에서 도서관 자료의 접근 외연을 확장하고 있다. 또한 정보기술의 발전으로 학교도서관의 관내 자원 및 관외 자원을 이용할 수 있을 뿐 아니라 학교 근무시간 및 학사일정의 기간 범위를 넘어서 하루 24시간 일주일에 7일 연중무휴로 학교도서관에 접근할 수 있게 되었다. 학교도서관의 시설, 장비, 장서는 학생과 교사의 교수학습 요구 변화에 부응하여 지속적으로 개선할 필요가 있다.

4.2 시설

학교 건물의 신축계획 시 또는 기존 건물의 개선 시 학교도서관의 기능과 이용자의 편의를 고려하는 것은 기본적으로 중요한 사항이다. 학교 시설의 설계에 반드시 학교도서관의 교육적 역할을 반영해야 한다. 오늘날 많은 학교도서관들은 '참여문화'의 공간으로서 이용자들의 의견을 반영, "공동학습의 장"으로 설계해야 하며, 정보 소비자로서의 이용자, 나아가 정보 창조자로서의 이용자로 그 역할 범위를 확대해야 한다. 도서관에서의 공동학습을 위해서는 전통적인 교수학습 공간은 물론 새로운 지식정보 창출을 위한 시설과 장비를 제공해야 한다.

4.2.1 위치 및 공간

학교도서관 시설의 규모 및 디자인에 대하여 국제적으로 보편적인 기준은 존재하지 않는다. 그러나 설계 시 가장 기본이 되는 기준을 따르는 것이 좋다. 일반적으로 도서관들은 자료 중심 모델에서 학습자 중심 모델로 변화되고 있다. 학교 및 대학도서관들은 종종 학습공유센터로 설계된다. 학교도서관의 시설계획에 고려할 사항은 다음과 같다.

- 가능하면 학교 건물 1층 중앙에 위치할 것

- 교실과 인접하여 접근하기 좋은 곳
- 소음요인, 적어도 도서관의 일부는 외부 소음이 들어오지 않는 곳
- 자연광 및 전등, 적정하고 충분한 조명
- 장서보존은 물론 연중 업무 및 학습에 알맞은 적정 실내온도(예: 에어컨, 온풍기) 유지
- 이용자의 특수 요구를 고려한 적정한 실내 디자인
- 적정규모의 공간배치, 즉 소설, 비소설, 양장본, 지장본, 신문잡지, 비도서 자료 공간 등 정보자료 공간, 학습 공간, 독서 공간, 컴퓨터 워크스테이션, 전시 공간, 직원 업무 공간
- 미래 교과과정 및 정보기술 변화에 따라 복합적 활동이 가능한 공간 활용의 신축성

4.2.2 공간의 구성

공간 구성은 다음과 같은 기능적 요소를 고려하여야 한다.

- 학습 및 연구 공간 - 정보이용 데스크, 목록, 온라인 데스크, 학습 연구 테이블, 참고자료 및 기본 자료 비치 공간
- 개인 독서 공간 - 리터러시, 평생 학습, 오락 독서용 도서 및 정기간행물 비치 공간

- 교육 공간 - 적정 교육 기자재 및 전시공간을 갖춘, 소그룹, 대그룹, 학급 단위 집합 교육을 할 수 있는 좌석 공간 (학생 수의 10% 좌석을 권장)
- 미디어 제작 및 단체 프로젝트 수행 공간 - 개별, 팀 및 학급단위 프로젝트 수행 공간(실험실 또는 제작 공간).
- 사무 공간 - 대출 데스크, 사무실, 도서관 미디어 자료처리, 장비, 소모품, 각종 재료 보관 공간

4.2.3 물리적 및 디지털 자료 접근성

도서관의 물리적 자료와 디지털 자료 접근을 극대화해야 한다. 정보기술과 더불어 학교도서관 정보 자료에 대한 디지털 접근은 학교 안팎에서 하루 24시간 일주일에 7일 연중무휴로 가능해야 한다. 직원이 부족한 도서관에서는 훈련받은 학생들 및 학부모 자원 봉사자를 포함한 전체 도서관 시스템을 고려해야 한다.

4.3 장서개발 및 관리

학교도서관은 연령, 언어, 인구 통계적 특성에 따른 이용자들의 수요를 충족시키기 위하여 물리적 자료 및 디지털 자료에 대한 광범위한 접

근을 제공해야 한다. 장서는 이용자들이 언제나 새로운 자료에 접근할 수 있도록 지속적으로 개발해야 한다. 장서관리정책은 장서의 목적, 범위, 내용을 정의함은 물론 양질의 광범위한 외부 자원 접근을 규정해야 한다. 점차적으로 e-book(참고자료, 소설, 비소설), 온라인 데이터베이스, 온라인 신문과 잡지, 비디오 게임, 멀티미디어 학습자료 등과 같은 디지털 자료는 이제 도서관에서 실질적인 중요 자료가 되고 있다.

학교도서관은 학생들의 학습용 자료를 충족하는 장서에 더하여 전문장서, 즉 교사용 자료(예: 교육학 자료, 주제전문자료, 새로운 교수학습 스타일과 방법에 관한 자료), 그리고 학부모와 돌봄 선생님을 위한 자료, 도서관 직원을 위한 자료도 구비해야 한다.

〈사례〉

이탈리아 로마의 초등학교도서관은 "학부모 서가"를 개설하고 아동심리학, 교육학, 어린이들의 불안감 및 자아존중감 등 특수 주제 분야의 자료를 구비하여 이용에 제공하고 있다.

4.3.1 장서관리정책 및 절차

학교도서관 사서는 학교 경영 관리자 및 교사들과 협력하여 장서관리정책을 개발해야 한다. 장서관리정책은 교과과정 및 학교 공동체의 특수한 요구와 관심에 기초를 두어야 하며, 학교 밖 지역사회의 다양성을 반영해야 한다.

장서관리정책에는 다음과 같은 요소가 포함되어야 한다.

- IFLA/UNESCO의 학교도서관 선언에 맞는 학교도서관의 사명
- 지적 자유 및 정보의 자유에 대한 언급
- 장서관리정책의 목적, 교과과정과의 연관성, 국가적, 윤리적, 문화적 언어적 연관성, 이용자들의 토착적 고유성
- 각 자원에 대한 장단기 목표
- 장서관리 의사결정의 책임 소재

장서관리정책에는 주제전문가로서 학생들에게 필요한 지식의 가치를 알고 있는 교사들과 협동적 노력으로 장서를 구성해야 하며, 교사들이 도서관의 장서 구성에 중요한 역할을 해야 한다는 점을 명백히 규정해야 한다. 장서관리정책에는 지적자유의 원칙과 어린이의 알권리 보장의 원칙에 부합하는 자료심사 방법을 규정해 두어야 한다. 장서관리정책은 또 학교도서관 사서는 정보자원에 대한 수서의 제한 및 정보 접근의 제한 등 어떠한 자료검열 요구에도 항거할 책임이 있음을 분명히 해 두어야 한다.

학교도서관의 장서개발 및 관리에 대한 절차는 별건 문서로, 또는 장서관리정책의 부록으로 성문화해야 한다. 절차서와 매뉴얼은 자료의 선택과 수서, 정리 및 조직(분류, 목록, 서가배열), 유지관리, 수리, 폐기의 기준을 제시해야 한다. 매뉴얼에는 지역적, 국제적으로 자료를 획득하는 방법, 학교 공동체 구성원들의 특수성을 감안하여 국가적, 윤리적, 문화적, 언어적으로 부합되는 자료의 수집방법을 제시해야 한다. 매뉴얼은 또 쟁점이 되는 자료를 재심사하는 가이드라인을 제시해야 한다.

〈사례〉

프랑스에서는 학교도서관 사서가 학교의 교과과정 및 교육활동과 연계하여 학교 공동체 구성원들과 상의하여 10개 조항으로 요약되는 수서 정책을 개발하고 있다. 그 사이트는 다음과 같다.

www.cndp.fr/savoirscdi/centre-de-ressources/fonds-documentaire-acquisition-traitement/les-10-commandements-dune-politique-dacquisition.html

4.3.2 디지털 자원과 관련된 이슈들

학교도서관은 정보기반 사회로 접근하는 중요 포인트를 제공한다. 학교도서관은 교육과정에 관련된 디지털 자료뿐 아니라 이용자들의 관심과 그들의 문화에 관련된 디지털 자료도 접근할 수 있도록 해야 한다. 소셜 미디어에 의한 참여문화의 확대로 도서관은 이제 정보 소비자에서 정보 생산자로 그 역할 범위가 확대되고 있다. 그 결과 학교도서관 사서들은 학생들의 창조적 학습활동에 필요한 각종 장비 및 컴퓨터를 갖춘 "창조 공간"의 제공을 고려하지 않으면 안 되게 되었다. 이들 정보를 생산할 수 있는 도구들은 예를 들면 비디오 제작, 블로그 제작, 팟캐스트, 3D프로젝트, 포스터제작, 인포그래픽 장비 등이 있다.

디지털 자원 및 인터넷 자원의 접근 가능성이 증대됨에 따라 학교도서관 목록시스템도 학교도서관이 보다 넓은 광역 네트워크에 포함되어 이용을 원활하게 할 수 있도록 국가적, 세계적으로 통용되는 서지 표준에 의거 분류와 목록을 조정할 필요성이 제기되었다. 이제 세계의 많은 장소에서 학교도서관은 단일 또는 공유 목록시스템 안에 서로 연결됨으로써 그 편익을 누릴 수 있게 되었다. 그러한 협업을 통하여 자원의 선택, 목록, 자료처리 등에 품질과 효율성을 높임으로써 자원 활용의 효과를 극대화할 수 있게 하고 있다. 또한 세계 여러 곳에서 학교도서관은 상호 연대를 통하여 값비싼 상업 데이터베이스 및 온라인 참고자료의 공유를 용이하게 하려는 정부당국의 노력으로 많은 편익을 얻게 되었다.

〈사례〉

캐나다 앨버타 주 교육부는 온라인 참고정보센터(Online Reference Centre)를 통해 모든 학생들과 교사들에게 영어와 프랑스어로 된 양질의 온라인 정보자원을 제공하도록 운영비 전액을 지원하고 있다.

www.learnalberta.ca/OnlineReferenceCentre.aspx.

〈사례〉

프랑스에서는 학생들이 디지털 자원에 쉽게 접근, 이용할 수 있도록 300종이 넘는 출판물과 색인을 탑재하고 있는 코리리스 플랫폼(Correlyce platform) 사이트를 제공하고 있다. www.correlyce.fr

디지털 장서의 관리 기준은 인쇄본 장서의 관리기준과 유사하다. 하지만 고려해야 할 몇 가지 특수 조건들이 있다.

- 접근 - 인쇄본에 대하여 디지털 아이템을 선택함으로써 접근 효율성을 개선할 것인지?
- 재정적 기술적 문제 - 디지털 아이템의 라이선스 비용 또는 새로운 포맷의 변경 비용 등으로 디지털 자료 운영비가 장기적으로 과도하게 소요되지는 않는지?
- 법적 문제 및 라이선스 문제 - 저작권법 또는 디지털 자료의 이용

자 수 제한, 외부 액세스 문제, 이용자의 프라이버시에 대한 라이선스 계약조건

- 보안 - 자료 접근에 대하여 어떻게 보안조치를 할 것인지?

4.3.3 장서기준

오늘날 학교도서관 장서는 많은 디지털 자원과 외부 데이터베이스를 포함하고 있으므로 사이트 또는 외부 상업 데이터베이스 및 참고자료 라이선스 계약을 통하여 자료이용이 가능하다. 따라서 전통적인 방식으로 장서기준을 개발하여 적용하기는 어렵다. 국가 또는 지역의 장서기준을 이용하든 안 하든 장서개발에 대한 의사결정은 교과과정의 필요성 및 교육적 수요를 기반으로 이루어져야 한다.

현행 장서는 이용자들의 연령, 능력수준, 학습 스타일, 그리고 교육배경에 따라 균형을 맞출 필요가 있다. 장서는 실물 장서든 디지털 장서든 교과과정을 지원할 수 있어야 한다. 또한 학교도서관은 인기 그래픽 소설, 음악, 컴퓨터 게임, 영화, 잡지, 만화, 포스터 등 여가선용 목적의 자료도 수집해야 한다. 이러한 자료들은 학생들과 함께 협력하여 자료를 선택함으로써 그들의 관심과 문화를 반영해야 한다.

〈사례〉

미국 남 캐롤라이나주 교육부는 2012년 장서개발표준을 배포하였다. 이 기준에 따르면 학생 1인당 책 수는 "최소"(11권), "기본"(13권), "우수"(15권)로 되어 있다. 소설과 비소설 비율은 학년 등급에 따라, 특별 리터러시 프로젝트 또는 수요에 따라 다르다.

4.3.4 자원공유

학교도서관은 상호대차 및 자원공유를 통하여 이용자들의 자료 접근을 편리하게 해야 한다. 하지만 이는 학교도서관의 전통적 기능이 아니기 때문에 아직 자원공유를 쉽게 하는 잘 정비된 시스템이 드물다. 상호대차 및 자원공유는 학교도서관을 유니온 카탈로그로 서로 연결하고, 온라인 데이터베이스와 디지털 참고자원의 접근을 공유함으로써 보다 쉽게 자원을 이용할 수 있다.

〈사례〉

이탈리아 비첸차에서는 26개 고등학교도서관, 15개 종합학교(초등 및 중등), 2개의 개인 단체(재단 및 회사)가 도서관 자원 및 소프트웨어 네트워크를 구성하고 상호대차 서비스를 제공하고 있다.

www.rbsvicenza.org/index.php?screen=news&loc=S&osc=news&or

derby=Autore

〈사례〉

포루투칼에서는 학교와 공공도서관이 네트워크를 구축하고 자료 목록 및 자동화시스템을 공유하고 있다.

www.rbe.mec.pt/np4/home

〈사례〉

네덜란드와 플랑드르에서는 도서관을 "연합학교"[광역사회 학교]의 중심부에 두고 있다. 학교도서관은 통합적, 압축적, 포괄적 지식 센터로서, 광범위한 지역사회에 상호 도서관서비스를 제공한다(예: 유아, 초등학교, 체육관 등). www.bredeschool.nl/home.html

참고문헌

Bon, I., Cranfield, A., & Latimer, K. (Eds.). (2011). *Designing library space for children.* Berlin/Munich: De Gruyter Saur. (IFLA Publications; Nr 154.)

Dewe, M. (2007). *Ideas and designs: Creating the environment for the primary school library.* Swindon, UK: School Library Association [UK].

Dubber, G., & Lemaire, K. (2007). *Visionary spaces: Designing and planning a secondary school library.* Swindon, UK: School Library Association [UK].

Durpaire, J-L. (2004). *Politique d'acquisition in Les politiques documentaires des Etablissements scolaires* [The acquisition policy within a school's policy] (pp. 34-36). Paris: Inspection Generale de l'Education Nationale.

La Marca, S. (Ed). (2007). *Rethink! Ideas for inspiring school library design.* Carlton, Victoria, Australia: School Library Association of Victoria.

Landelijk Steunpunt Brede Scholen. (2013). *Verschijningsvormen Brede Scholen* 2013. [Examples of Community Schools 2013] (2nd ed.). Den Haag,

Netherland: bredeschool.nl. Retrieved from

www.bredeschool.nl/fileadmin/PDF/2013/2013-05-28__13_170_LSBS_gew_herdruk_brochure_Verschijningvormen_4.pdf

Latimer, K., & Niegaard, H. (2007). *IFLA library building guidelines: Developments and reflections.* Munich: K.G. Saur.

Loertscher, D., Koechlin, C., Zwann, S., & Rosenfield, E. (2011). *The new learning commons: Where the learners win!* (2nd ed.) Clearfield, UT: Learning Commons Press.

Marquardt, L. (2013). La biblioteca scolastica, ambiente e bene comune per l'apprendimento [school libraries, learning environments and commons]. In M. Vivarelli (Ed.). *Lo spazio della biblioteca ...* [The Library Space …]. Milano: Editrice Bibliografica. [See Chapter 4.6, pp. 299-334, and case study pp. 400-401.]

Molina, J. & Ducournau, J. (2006). Les 10 commandements d'une politique d'acquisition. [The 10 Commandments of an acquisition policy]. Retrieved from www.cndp.fr/savoirscdi/metier.html

OSLA (Ontario School Library Association). (2010). *Together for learning:*

School libraries and the emergence of the learning commons. A vision for the 21st Century. Toronto, Canada: OSLA, 2010. Retrieved from www.accessola.com/data/6/rec_docs/677_olatogetherforlearning.pdf

Pavey, S. (2014). *Mobile technology and the school library.* Swindon, UK: School Library Association [UK]

Preddy, L. B. (2013). *School library makerspaces: Grades 6-12.* Westport, CT: Libraries Unlimited.

South Carolina Department of Education. (2012). *South Carolina standards for school library resource collections.* Columbia: SCDE. Retrieved from http://ed.sc.gov/agency/programs-services/36/documents/Standards_School_Library_Resource_Collections.pdf

제5장

학교도서관의 프로그램 및 제반 활동

학교도서관은 교육과정에 통합적 기능을 수행한다.

-학교도서관 선언에서

5.1 개관

학교도서관이 그 교육적 사명을 다하기 위해서는 잘 기획된 교육 프로그램 및 도서관 서비스 활동을 통하여 해당 교육공동체에 능동적으로 참여하지 않으면 안 된다. 학교도서관이 제공하는 프로그램 및 활동은 해당 지역사회 및 학교의 교육목적에 부합해야 하기 때문에 세계적으로 지역에 따라 다양하게 나타난다(3.5.4 지역사회 협력 참조).

학교도서관 프로그램 및 활동에 사용되는 용어들도 세계적으로 다양하다. 예를 들면 독서능력 개발에 대해서도 '독서 증진', '독서 확장', '자발적 독서', '여가선용 독서', '취미 독서' 등의 용어가 있다. 그러나 용어를 어떻게 사용하든 독서 동기가 부여된 유능한 독자를 개발하는 일은 세계적으로 학교도서관 프로그램 및 활동의 중요한 부분이다.

〈사례〉

아프리카 나미비아의 독서 마라톤 프로그램은 어린이들에게 자신의 언어(나미비아에는 13종의 문어 언어가 존재함)로 된 이야기를 제공함으로써 독서문화를 증진시키고 있다. 또한 각 학교와 도서관을 위해 각 언어로 된 어린이책의 출판을 장려하고 있다.

다른 지역에서 이루어지는 용어관련 텍스트도 정보 이용과 관련이 있다. 그러한 활동은 예전에는 서지 교육(도서관의 텍스트와 시스템 이용방법에 관한 교육), '이용자 교육'(이용자들에게 도서관 및 서비스를 이해하도록 돕는 여러 수단과 방법)이라고 불렀으며, 지금은 '정보 리터러시', '정보 조사'와 관련하여 더욱 확대되고 있다. 지금까지 도서관과 관련된 전형적인 정보 이용교육은 시대를 내려오면서 변화되어왔다. 즉, 1960년대와 1970년대에는 소스자료 접근, 1980년대 까지는 검색 루트 탐색, 1990년대 초 까지는 과정(프로세스) 접근 등으로 변화되었다(Kuhlthau, 2004). 과정접근은 문제해결이라는 관점에서 정보에 대한 사고(思考)와 정보의 이용을 강조한 것이다. 이는 도구적 지식, 정보 소스, 탐색 전략과 같은 이전의 여러 접근방법에 대한 지식을 폐기하는 것이 아니라, 사고력 향상 및 문제해결 능력의 측면에서 최적 탐색 방법에 대한 지식을 강화하는 것이다.

5.2 프로그램 및 활동

학교도서관은 학교의 교수 학습에 필수적인 요소이다. 학교도서관은 또한 학생들의 연대의식, 다양한 학습 참여, 공동체와의 폭넓은 관계 형성 등 학교의 교육사회적 목적에 기여한다. 학교도서관의 목적은 리터러시 향상, 교과과정 기반 학습, 시민 정신 배양 등 학교의 목적과 맥을 같이해야 한다. 학교도서관이 학교의 교육목적에 기여하는 정도는 학교도서관의 접근 가능한 자료와 인력에 달려있다.

〈사례〉

헝가리에서는 도시 근교에 살면서 시내에서 공부하는 많은 학생들을 위해 학교와 가정 간 "셔틀"을 운영한다. 대중교통이 불편하면 학생들은 등·하교를 전후하여 기다리는 시간이 많게 된다. 많은 학교도서관들은 이러한 상황을 해소하기 위해 학교 수업 시작 전과 종료 시간 후에도 학생들이 이용할 수 있도록 도서관을 연장 운영하고 있다. 그 결과 학생들은 도서관이라는 문화 공동체 안에서 안전하게 시간을 보낼 수 있다. 이는 또한 사서교사와 학생들 사이의 인간관계를 돈독하게 하는 기회를 제공해 준다.

도서관 서비스와 활동은 학교도서관 전문사서가 교장, 부장교사, 수석교사, 기타 교내 교육 전문가, 담임교사, 지원 인력 및 학생들과 협력하여 설계해야 한다. 학교도서관 전문사서가 자료 기반의 교육 설계와 적정 교육 자료의 선택에 있어 담임교사들과의 협력하지 않는다면 문헌 조사연구를 요하는 학생들의 학업성취를 도울 수 없게 된다.

학교도서관 전문사서의 교육적 업무는 다음과 같은 핵심적 활동에 초점을 맞추어야 한다.

- 리터러시 및 독서능력 향상
- 미디어 및 정보 리터러시(예: 정보 리터러시, 정보기술, 정보경쟁력, 정보 달인, 미디어 리터러시, 트랜스 리터러시, 트랜스미디어 리터러시)
- 탐구기반 학습(예: 문제기반 학습, 비판적 사고)
- 정보기술 통합
- 교사들을 위한 전문성 개발
- 문학 및 문화 감상능력

학교도서관의 핵심적 활동에 관련한 조사 연구는 학교도서관 활동의 기본 틀을 제시하고 있다. 학교도서관의 핵심적 교육활동은 학교의 프로그램 및 그 우선순위에 달려 있으며 각 학년별 교과과정의 진행정도를 반영해야 한다.

5.3 리터러시 및 독서능력 증진

학교도서관은 학생들의 문자해독 능력과 독서능력 개발을 지원해야 한다. 독서 수준과 학습의 결과 사이에는 직접적 연관성이 있고, 읽기 자료의 접근성은 독서 능력 향상의 핵심적 요소임이 밝혀졌다(Krashen, 2004). 학교도서관 사서들이 이용자에게 읽기자료를 제공할 때는 독자들의 개인적 선호, 독자들의 자료선택권을 인정하고 실용적이고 융통성 있게 안내해야 한다. 스스로 자신이 읽을 자료를 선택할 기회가 있는 학생들이 장기적으로 시험성적이 향상된다는 것이 밝혀졌다. 읽기 자료를 스스로 선택할 때 어휘, 문법, 글쓰기, 말하기 능력이 향상된다. 제2외국어를 배우는 학생들은 해당 외국어에 관한 좋은 책들에 접근할 수 있을 때 언어에 대한 이해력이 풍부해진다. 오디오 북과 같은 대안적 읽기 자료에 접근할 수 있는 독자들은 독서능력이 향상되고, 독서에 대한 태도가 개선된다.

책 읽기에 장애를 가진 학생들에게는 대안자료가 필요하며, 경우에 따라서는 특수 독서 장비가 필요하다. 학교도서관 사서는 이러한 학생들의 독서 수요를 지원하기 위하여 특수교육 전문 교사들과 협력해야 한다. 학교도서관 사서는 또한 일반 교과교사들과 협력하여 지역적, 국가적 표준을 충족할 수 있는 교실 독서를 지원해야 한다(예: 독서 프로젝트에서 지정하는 추천도서 및 나라의 언어 표준에 적합한 추천도서).

학교도서관은 다양한 인쇄자료 및 디지털 자료를 보유함으로써 심미적이고도 자극적인 독서환경을 제공해야 하며, 묵독에서부터 그룹토론 및 창의적 작업에 이르기까지 광범위한 지적 활동의 기회를 제공해야 한다. 학교도서관 사서는 자유로운 대출이 가능하도록 정책적으로 보장해야 하며, 가능한 한 지연 반납 또는 자료 분실에 대한 벌금이나 페널티를 부과하지 않는 것이 좋다.

리터러시 기반의 독서 장려 및 미디어를 즐기도록 격려하는 활동은 학생들을 학습은 물론 사회문화적 활동에 참여하게 하는 것이다. 학교도서관 장서는 지역적, 국제적 측면에서 인쇄자료 및 창작 자료를 포함, 학교 공동체 구성원들의 국가적, 문화적, 윤리적 정체성을 반영하는 자료를 구비하도록 노력해야 한다. 학교도서관 사서는 학생들이 교실 및 도서관에서 스스로 읽기 자료를 선택하고, 그들이 읽은 바를 상호 토론하고 공유하는 기회를 갖도록 이끌어야 한다. 신간 소설, 비소설 자료는 북 토크, 도서관 전시, 웹페이지 탑재 등을 통하여 교사들과 학생들에게 적극 알려야 한다. 리터러시와 독서 능력 증진을 위한 특별 행사는 도서관 내에서 또는 학교 전체적으로 전시, 작가 방문, 국제 리터러시의 날 등과 같은 여러 항목의 프로파일로 개최할 수 있다. 이러한 특별 활동을 통하여 학부모들은 학교행사에 참여할 기회를 갖게 된다. 학부모들은 가정 독서 프로그램 및 낭독 프로그램을 통하여 자녀들의 리터러시 개발 활동에 참여할 수 있다.

〈사례〉

프랑스에서는 바벨리오 챌린지 프로그램으로 책읽기를 독려하고 사회적 문자해독 네트워크를 통하여 어린이들의 독해력을 개발하고 있다. www.babelio.com

〈사례〉

영국의 공인 도서관정보 전문교육원(CILIP)에서 주관하는 카네기 및 그리너웨이 메달은 숨어 있는 좋은 독서증진 프로그램으로 매년 선정된 책과 관련, 포상을 시행함으로써 영국 전역에 걸쳐 독서활동을 독려하고 있다.

www.carnegiegreenaway.org.uk/shadowingsite/index.php

〈사례〉

이탈리아에서 2004년 하멜린 문화협회가 설립하고 볼로냐의 "살라 보사(Sala Borsa)"도서관이 후원하는 재너두 프로젝트(the Xanadu Project)는 고등학교 학생들(13~16세)을 대상으로 개발한 독서프로젝트로 최근에는 이탈리아의 다른 지역에서도 8학년까지 시행되고 있다. 이 프로젝트는 독서에 대한 자극과 반응, 사고력 극대화, 네트워킹, 도서, 만화, 영화, 음악 감상 등을 지원한다.

www.bibliotecasalaborsa.it/ragazzi/xanadu2014/biblio.php

5.4 미디어 및 정보 리터러시 교육

학교도서관이 두 번째로 해야 할 일은 끊임없이 변화하는 세계 속에서 학생들에게 학습자 및 시민으로서 정보에 대한 책임의식과 윤리의식을 확립하도록 돕는 것이다. 2007년도 유네스코 문서, 정보 리터러시의 이해: 정책 결정자를 위한 독본(Forest Woody Horton, Jr. 작성)은 정보 리터러시에 관한 개념 및 정의에 대하여, 그리고 정보 리터러시가 비공식, 공식학습에서 수행하는 역할에 대하여 알기 쉽게 설명하고 있다. 유네스코는 또한 미디어와 정보 리터러시(MIL)의 개념, 우리의 개인생활 및 민주주의 사회에서 미디어와 정보자원의 중요성에 대한 인식을 제고시키고 있다. 2011년도 유네스코 문서, 교사를 위한 미디어 및 정보 리터러시 커리큘럼[MIL]은 미디어 리터러시와 정보 리터러시가 동시에 고려되어야 하는 이유를 설명하고 있다. 교사를 위한 커리큘럼의 기본 틀은 교수와 학습에 있어 다음과 같은 영역이 있음을 설명하고 있다.

1) 민주적, 사회적 참여를 위한 정보와 미디어의 이해
2) 미디어의 텍스트 및 정보원의 평가(누가 누구를 위해 창안했으며 어떤 메시지를 담고 있는지)
3) 미디어 및 정보의 생산과 이용

학교도서관 사서들은 교수학습용 미디어 및 정보기술에 대하여 체계적인 기본지식을 갖추는 것이 중요하다는 것을 인정하고 있다. 그들은 또한 교과교사들과의 협업을 통하여 학생들의 정보기술능력을 향상시킬 수 있다. 미디어 및 정보 리터러시 커리큘럼을 기반으로 한 교육프로그램의 목적은 학생들을 정보사회에서의 책임감과 윤리의식을 갖추도록 개발하는 것이다. 정보 리터러시를 갖춘 학생들은 자기 주도적 학습능력을 갖게 된다. 학생들은 정보의 필요성을 인식하고 아이디어의 세계에 능동적으로 참여할 수 있어야 한다. 그들은 문제를 해결하는데 자신감을 갖고 신뢰성 있는 관련 정보를 찾아서 활용하는 방법을 터득할 수 있어야 한다. 그들은 정보의 접근 및 학습커뮤니케이션을 위한 정보기술도구를 운용할 수 있어야 한다. 그들은 복잡한 해답을 요하는 문제 또는 정답이 없는 문제 상황에서도 정보기술을 원만하게 이용할 수 있어야 한다. 그들은 수준 높은 작업을 수행하면서 우수한 학습결과물을 만들어 낼 수 있어야 한다. 정보 리터러시를 갖춘 학생들은 유연해야 하고, 변화 적응능력이 있어야 하며, 개별 또는 그룹 활동 모두 저마다 기능을 발휘할 수 있어야 한다.

〈사례〉

프랑스에서는 학생들이 인터넷을 책임감 있게 이용하도록 훈련을 받는다.
http://eduscol.education.fr/internet-responsable

〈사례〉

프랑스에서는 학교도서관 사서를 위한 교육훈련과정에서 미디어 및 정보 리터러시에 대한 벤치마킹 및 실행과정이 있다.

http://media.eduscol.education.fr/file/Pacifi/85/4/Reperes_Pacifi_157854.pdf

5.5 탐구기반 학습모델

여러 나라, 여러 지역, 많은 학교도서관들은 수요조사에 바탕을 두고 수요자의 맥락에서 미디어 및 정보 리터러시를 개발하는 교육모델을 성공적으로 수립해왔다. 탐구에 기반을 둔 학습모델을 창안하기 위해서는 다년간 연구, 개발, 실험을 거쳐야 한다. 교육당국이 추천한 모델이 없는 학교들은 자체적으로 모델을 개발하기보다 그들 커리큘럼의 목적 및 학습결과에 가장 근접하는 모델을 선택하는 것이 좋다. 탐구기반 학습에 바탕을 둔 교육모델의 사례는 부록 C에 제시되어 있다.

탐구기반 교육모델은 학생들에게 콘텐트의 각 영역 간, 그리고 학술환경에서 실제 생활로 전환이 가능한 학습과정을 제공하기 위하여 주로 과정적 접근법을 이용한다. 이 모델에는 몇 가지 유의해야 할 개념들이 있다.

- 학생이 정보로부터 의미를 구축할 것
- 학생이 과정적 접근법을 통해 양질의 학습결과물을 만들어 낼 것.
- 학생이 독립적으로(자기 주도적으로) 그리고 그룹의 일원으로 작업하는 방법을 터득할 것.
- 학생이 정보와 정보기술을 책임감 있게 윤리적으로 이용할 것.

탐구기반 교육모델은 학습 필요성 탐구 및 평생학습 능력, 즉 기획, 자료 수집, 자료의 선택 및 조직화, 작업과정, 표현 및 공유, 그리고 평가 기술을 통합하는 과정이다. 과정 기반 학습모델은 자기 주도적 학습능력(예: 메타 인지능력) 및 협업능력을 길러준다. 이러한 능력은 주제별 맥락 속에서 교과과정에서 도출된 토픽과 문제들을 해결하는 최선의 능력이다.

기획능력은 어떠한 조사연구나 업무, 프로젝트, 에세이 쓰기, 토픽 해결 등에 필수적인 능력이다. 탐구의 시작 단계부터 기획활동은 적절한 질문의 구성, 정보 자원의 인식, 정보 탐색 전략, 그리고 합리적인 타임라인 구성 등을 정하는 일이다. 이러한 조사과정을 통해 학생들은 예기치 못했던 도전 및 장애요인에 대응하여 계획을 수정할 수 있을 것이다.

자료수집 능력은 정보검색의 기본능력이다. 여기에는 문자와 숫자의 이해능력, 컴퓨터 데이터베이스와 온라인 인터넷에서 여러 가지 다른 정보에 대해 탐색 전략을 구사하는 능력, 색인이나 정보원을 이용하는 능력이 포함된다. 정보원 연구에 더하여 정보를 생산하는 능력은 조사, 인터뷰, 실험, 관찰을 포함한다.

자료의 선택 및 조직화 능력은 판단 능력과 사고 능력이라 할 수 있다. 선택행위는 요구에 초점을 두고 관련되는 적정 정보를 찾아내는 능력이다. 자료의 권위, 완전성, 적시성, 정확성, 관점 등과 같은 기준은 학생들이 정보를 찾는데, 그리고 찾은 정보에 대하여 윤리적 의사결정을 내리는 데 도움을 준다.

정보처리과정은 다양한 정보원을 이용하여 통합하고, 추론하고, 결론을 도출하여 선행 지식에 추가적 연관관계를 구축하는 것이다. 이러한 과정을 통하여 학생들은 그들이 수집한 정보를 이해하고, 변형하여 자신의 지식으로 종합하는 능력을 개발하게 된다.

표현과 공유를 통해 아이디어를 명쾌하게 소통하는 창의적인 결과물, 설정한 목적이 반영된 결과물, 청중의 이해를 효과적으로 끌어내는, 발표를 감안한 높은 수준의 결과물을 도출할 수 있다.

평가 능력은 조사연구의 과정과 결과를 아울러 평가하는 것을 말한다. 학생들은 그들의 노력과 성취목표에 대하여 임계점까지(끝까지) 생각할 수 있는 능력을 갖추어야 한다. 학생들은 본래의 계획대비 그들이 이룩한 결과물을 연계시킬 수 있어야 하며, 그 결과물이 목표를 달성했는지, 그 학습계획의 강점과 약점은 무엇인지, 개선할 점은 무엇인지, 향후 과제에 대한 시사점은 무엇인지 판단할 수 있어야 한다.

자기주도 학습능력은 평생학습능력 개발의 핵심요소이다. 학생들은 조사연구의 과정을 통해서 사고능력과 학습과정을 터득하고(예: 메타인지능력), 자신이 터득한 지식을 활용하여 학습의 목표를 설정하고, 그 목표를 달성하도록 학습과정을 관리할 수 있다. 자기주도 학습자는 자신의 필요에 따라 정보미디어를 활용할 수 있고 의문에 대한 해답을 찾을 수 있으며 대안을 모색하고 다른 관점들과 비교하여 평가할 수 있다. 그들은 정보와 정보원 그리고 도서관의 복잡한 조직구조를 인지하고 필요할 경우 도움을 요청할 수 있다.

협업능력은 학생들이 다른 친구들과 다양한 정보원 및 기술을 활용하여 집단적 학습을 함께 수행할 때 개발된다. 학생들은 다양한 의견을 건설적으로 평가하는 방법과 서로의 의견을 반영하여 조정하는 방법을 배우게 된다. 학생들은 여러 가지 다른 의견들을 인지하고 다른 사람의 의견 및 학습 스타일을 존중하는 태도를 보인다. 학생들은 그들 사이의 다른 점을 반영하여 함께 프로젝트를 창안하고, 개인들의 과업을 종합하여 완성된 프로젝트를 만드는데 기여한다.

탐구기반의 학습과정은 정보의 이용에 있어 단순히 정보의 짜깁기나 특정주제에 대한 증거 탐색 및 특정 질문에 대한 해답을 구하는 정도를 넘어선다. 이는 정보 탐색의 과정은 물론 조사연구의 결과물을 창출하는 과정, 즉 정보를 종합적으로 인지하는 과정이다. 정보 조사학습은 일상적이고 표준화된 작업이 아니라 매우 심사숙고하는 인지적 영역이라 할 수 있다.

탐구기반의 학습법을 활용하고자 할 경우 학교도서관 사서들과 교사들은 도서관의 규모나 장서의 성격 및 정보기술 수준에 관계없이 조사연구학습의 영향, 방향, 학습 호기심을 유발하는 발견 학습에 대한 동기부여 방법 등 제반 문제에 직면하게 된다. 과정 기반 모델은 학생들에게 탐구기반학습이라는 시각을 열어 줌으로써 발견학습 및 개인능력 성장의 경험과 기회를 제공해 준다. 이 방법을 효과적으로 수행하면, 조사연구를 통하여 배우는 학생들은 탐험 및 위험관리, 호기심과 동기부여, 적극적 창의적인 사고력, 실제생활과의 연계 능력 및 대중에 대한 설명능력을 갖출 수 있다.

학습과정 모델은 교육학 및 문헌정보학 분야 연구에 바탕을 두고 있다. 교육학 분야로부터는 학습이론을 이용하고, 문헌정보학으로부터는 정보추구행태이론을 이용한다. 예를 들면 교육학에서는 다양한 학습자들의 호기심, 학생들의 인지능력 및 그들의 기존경험과 지식을 끌어내는 방법적 지식을 이용할 수 있다. 또한 학습자들이 지식을 능동적으로 축적하고 구성해 나간다는 구성주의 학습개념과 학습자들이 정보를 활용하여 그들의 사고방식과 경험에 변화를 일으킨다는 경험주의 교육개념을 원용할 수 있다. 문헌정보학에서는 이용자들이 정보이용과정에서 수준별 막연한 정보 필요성 개념으로부터 질문과 요구를 구체화하는 정보탐색과정에 대한 지식, 이용자들이 탐색과정에서 그들의 정보문제와 도서관 정보시스템의 실제를 이해하고 보다 성공적으로 정보를 탐색하도록 하는 기법들을 이용할 수 있다.

학교에서 이루어지는 여타 학습프로그램과 마찬가지로 탐구기반 학습활동은 학생들이 학습을 순차적이고 지속적으로 개선해가도록 설계해야 한다. 학교도서관 사서는 학교에 존재하는 총체적 미디어와 정보기술 및 전략에 따라 조사연구과정 학습지도를 체계적으로 할 수 있도록 주도적인 역할을 해야 한다.

탐구기반 교수학습 모델을 도입하지 않은 국가나 지역의 학교도서관 사서는 교과교사들과 협력하여 학교 경영자에게 그러한 교수학습 모델의 도입을 요청해야 한다. 교사들과 학생들은 그들이 원하는 모델을 적용함으로써 학교의 목적과 지역사회의 요구에 부응할 수 있다. 하지만, 어떤 모델을 적용할 경우라도 주의할 것은 반드시 충분한 사전 연습을 해야 한다는 것이다. 학습모델에 대한 이론적 근거를 이해하지 못한 상태에서 어떤 학습모델을 적용한다면 그 모델은 효력을 발휘할 수 없을 것이다.

〈사례〉

스웨덴의 웁살라에서는 중등학교학생들이 환경오염에 대한 이야기를 읽음으로써 탐구기반 프로젝트를 시작한다. 그 이야기는 독서 그룹별 토론을 거친다. 학생들은 각기 그 책으로부터 환경감시, 지구온난화, 질병과 같은 주제를 조사한다. 학생들은 처음에는 광범위한 정보를 탐색하고, 이어서 심도 있는 정보를 탐색하여 각기 초점이 다른 특수한 토픽에 대하여 조사연구결과를 구성한다(예: 정부는 스마트폰을 통해 사람들을 어떻게 모니터할 수 있는지와 같은 아주 구체적인 환경감시에 관한 것). 그 프로젝트의 최종 결과물은 학생들이 수집한 자료와 포트폴리오 파일을 이용하여 일종의 과제물로 쓰는 에세이이다.

5.6 교수학습 기술의 통합적 적용

지금까지 학교도서관에 관한 연구는 도서관의 역할이 정보기술 도구 및 정보기술을 활용한 교육인프라를 제공하는 점에서 매우 중요하다는 것을 밝히고 있다. 정보기술은 도서관 및 자료의 범위를 교실과 교실 밖으로 확장하는데 도움을 준다. 학교도서관 사서는 학생들이 온라인을 이용하여 인터넷 정보원을 이용하도록 도와주고, 데이터베이스와 그 생산 도구들을 이용하여 학습할 수 있도록 도와주어야 한다. 학교도서관 사서는 학교 내 정보기술 전문가가 있을 경우 그 전문가와 협업하여 사서와 정보기술전문가의 역할을 분명히 정의하고 학교 내에서 교사들과 학생들에게 정보기술을 활용한 도서관 서비스와 프로그램을 제공하는데 빈틈이나 불편이 없도록 해야 한다.

5.7 교사의 전문성 개발

학교도서관은 교사들에게 새로운 자료와 정보기술, 새로운 교과과정, 그리고 새로운 교육전략과 관련한 전문성 개발 기회를 제공함으로써 교사들을 지원해야 한다. 학교도서관 사서는 동료교사들과 파트너로서 업무를 수행하면서 여러 가지 방법으로 교사들의 전문성 개발을 비공식적으로 지원할 수 있다.

- 교사들에게 주제 지식을 확장하고 교수방법을 개선할 수 있는 정보원 제공
- 여러 가지 다른 교육 평가에 관한 정보자료 제공
- 교실 또는 도서관 수업에서 행하는 수업기획에 함께 일함.
- 도서관을 접근점으로 하여 도서관 상호대차나 디지털 네트워크를 통해 보다 광범위한 정보 자료 제공

5.8 학교도서관 사서의 교육적 역할

학교도서관 전문사서가 학생들에게 최적 학습경험을 제공하기 위해서는 교과교사들과 협력수업을 시행하는 것이 좋다. 사서와 교사의 협력수업은 각 교사 팀원들이 각기 전문영역을 담당하여 전체 교수 학습활동을 설계하고 실행하는 것이 바람직하다.

학교도서관 사서와 교과교사들이 협업하는 방법으로는 학습지원, 병렬학습, 보완학습, 팀티칭 등 4가지 방법이 있다.

1) 학습 지원 - 한 교사가 리더의 역할을 맡고, 다른 교사는 학습자 주

변에 머물면서 1대 1로 학생들을 보조적으로 가르친다. 한 사람은 가르치고 한사람은 보조하는 방식이다.

2) 병렬학습 - 둘 또는 그 이상의 교사들이 협업하여 교실 또는 도서관에서 여러 다른 파트의 학생집단을 동시에 맡아 순차적으로 진행하는 방법이다. 일명 '정거장 학습법'으로 알려진 방법이다.

3) 보완학습 - 한 교사가 다른 교사들이 가르친 내용을 보다 더 강화시켜주는 방법이다. 예를 들면 한 교사가 다른 교사가 설명한 내용을 표현을 달리하여 또는 모범 노트 기법을 이용하여 설명하는 방식이다.

4) 팀티칭 - 둘 또는 그 이상의 교사들이 협업하여 교실 또는 도서관에서 전체 학생들을 대상으로 수업설계, 수업진행, 평가, 그리고 책임을 분담하는 방식으로 수업책임, 리더십, 비용 등 책임을 동등하게 분담한다.

협력수업에 대한 이러한 접근법은 각기 수업의 콘텐트, 전달, 평가와 관련하여 참여 교사들이 협업하여 계획함으로써 협력학습의 효과를 강화하는 방법이다. 학교도서관 사서와 교과교사들 간 수업계획의 협업은 또한 어떤 상황에서는 교육의 질을 강화시킬 수 있으며, 학교도서관 사서는 도서관이나 교실에서 학생들의 단독 교사로서 역할을 수행할 수 있다. 통합교과적인 또는 학생들의 흥미와 요구에 관련되는 미디어와 정보 리터러시 수업에는 협업이 필수적이다.

참고문헌

Asselin, M., & Doiron, R. (2013). *Linking literacy and libraries in global communities.* London: Ashgate.

Gordon, C., & Lu, Y-L. (2008). "I hate to read-Or do I?": Low achievers and their reading. *School Library Research*, 11. Retrieved from www.ala.org/aasl/slmr/volume11/gordon-lu

Hughes-Hassell, S., Barkley, H. A., & Koehler, E. (2009). Promoting equity in children's literacy instruction: Using a critical race theory framework to examine transitional books. *School Library Research*, 12. Retrieved from www.ala.org/aasl/slmr/volume12/hughes-hassell-barkley-koehler

Krashen, S. D. (2004). *The power of reading: Insights from the research* (2nd ed.). Westport, CT: Libraries Unlimited.

Kuhlthau, C.C. (2004). *Seeking meaning: A process approach to library and information service* (2nd ed.). Westport, CT: Libraries Unlimited.

Markless, S. (Ed.). (2009). *The innovative school librarian: Thinking outside the box.* London: Facet Publishing. [See Chapters 7, pp.127-142 Becoming integral to teaching and learning.]

Eduscol [Ministry of Education, France]. (2012). *Vademecum vers des centres de connaissances et du culture* [Short guide to knowledge centres and culture]. Retrieved from http://eduscol.education.fr/cid60332/-vers-des-centres-de-connaissances-et-de-culture-le-vade-mecum.html

Trelease, J. (2013). *The readaloud handbook* (7th ed.). New York: Penguin Books.

Villa, R. A., Thousand, J. S., & Nevin, A. I. (2008). *A guide to co-teaching: Practical tips for facilitating student learning* (2nd ed.). Thousand Oaks, CA: Corwin Press/Council for Exceptional Children.

제6장

학교도서관의 평가 및 홍보

학교도서관은 문맹퇴치, 교육, 정보, 그리고 경제, 사회, 문화발전을 위한 모든 장기적 전략수립에 필수적인 요소이다.

-학교도서관 선언에서

6.1 개관

많은 연구에서 정보 자원이 잘 구비된 학교도서관과 유능한 사서들이 근무하는 학교도서관은 학생들의 학업 성취에 긍정적인 영향을 미치는 것으로 나타났다. 예로는 LRS(2015) 미국 학교도서관의 영향에 관한 연구(www.lrs.org/data-tools/school-libraries/impact-studies) 및 윌리엄스와 모리슨(2013)의 영국 학교도서관의 영향에 관한 연구(www.scottishlibraries.org/storage/sectors/schools/SLIC_RGU_Impact_of_School_Libraries_2013.pdf)가 있다. 하지만 이 연구들은 학교도서관계에 널리 알려져 있지 않아 전반적인 공감을 얻지 못하고 있다. 이에 따라 세계 도처의 수많은 학교도서관들은 계속적인 운영 축소 압력에 직면하고 있다. 학교도서관의 감축으로 도서관 전문사서가 퇴출되기도 한다. 전문사서가 없으면 교육의 개선과 학생들의 학업성취 촉진제로서 학교도서관의 잠재력은 사라지게 된다.

지난 10여 년 간 학교도서관이 미치는 영향에 관한 연구들은 전일제 학교도서관 전문사서가 근무하는 학교도서관이 학생들의 학업 성취에 강력한 영향을 미친다는 것을 증명해주고 있다. 학생들의 학업 성취에 미치는 학교도서관의 긍정적인 영향으로는 빈곤층, 소수자, 장애학생들의 학업성취에 격차를 줄여준다는 것이다. 학생들의 학업 성취와 관련되는 전문사서의 활동에는 교사와의 협업, 강의, 일정 관리, 이용접근문제, 정보기술 습득, 장서, 예산, 전문성 개발 등이 포함된다. 정보 자원이 잘 갖추어진 학교도서관은 언제든지 학생들과 교사들에게 온라인으로 정보와 서비스에 접근할 수 있도록 해주기 때문에 향후의 도서관 연구에서는 도서관이 어떻게 공간과 시간을 배치할 것이며, 이용을 위한 디지털화의 가능성을 어떻게 평가할 것인가에 대하여 그 방법을 개발할 필요가 있다.

평가는 학교도서관의 프로그램 및 서비스 실행에 필수적인 과정이다. 평가는 의사결정 또는 문제해결(회계책임 관련)의 길을 제시해 준다. 또한 학교도서관에 대한 관련자들의 인식에도 영향을 미치며, 학교도서관(도서관의 변화 발전 관련)에 대한 지원을 끌어낼 수 있다. 평가의 과정은 도서관의 발전방향을 결정하는 데 도움을 주며, 미래 학교도서관의 새로운 비전을 창안하는 데도 영감을 줄 수 있다.

사실 학교도서관의 평가는 학교의 교육계획과 분리하여 실행할 수 없다. 평가 역시 학교 계획과정의 일부이므로 전체적으로 학교경영의 품질보증계획에 포함 되어야 마땅하다.

6.2 학교도서관의 평가 및 실증적 평가 실행

학교도서관과 학교도서관 사서들은 체계적이고 일관된 평가를 받는 일이 별로 없다. 하지만 평가는 도서관의 프로그램과 서비스가 학교의 목적 달성을 지원했는지를 증명하는 데 유용하다. 평가는 학생들과 교사들이 도서관의 프로그램과 서비스가 얼마나 유익한지, 즉 도서관의 유용성을 인지하는 정도를 나타내준다. 또한 평가는 도서관 직원들과 이용자 모두를 위해 도서관 프로그램과 서비스를 설계하는데 도움이 되고 그러한 프로그램과 서비스를 실천하는 촉진제가 될 수 있다.

실증적 평가 실행은 실무 개선을 위한 데이터 수집 및 분석에 초점을 맞추고 있다. 실증적 평가는 일반적으로 그 범위가 좁고, 학교 급별 평가 담당자에 의해 수행되며, 그 결과 실천을 위한 제안사항들이 도출된다. 실증적 평가를 위한 데이터의 수집 및 분석 자료는 온라인 대출목록시스템(OPAC)의 기록, 교육의 형식, 학급, 학년, 주제(실행증거 - 의사결정 데이터), 학생들의 학습 결과물, 학생 및 교사에 대한 설문조사, 학부모(활동실행 증거, 도서관에 영향을 미치는 데이터) 등과 같은 다양한 자료에서 얻는다.

6.3 학교도서관의 평가 방법

학교도서관 평가는 해당 도서관의 환경과 맥락을 고려해야 한다. 전체적 프로그램의 질에 초점을 둔 학교도서관 평가는 대체로 그 평가 분야가 광범위하고, 외부 전문가에 의하여 평가가 이루어지며, 그 결과 품질 등급 순위가 매겨진다(부록 D: 학교도서관 평가 체크리스트 샘플 및 부록 E: 학교장을 위한 학교도서관 평가 체크리스트 참조). 대부분의 학교도서관 평가는 학교도서관 사서에 의한 자체 평가연구를 포함한다. 학교도서관의 평가에는 또 기타 여러 가지 요소들이 포함되는데, 프로그램의 질 뿐 아니라 이해관계자들의 인식, 프로그램의 내용, 프로그램이 미치는 영향 등이다. 학교도서관의 평가에서 언제나 기본이 되는 것은 평가를 뒷받침하는 실증자료이다.

6.3.1 프로그램의 질

전체적인 프로그램의 질에 초점을 두는 학교도서관 평가는 보통 장기 프로젝트로 수행되며, 때로는 수년간에 걸친 여러 가지 다양한 활동을 대상으로 한다. 프로그램의 질 평가는 원래 학교의 인정과정이나 주 또는 국가의 표준 문서 등 교육활동의 기본 틀을 짜기 위해 시작된 것이다. 종합 프로그램 평가는 강력한 행정력의 뒷받침과 그 지역의 상담 전문가와 같은 외부 전문가의 참여로 수행되어야 한다. 하지만 평가의 가치는 소요 자원의 한계를 사려 깊게 기획한 부분적 프로그램의 평가로부터 도출될 수 있다. 예를 들면 자체 평가연구에서 학생과 교사들이 도서관 기반의 교육활동에 참여한 비율을 알아보기 위해서는 단기 또는 한 학년도에 걸친 도서관의 교육활동 범위를 살펴보아야 한다. 어떤 기준치 대비 비교연구는 도서관 프로그램 또는 장서나 시설과 같은 서비스의 한 측면에 한정할 수 있다.

6.3.2 이해관계자들의 인식

여러 연구들은 이해관계자들의 인식 평가에 대하여 의미있는 종합적인 사례들을 제시하고 있다. 학교나 교육구청을 넘어서는 연구들이 있는가 하면, 더욱 간단한 대안 연구들도 있다. 그 각각의 예로는 a)지역

교육구내 만족도 조사, b)단위 학교 기반의 조사 및 피드백 활동이 있다.

대부분의 교육구청이나 교육행정당국은 학생, 교사, 학부모를 대상으로 연간 만족도를 조사하여 제시하고 있다. 이는 도서관의 프로그램과 서비스에 관련된 문제점을 발견하는데 매우 유용하다. 처음부터 조사 연구 노력이 성공을 거두기는 어렵겠지만, 이러한 지역 조사활동을 통한 문제점의 도출은 지역 교육구내 학교도서관의 프로그램 및 서비스에 대한 이해관계자들의 인식과 이해를 촉진하는데 매우 중요한 가교의 역할을 할 수 있다.

도서관에 대한 학생들의 인식도 조사는 교내 각 학급단위 조사에 대하여 교장선생님의 협조를 받아야 하며, 조사의 시작 단계에서는 "우리 학교도서관의 좋은 점이 무엇인지?" 그리고 "더 좋은 도서관을 만들기 위하여 우리는 무엇을 해야 하는지?"와 같은 질문을 던져본다. 조사에서 얻은 데이터의 분석 결과는 교사, 경영관리자, 학부모들과 공유해야 한다. 중등학교 수준에 알맞은 접근법은 각 학급별 학생들의 대의원 회의를 구성하여 학교도서관의 서비스와 자원에 대하여 피드백을 받아보는 방법이 있다. 여러 가지 피드백의 과정을 통하여 학생들은 학교도서관에 대하여 더 좋은 것 또는 별로인 것이 무엇인지, 어떻게 하면 학교도서관이 학생들을 위하여 더 좋은 공간이 될 것인지에 대하여 당면 이슈를 인식하고 표현할 수 있는 안목을 갖게 될 것이다. 이 두 가지 방법 모두 도서관의 프로그램과 서비스의 특수한 한 부분으로서 도서관 평가에 손쉽게 적용할 수 있을 것이다.

6.3.3 프로그램의 내용

프로그램의 내용에 초점을 둔 학교도서관 평가는 넓은 범위이거나 좁은 범위에서 1회 또는 지속적으로 수행할 수 있다. 자체평가는 도서관을 통한 교육활동을 한 학기 또는 몇 년에 걸쳐 학습 결과를 분석할 수 있도록 설계할 수 있을 것이다. 도서관의 교육활동을 통한 학습의 결과는 하나 또는 그 이상의 교과과정에서 나온 학습결과와 비교해 볼 수 있을 것이다.

또 다른 접근방법은 교과교사의 핵심 그룹이나 주제별 담당 부서장들이 도서관 기반의 교육활동을 통해 달성하고자 하는 학습결과물이 무엇인지를 조사하는 것이다. 최선의 결과를 도출하기 위해서(예: 풍부한 토론 및 진지한 관찰), 최선의 핵심 그룹을 조직하고, 학교도서관 사서가 아닌 제3의 인사의 도움을 받아, 즉 다른 학교의 사서 또는 교육청의 장학관과 같은 인사의 도움을 받아 평가를 하는 것이다.

6.3.4 프로그램의 영향평가

학교도서관의 영향평가는 교육의 '부가 가치'라는 개념에 초점을 두고, 학교도서관 활동이 학생들의 학습에 기여하는 정도를 알아낼 수 있도록 설계해야 한다. 여기서 학생들로부터 그들이 무엇을 배웠는지를 알아내는 것이 중요하다. 예를 들면 조사평가에서는 학생들의 학습 주제에 대한 이해의 정도, 조사연구 진행방법에 대한 그들의 인지도, 그들의 학습 중요성에 대한 인식 등을 알아낼 수 있어야 한다. 또한, 학습연구 프로젝트가 학생들의 학습에 어느 정도 영향을 미치는지를 파악하기 위해서는 도서관 파워 프로젝트(the Library Power project)(Oberg, 1999)에서와 같이 초등학교 학생들을 대상으로 1학년부터 6학년까지 프로젝트 수행 종료 시에 다음과 같은 질문으로 인터뷰를 하는 것이 좋다.

- 네가 참여한 프로젝트에 대하여 말해주겠니? 책과 컴퓨터는 어떻게 이용했니? 잘 된 점은 무엇이고, 문제점은 무엇인지?
- 시작은 어떻게 했어? 중간에는 무얼 했지? 어떻게 끝마쳤어? 시작, 중간, 끝날 때 각각 어떻게 느꼈어?
- 무엇을 배웠니; 무엇이 기억에 남니? 학교 밖 프로젝트에도 참여했니? 학교 밖 프로젝트는 어땠었니?

이와 비슷하게 중등학교에서 사용하는 접근방법으로는 학교도서관의 영향 측정(SLIM: the Student Learning Impact Measure(Todd, Kuhlthau & Heinstrom, 2005)이라는 질문지가 있다. 프로젝트의 시작, 중간, 종료의 3시점에서 학생들에게 다음과 같은 질문에 답하도록 한다.

- 해당 주제에 대하여 생각해 보고, 아는 바를 쓰시오.
- 이 주제에 얼마나 관심이 있는지?
- 이 주제에 대하여 얼마나 알고 있는지?
- 지난 연구 프로젝트에서 가장 쉽게 알아낸 것은 무엇인지?
- 지난 연구 프로젝트에서 가장 수행하기 어려웠던 점은 무엇인지?
- 이 프로젝트를 수행하면서 배운 점은 무엇인지?(이 질문은 프로젝트가 끝났을 때 할 것)

또한 다음과 같은 학생들의 학습에 대한 또 다른 측면들도 인터뷰, 질문지, 학습기록, 또는 조사 집단을 통하여 알아볼 수 있다.

- 자료 찾기, 신뢰성, 가치, 정보의 연관성을 인지하는 능력
- 신뢰성 있는, 잘 정보화된 결과물을 창안하는 능력
- 다른 사람의 디지털 자료를 책임성 있게 활용하는 능력

인터뷰 질문 응답 또는 질문지를 통한 학생들의 응답을 분석하는 일은 학교도서관 사서 및 교사들에게 시간 소모적인 일일 것이다. 그러나 이러한 작업은 학생들이 어떻게 지식을 습득하고, 교육과정의 내용을 어떻게 이해하는지 평가할 수 있을 뿐 아니라 학교 및 학교를 넘어서는 학교 밖 업무처리에도 중요한 정보취급 및 정보처리 과정 능력을 가늠해 볼 수 있을 것이다. 탐구학습 과정에서 토론에 참가하는 학생들은 그들 서로간의 이해를 도울 수 있고, 서로 모니터함으로써 각자 자신의 학습과정에 적용해볼 수 있다.

6.3.5 실증적 평가 실행

실증적 평가 실행은 의사결정을 위한 데이터 이용에서 전반적으로 적용되는 통합적인 접근방법이다. 학교도서관에서는 세 가지 종류의 증거 데이터를 종합할 수 있는데, 첫째는 'FOR practice', 즉 수행을 위한 데이터로 수행을 위한 정보를 공식적으로 조사 연구하여 얻는 데이터이고, 두 번째로는 'IN practice', 즉 실제 수행과정에서 실행을 진행하는 가운데 산출되는 부분적 데이터이며, 세 번째는 'OF practice', 즉 실행 후의 증거들, 이용자 보고, 이용자가 작성한 데이터로 학교도서관 사서들의 수행결과를 나타내는 데이터들이다(Todd, 2007).

학교도서관 사서들은 그들의 전문교육을 통하여, 그리고 학교도서관의 연구결과 발표된 많은 요약보고서들(예: Haycock, 1992; Kachel et al, 2013)로부터 'FOR practice', 즉 수행을 위한 데이터를 습득한다. 또 학교도서관 사서들은 대출 기록 및 교육활동, 의사결정을 위한 교육활동 스케줄 등 'IN their practice', 즉 업무수행 중에 생성되는, 예를 들면 독서활동 증진을 위한 자료원의 구입 및 모든 학생들에게 탐구학습 기회를 보장하는 계획 수립과 관련한 교육활동 중에 생성되는 증거자료를 이용한다.

6.4 학교도서관 평가의 효과

평가는 지속적인 업무개선 사이클에서 매우 중요한 부분이다. 평가는 도서관의 프로그램 및 서비스를 학교의 목적에 일치하도록 해준다. 평가는 학교도서관의 프로그램과 서비스에서 도출되는 편익이 무엇인지를 학생, 교사, 도서관 직원, 그리고 해당 지역사회에 드러내 보여준다. 평가를 통하여 프로그램 및 서비스 개선에 필요한 실증자료를 확보하고, 도서관 직원들과 이용자들 모두에게 프로그램과 서비스의 가치를 이해할 수 있도록 해준다. 성공적인 평가를 통하여 새로운 프로그램과 서비스를 개발할 뿐 아니라 기존의 프로그램과 서비스를 개선할 수 있다. 평가는 또한 공공관계의 유지 및 도서관의 권익 확보에도 필수적인 과정이다.

6.5 학교도서관의 홍보

홍보의 개념은 도서관과 공중 사이에 호혜적인 관계를 쌓아가는 장기적인 상호 작용 및 전략적 소통에 초점을 맞춘 것이다. -학교도서관과 이해관계자들 사이에서(3.5.4 지역사회 협력 참조)

마케팅 및 이용 촉진은 도서관 이용자들의 욕구와 필요를 충족시키는 보다 직접적인 프로그램 및 서비스에 초점을 맞춘다. 반면에 도서관의 권익 확보는 기본적으로 도서관의 변화대응 조치 및 아이디어와 이슈거리의 발굴 및 개발에 관한 것이다. 장기적으로는 학교도서관의 이해관계자 그룹 및 지원자들(supporters)과 우호적 상호관계를 쌓아갈 필요가 있다. 이것이 곧 학교도서관의 권익을 유지하는 길이다. 이용 촉진, 마케팅, 그리고 권익 옹호를 위해서는 체계적인 계획과 실천이 필요하다. 이용촉진 및 마케팅은 학교도서관 사서들의 업무 중 일부분이다. 또한 학교도서관 사서는 도서관의 권익 옹호에 대한 역할의 일환으로 학교도서관 관련 협의회 같은 단체를 계획하고, 실행하는 일을 수행해야 한다. 학교도서관 이용촉진 및 마케팅의 기본 초점은 도서관의 이용자에게 맞추어야 한다. 학교도서관 권익 옹호의 초점은 의사결정자들 및 의사결정자들에게 영향을 미치는 사람들에게 있으며, 이는 주로 도서관에 대한 재정지원 및 학교도서관 사서의 업무를 지원하는 데 관련된 것이다.

6.5.1 홍보 및 마케팅

이용촉진 홍보는 도서관이 제공하는 서비스에 관하여 이용자에게 알리는 일방향 커뮤니케이션이다. 반면, 마케팅은 도서관 서비스를 잠재 이용자들의 선호와 필요에 맞추고자 하는 쌍방향 커뮤니케이션이다. 학교도서관이 제공하는 서비스와 시설을 능동적으로 개선, 홍보하고 마케팅을 실행함으로써 대상 이용자 집단(학교와 지역사회)이 도서관을 그들의 학습 파트너로, 바람직한 서비스 및 자원제공자로 인식하도록 해야 한다.

학교도서관은 이해관계자들과 협력하여 홍보 및 마케팅계획을 수립해야 한다. 그 계획에는 홍보 마케팅의 목적, 목표달성을 나타내는 세부활동계획, 홍보 및 마케팅활동의 성공여부를 평가하는 방법 등을 포함한다. 이러한 홍보 및 마케팅계획은 매년 평가, 재검토, 개정하여야 한다. 이 계획은 학교도서관의 사서와 학교행정담당자가 적어도 2년에 한 번 전체적으로 철저히 논의하고 재검토해야 한다.

6.5.2 우호적 관계 유지

우호적 관계를 유지하기 위해서는 시간이 경과함에 따라 계획적이고도 끊임없는 노력이 필요하다. 우호적 관계는 홍보 마케팅과도 관련된다. 학교도서관의 우호적 관계 활동은 도서관에 대한 이해를 증진시켜 의사결정자들로부터 지지와 지원을 이끌어내는 것이다. 즉, 도서관에 대한 인식과 이해를 증진시키는 일로 다소 시간이 걸리며 계획적인 노력이 필요하다. 학교도서관의 우호관계 유지 노력은 학교도서관의 이용자라기보다는 의사결정자들 및 그들에게 영향을 미치는 사람들에게 초점을 맞추어야 한다.

우호관계란 지역사회에 관계를 쌓아가는 것이다.

우호관계는 타인들에게도 영향을 준다. 한 연구는 타인에게 영향을 미치는 여섯 가지 일반 원칙을 제시한 바 있다((Cialdini, 2006). 설득의 원칙이라고 불리는 이 원칙은 성공적인 우호관계 유지에 필수적인 사항들로 상호주의, 관심, 권위와 권한, 사회적 물증, 일관된 약속이행, 희소성 등이다.

상호주의와 관심은 인간관계의 형성에 관한 것이다. 사람들은 다른 사람들이 그들을 위해 무언가 일을 해주기 때문에, 또는 서로 호감이 가기 때문에 다른 사람들을 위해 일을 한다. 권위와 권한 그리고 사회적 물증이란 의사결정의 시간적 불확실성에 관한 것이다. 사람들은 보통 권위 있는 사람이 추천한 일이나 다른 사람들이 좋아하는 일이면 그 일을 수행한다. 일관된 약속의 이행과 희소성은 사람들의 행동을 유발하는데 관한 것이다. 사람들은 어떤 일이 그들의 가치관과 일치할 때, 그러한 행동이 그들이 생각하는 가치에 손실을 방지한다고 인식할 때 기꺼이 그 일을 하고자 한다.

우호관계 유지를 위한 프로그램 설계 시 이러한 보편적 원칙을 염두에 두는 것이 좋다. 예를 들면 학교도서관 사서들은 전국도서관협회 소속의 다른 사서들을 살펴보고 그들의 학교도서관 정책 이슈를 이끌어낼 필요가 있다. 다음은 우호관계 유지 계획 수립에 도움이 될 만한 질문들이다.

- 희소성: 학교도서관 사서들이 지원하지 않으면 다른 사서들은 무엇을 잃는가?
- 일관된 약속이행: 그들과 공유하는 가치는 무엇인가?
- 권위와 권한: 그들은 누구의 의견을 존중하는가?
- 사회적 입증: 다른 전국단위 협회소속 사서들은 학교도서관 정책에 무엇을 지원해왔는가?
- 상호주의: 학교도서관 사서는 다른 사서들에 대하여 어떤 문제들을 지원하는가?
- 호감: 다른 사서들에게 얼마나 호감을 갖고, 그 호감을 어떻게 보여줄 수 있는가?

우호관계 유지는 학교도서관 사서들과 그들의 협력그룹이 함께 계획된 길로 나아가는 과정이다. IFLA의 온라인 학습 플랫폼(www.ifla.org/bsla)은 도서관의 우호관계 유지에 관한 자료 및 그 방법에 관한 많은 자료를 제공하고 있다. 이 사이트는 학교도서관의 네트워크 형성에 관한 사례연구, 학교도서관의 법제 변화, 교육개혁 강화기제로서의 학교도서관 개발 등 학교도서관의 우호관계 유지에 관한 특화자료를 포함하고 있다. 우호관계 유지는 학교도서관의 유지 발전에 필수적이다. 우호관계 유지 및 도서관평가는 학교의 모든 구성원들에게 교수 학습의 성과 및 개선을 위한 지원의 필요성을 이해시키는 과정이다.

참고문헌

American Association of School Librarians. (2014). *Advocacy.* Retrieved from www.ala.org/aasl/advocacy

Cialdini, R. B. (2006). *Influence: The psychology of persuasion* (Rev. ed.). New York: Harper Business Books.

Department for Education and Office for Standards in Education, Children's Services and Skills [UK]. (2006). *Improving performance through school self-evaluation and improvement planning.* Retrieved from http://dera.ioe.ac.uk/5986/1/Improving_%20performance%20through%20school%20self-evaluation%20and%20improvement%20planning%20(PDF%20format).pdf

Department for Education and Skills and the School Libraries Working Group [UK]. (2004). *Self-evaluation model: School libraries resource materials.* Retrieved from www.informat.org/schoollibraries/index.html

FADBEN. (2012). *The FADBEN manifesto: Teaching information-documentation and information culture.* Retrieved from http://fadben.asso.fr/2012-FADBEN-Manifesto.html

Haycock, K. (1992). *What works: Research about teaching and learning through the school's library resource center.* Seattle, WA: Rockland Press.

Kachel, D. E., et al. (2013). *School library research summarized: A graduate class project.* Mansfield, PA: Mansfield University. Retrieved from http://sl-it.mansfield.edu/upload/MU-LibAdvoBklt2013.pdf

LRS (Library Research Service, Colorado State Library, Department of Education). (2015). *School libraries impact studies.* Retrieved from www.lrs.org/data-tools/school-libraries/impact-studies/

Mollard, M. (1996). *Les CDI àa l'heure du management* [CDI on time management]. Paris: ÉEcole nationale supéerieure des sciences de l'information et des bibliothèeques.

Oberg, D. (2009). Libraries in schools: Essential contexts for studying organizational change and culture. *Library Trends*, 58(1), 9-25.

Todd, R. (2007). Evidence based practice and school libraries: From advocacy to action. In S. Hughes-Hassell & V. H. Harada (Eds.), *School reform and the school library media specialist* (pp. 57-78). Westport, CT: Libraries Unlimited.

Todd, R. J., & Kuhlthau, C. C. (2005a). Student learning through Ohio school libraries, Part 1: How effective school libraries help students. *School Libraries Worldwide,* 11(1), 63-88.

Todd, R. J., & Kuhlthau, C. C. (2005b). Student learning through Ohio school libraries, Part 2: Faculty perceptions of effective school libraries. *School Libraries Worldwide,* 11(1), 89-110.

Todd, R., Kuhlthau, C., & Heinstrom, J. (2005). SLIM Toolkit. New Brunswick, NJ: Center for International Scholarship in School Libraries, Rutgers University. Retrieved from http://cissl.scils.rutgers.edu/index.html

Todd, R. J., Kuhlthau, C. C., & OELMA. (2004). *Student learning through Ohio school libraries: The Ohio research study.* Columbus, OH: Ohio Educational Library Media Association. Retrieved from www.oelma.org/studentlearning/default.asp

Williams, D., Wavell, C., & Morrison, K. (2013). *Impact of school libraries on learning: Critical review of published evidence to inform the Scottish education community.* Aberdeen, Scotland: Robert Gordon University, Institute for Management, Governance & Society (IMaGeS). Retrieved from www.scottishlibraries.org/storage/sectors/schools/SLIC_RGU_Impact_of_School_Libraries_2013.pdf.

용어해설

본 용어해설은 학교도서관 가이드라인의 검토 및 작성에 기여한 여러 전문가들의 의견에 기초하여 작성한 것임. 도서관 용어에 관련되는 더 많은 정보는 Joan M. Reitz가 작성하고, ABC-CLIO (www.abc-clio.com /ODLIS/odlis_l.aspx)에서 펴낸 ODLIS(Online Dictionary for Library and Information Science) 사전을 참조하기 바람. Libraries Unlimited 출판사에서 펴낸 이 사전의 양장본 및 지장본도 이용가능함.

우호적 관계: 시간 경과에 따라 끊임없는 지원과 이해를 이끌어내기 위한 계획적이고 지속적인 노력

서지교육: 이용자에게 도서관 자료와 시스템을 이용하는 방법을 가르치는 것으로 "BI"라고도 함(도서관 교육; 미디어 및 정보 리터러시; 이용자 교육 참조)

목록: 정보원을 기술하고, 목록에 들어갈 엔트리를 선정하는 과정. 보통

은 서지 기술, 주제 분석, 분류기호 지정, 서가 배열을 위한 도서의 물리적 장비와 관련되는 활동을 포함한다.

자료 순환: 도서관자료의 대출과 반납의 과정. 일정 기간 동안의 대출 총수, 일정 기간 동안 대출된 아이템의 총 대출 회수를 나타내며 보통은 1년을 단위로 한다.

시민 정신: 공동체의 구성원으로서(예: 시민) 권한, 의무, 특권을 가지고, 법적, 정치적으로 인정받은 시민이 지녀야 할 정신. 인간으로서의 기본권 및 책임에 더하여 공동체 내에서의 개인의 품위 및 행동방식까지 포함하는 개념이다.

시민 참여: 공공관심사에 대하여 이슈가 되는 문제들을 인지하고 의견을 표출하는 개인적 또는 집단적 행동을 말함; 즉 공동체의 삶의 질에 있어서 개성을 가지고 살아가는데 필요한 지식, 기능, 가치, 동기 등을 개발하는 것.

윤리 기준: 사서, 도서관 직원, 기타 정보전문직에 종사하는 사람들의 행위와 판단을 가늠하는 일련의 윤리 표준. 보통은 접근에의 평등성, 지적 자유, 비밀 보장, 지적 재산권의 존중, 지적 탁월성, 정확성, 통합성,

공평성, 정중함, 동료 및 이용자에 대한 존중 등을 포함한다.

장서: 도서관이 수집, 조직, 이용에 제공하는 모든 자료. 보통은 물리적 실물자료와 디지털자료를 포함하며, 때로는 "소장 자료"라고도 부른다. 장서는 실물자료와 디지털자료, 인쇄자료와 비인쇄지료, 보유자료와 원격자료, 도서관이 소유하는 자료와 도서관을 통하여 수수료를 지불하거나 무료로 다른 기관들에 접근할 수 있는 자료 등이 있다.

정보문화: 학생들이 정보의 성질을 이해하고, 정보통신산업의 기본 메커니즘에 대한 이해를 밝게 하며, 인류의 끝없는 기술 혁신 및 기록을 위한 최선의 접근 방법을 개발하고, 이에 맞게 개인의 데이터를 이용하는 능력을 개발하는 등 제반 정보문화를 창조하는 데 필요한 방법적 지식의 실체. 여기에는 정보의 이용에 따른 윤리와 책임도 포함된다(미디어 및 정보 리터러시 참조).

큐레이션: 박물관, 미술관, 기타 전시 공간에서 소장 컬렉션 및 자료를 개발, 보호, 조직, 감독하는 일. 여기에는 웹사이트와 같은 디지털 컬렉션도 포함한다. 이러한 특수 컬렉션을 담당하는 사람(큐레이터)은 좋은 전시아이템의 선별, 전체 컬렉션에서 각 아이템의 위치설정 및 그 해석 등에 관한 특수지식과 경험을 갖추어야 한다.

데이터베이스: 레코드 형식으로 신속하게 검색할 수 있게 구성되며 정기적으로 업데이트되는 거대한 자료파일로서 데이터베이스 시스템관리 소프트웨어로 관리한다. 학교도서관에서 자주 이용하는 데이터베이스는 목록, 정기간행물 색인, 초록, 전문(full-text) 참고자료 등이 있으며, 매년 라이선스계약으로 임대하여 이용하고, 도서관 회원 및 직원들에게만 접근이 허용된다.

원주민: 토착민을 지칭하는 용어로, 경우에 따라 고유의 언어 또는 부족 특성을 나타낼 때 선택적으로 사용한다. 때로는 Native(원주민), Native American(아메리카 원주민), Aborigine(토착민), First Nation(제1 민족)등으로 사용한다.

정보 리터러시: 정보를 효과적으로, 책임성 있게, 목적에 맞도록 접근, 평가, 활용하는데 필요한 일련의 기술, 태도, 지식이다. 여기에는 문제 해결이나 의사결정에 필요한 지식, 그러한 필요를 알아내고, 정보를 찾아 활용하고, 필요한 경우에는 정보를 공유하고, 문제에 적용하거나 의사결정을 내릴 수 있는 능력을 포함한다. "information competence정보 능력", "information fluency정보 숙달"로도 사용한다(미디어 및 정보 리터러시 참조).

도서관 교육, 탐구기반 접근: 문제 해결이라는 관점에서 정보에 관한 사고 방식 및 정보 활용방법을 가르치는 것으로, 문제해결을 위한 여러 가지 정보도구, 정보자원, 정보검색 전략에 대한 지식을 통합적으로 다룬다. 이 접근방법은 1990년대 들어 강조되기 시작했다.

도서관 교육, 정보원 접근법: 도서관의 도구와 자원, 특히 참고자료 텍스트와 정보 검색을 위한 색인 등의 특성 및 이용에 관하여 이용자들을 가르치는 것. 이 방법은 1960년대와 1970년대에 강조되었다.

도서관 교육, 패스파인더 접근법: 이용자에게 어떻게 탐색 전략을 이용할 것인지, 즉 전문가의 실무관행에 기초한 논리적 패턴의 이용, 도서관의 검색도구 및 정보원의 접근 등을 다룬다. 탐색 전략은 "pathfinders 경로인자" 또는 "guides to the literature 문헌 가이드" 라는 명칭으로 각종 안내서에 등장하였다. 이 방법은 1980년대에 강조되기 시작했다.

도서관 교육, 과정접근법: 이용자에게 정보이용에 있어 지식개발 및 문제해결을 위해 감정, 인식, 체감(느낌, 생각, 행동)을 통하여 어떻게 개인 학습과정을 개발하는지를 가르치는 것. 정보탐색과정 연구(Kuhlthau, 1985)에 기초한 이 접근법은 1990년대에 강조되기 시작했다.

도서관 프로그램: (학교도서관 프로그램을 볼 것.)

미디어 리터러시: (미디어 및 정보 리터러시를 볼 것.)

미디어 및 정보 리터러시: 여러 가지 미디어 형태로 유통되고 있는 정보를 이용함에 있어 여러 다른 종류의 미디어와 포맷을 이해하고 활용하는 데 필수적인 일련의 기술, 태도, 지식을 말함. 여기에는 "정보와 미디어는 인간에 의해, 개인, 사회, 정치, 경제적 목적으로 창조되는 것으로 본질적으로 편파적"이라는 개념을 내포하고 있다.

패스파인더: 도서관의 검색도구 및 자료원에 접근하기 위해 권장하는 탐색 전략. "도서관 가이드" 또는 "문헌 가이드"라고도 부른다.

프로그램: (학교도서관 프로그램을 볼 것.)

학교도서관 사서: 학교도서관의 프로그램, 서비스, 각종 활동을 주도적으로 수행할 책임을 지는 사람으로 문헌정보교육을 받은 사서교사. 학교도서관 사서는 도서관의 일상적 운영에 더하여 장서개발, 각 학년 수준에 맞는 미디어 및 정보 리터러시 스킬 교육, 학생들에게 그들의 독서 수준에 적합한 독서 자료 선택지도, 교과 교사의 교육 프로그램에 도서

관 자료와 서비스 통합 지원 등으로 교육과정을 지원한다. 학교도서관 사서는 여러 가지 명칭으로 알려져 있다(사서 교사, 도서관 미디어 전문가, 학습 자원 교사).

학교도서관: 공·사립 초·중등학교에서 학생들의 정보수요 및 교직원의 커리큘럼 수요에 대응하여 서비스를 제공하는 학습공간으로서 실물자료 및 디지털 자료공간을 포함한다. 학교도서관은 해당 학교의 급별 수준에 적합한 교육자료 컬렉션을 제공한다. 학교도서관은 학교도서관 사서가 경영한다. 학교도서관 사서는 독서 및 조사연구와 관련된 제반 활동과 서비스를 통하여 학생들과 교사들에게 인지능력, 개인적, 사회적, 문화적 성장을 도와주는데 헌신해야 한다. 학교도서관은 여러 가지 명칭으로 알려져 있다(예: 학교도서관 미디어센터, 문서 정보센터, 도서관 자원센터, 도서관 공동학습센터).

학교도서관 프로그램: 학생들의 미디어 및 정보 리터러시 능력, 조사연구 능력, 독서능력, 디지털 기술, 기타 리터러시 및 커리큘럼 운영에 알맞게 설계한 교수 학습활동에 제공하는 도서관의 종합 계획.

이용자 교육: 이용자에게 도서관, 자료 및 시스템, 서비스를 이해하도록 도와주는 여러 가지 수단으로서 직접 안내는 물론 도서관 사인 표지,

유인물, 문헌 안내 등을 포함한다(서지 교육; 도서관 교육; 미디어 및 정보 리터러시도 볼 것).

참고문헌

본 가이드라인의 각 장 말미에는 해당 주제에 관련되는 유용한 정보들을 제시하였다. 본 참고문헌은 이 가이드라인의 개정작업을 진행하는 동안 참고한 자료와 본 가이드라인을 평가 검토하고 기여한 여러 연구자들이 추천한 자료들이다. 따라서 여기서는 앞서 각 장 말미에 제시한 참고문헌들은 제외하였다.

Alexandersson, Mi., & Limberg, L. (2004). *Textflytt och sökslump: Informationssöokning via skolbibliotek* [Moving text and searching by chance: Information retrieval through the school library]. Stockholm, Sweden: Myndigheten föor Skolutveckling.

American Association of School Librarians. (2009). *Empowering learners: Guidelines for school library programs.* Chicago: American Library Association.

American Association of School Librarians. (2008). *Learning 4 life: A national plan for implementation of Standards for the 21st-Century Learner and Guidelines for the School Library Media Program.* Chicago: ALA. Retrieved from www.ala.org/aasl/learning4life.

American Association of School Librarians. (2009). *Standards for the 21st-century learner in action.* Chicago: AASL.

Asselin, M., & Doiron, R. (2013). *Linking literacy and libraries in global communities.* Farnham, England: Ashgate Publishing.

Barrett, H., et al. (2010). *Skolbibliotekets májligheter: Frán fárskola till gymnasium* [The possibilities of the school library: From pre-school to senior high school]. Lund, Sweden: BTJ F?rlag.

Capra, S., & Ryan, J. (Eds.). (2002). *Problems are the solution: Keys to lifelong learning.* Capalaba, Australia: Capra Ryan & Associates.

Chapron, F. (2012). *Les CDI des lycéees et collèeges: De l'impriméе au numéerique* [CDI or school libraries in high schools and junior high schools: From print to digital] (nouvelle éedition). Paris, France: Presses universitaires de France.

Coatney, S. (Ed.). (2010). *The many faces of school library leadership.* Santa Barbara, CA: Libraries Unlimited.

Connaway, L., & Powell, R. (2010). *Basic research methods for librarians.* Westport, CT: Libraries Unlimited.

Cook, D., & Farmer, L. (Eds.). (2011). *Using qualitative methods in action research.* Chicago, IL: American Library Association.

Court, J. (Ed.). (2011). *Read to succeed. London* [UK]: Facet Publishing.

Crowley, J. D. (2011). *Developing a vision: Strategic planning for the school librarian in the 21st century* (2nd ed.). Santa Barbara, CA: Libraries Unlimited.

Das, L., & Walhout, J. (2012). *Informatievaardigheden en de mediathecaris* [Information literacy and the school media specialist]. Rapport 30. Heerlen, Netherlands: Open Universiteit, Ruud de Moor Centrum.

Erikson, R., & Markuson, C. (2007). *Designing a school library media center for the future* (2nd ed.). Chicago: American Library Association.

Farmer, L. (2014). *Introduction to reference and information and services in today's school library.* Lanham, MD: Rowman & Littlefield.

Farmer, L. (2011). *Instructional design for librarians and information professionals.* New York: Neal-Schuman.

Farmer, L., & McPhee, M. (2010). *Technology management handbook for school library media centers.* New York: Neal-Schuman.

Hughes-Hassell, & Harada, V. H. (2007). *School reform and the school library media specialist.* Westport, CT: Libraries Unlimited.

Gordon, C. (2000). *Information literacy in action.* Melton, Woodbridge, UK: John Catt Educational.

Guld?r, M., & Helinsky, Z. (2013). *Handbok fár skolbibliotekarier: Modeller, verktyg och praktiska exempel* [Handbook for school libraries: Models, tools and practical examples]. Lund, Sweden: BTJ Fárlag.

Hart, G. (2011). The "tricky business" of dual use school community libraries: A case study in rural South Africa, *Libri, 61(3)*, 211-225.

Hart, G. (2012). Teacher-librarians leading change: Some stories from the margins. *School Libraries Worldwide,* 18(2), 51-60.

Hoel, T., Rafste, E. T., & Sætre, T. P. (2008). *Opplevelse, oppdagelse og opplysning: fagbok om skolebibliotek* [Adventure, discovery and enlightenment: A textbook about school libraries]. Oslo, Norway: Biblioteksentralen.

Kelsey, M. (2014). *Cataloging for school librarians.* Lanham, MD: Rowman & Littlefield.

Kiefer, B., & Tyson, C. (2009). *Charlotte Huck's children's literature: A brief guide.* New York: McGraw Hill.

Kuhlthau, C. C., Maniotes, L. K., & Caspari, A. K. (2012). *Guided inquiry design: A framework for inquiry in your school.* Santa Barbara, CA: Libraries Unlimited.

Kuhlthau, C. C., Maniotes, L. K., & Caspari, A. K. (2015). *Guided inquiry: Learning in the 21st century school* (2nd ed.). Westport, CT: Libraries Unlimited.

Lester, J., & Koehler, W. (2007). *Fundamentals of information studies* (2nd ed). New York: Neal-Schuman.

Limberg, L. (2003). *Skolbibliotekets pedagogiska roll: En kunskapsöoversikt* [The pedagogical role of the school library: A systematic review]. Stockholm, Sweden: Statens skolverk.

Limberg, L., Hultgren, F., & Jarneving, B. (2002). *Informationssöokning och läarande: En forskningsöoversikt* [Information retrieval and learning: A research review]. Stockholm, Sweden: Skolverket.

Limberg, L., & Lundh, A. H. (Eds.). (2013). *Skolbibliotekets roller i fööräandrade landskap.* [The role of school libraries in changing landscapes]. Lund, Sweden: BTJ Föorlag. Retrieved from www.kb.se/Dokument/Bibliotek/projekt/Slutrapport 2013/Skolbibliotekets roller slutrapport 2013.pdf

Liquete, V. (Ed.) (2014). *Cultures de l'information* [Cultures of information]. CNRS Editions: Paris, France.

Malmberg, S., & Graner, T. (2014). *Bibliotekarien som medpedagog eller Varföor sitter det ingen i låanedisken?* [The librarian as co-pedagogue, or Why is nobody sitting at the library desk?]. Lund, Sweden: BTJ Föorlag.

Markuson, C., & European Council of International Schools. (2006). *Effective libraries in international schools.* Saxmundham, UK: John Catt Educational.

Morris, B. J. (2010). *Administering the school library media center* (5th ed.). Santa Barbara, CA: Libraries Unlimited. Available on the World Wide Web as an e-book.

Niinikangas, L. (1995). An open learning environment - new winds in the Finnish school library. *Scandinavian Public Library Quarterly 4*, 3-10.

Pavey, S. (2014). *Mobile technology and the school library.* Swindon, UK:

School Library Association UK. Series: SLA Guidelines Plus

Rosenfeld, E., & Loertscher, D. V. (Eds.). (2007). *Toward a 21st century school library media program.* Lanham, MD: Scarecrow Press.

Sardar, Z., & Van Loon, B. (2010). *Introducing media studies: A graphic guide.* London, England: Icon Books.

School Library Association [UK]. *Guideline series.* Retrieved from www.sla.org.uk/guidelines.php

Schultz-Jones, B. A., & Ledbetter, C. (2013). Evaluating students' perceptions of library and science inquiry: Validation of two new learning environment questionnaires. *Learning Environments Research*, 16(3), 329-348.

Shaper, S. (Ed). (2014). The CILIP *guidelines for secondary school libraries.* London, UK: Facet Publishing.

Schlamp, G.(Ed.). (2013). *Die schulbibliothek im zentrum: Erfahrungen, berichte, visionen* [The school library in the centre: Experiences, stories, visions]. Berlin, Germany: BibSpider.

Thomas, N. P., Crow, S. R., & Franklin, L. L. (2011). *Information literacy and information skills instruction: Applying research to practice in the 21st century school library* (3rd ed.). Santa Barbara, CA: Libraries Unlimited. Available on the World Wide Web as an e-book.

Tilke, A. (2011). *The International Baccalaureate Diploma Program and the school library: Inquiry-based education.* Santa Barbara, CA: Libraries Unlimited. Available on the World Wide Web as an e-book.

Tomlinson, C., & Lynch-Brown, C. (2009). *Essentials of young adult literature* (2nd ed.). Old Tappan, NJ: Pearson.

Wilson, C., Grizzle, A., Tuazon, R., Akyempong, K., & Cheung, C. K. (2012). *Education aux méedias et àa l'information: programme de formation pour les enseignants* [Media education and information: A training program for teachers]. Paris, France: UNESCO.

Woolls, B., Weeks, A. C. & Coatney, S. (2013). *School library media manager* (5th ed.). Westport, CT: Libraries Unlimited.

Zamuda, A., & Harada, V. H. (2008). *Librarians as learning specialists: Meeting the learning imperative for the 21st century.* Westport, CT: Libraries Unlimited.

부록 A: IFLA/UNESCO 학교도서관 선언(1999)

[www.ifla.org/publications/iflaunesco-school-library-manifesto-1999]

교수 학습을 위한 우리 모두의 학교도서관

학교도서관은 오늘날 지식정보사회에서 성공적으로 살아가는 데 필요한 기본정보와 아이디어를 제공해 준다. 학교도서관은 학생들에게 평생학습능력과 상상력을 길러주며 책임 있는 시민으로 살아갈 수 있는 능력을 길러준다.

학교도서관의 사명

학교도서관은 학교공동체의 모든 구성원들에게 모든 형태의 정보미디어를 효과적으로 이용할 수 있게 하고, 사고능력을 최대로 신장시키는 도서, 정보원 및 학습서비스를 제공한다. 학교도서관은 유네스코 공공도서관 선언의 원칙에 의거 광역 도서관 정보네트워크에 연결된다.

학교도서관 직원은 문학작품에서 사실자료, 인쇄자료에서 전자자료, 현장접근에서 원격접근에 이르기 까지 책과 정보원을 이용할 수 있도록 지원한다. 도서관 자료는 교수용 텍스트 및 교수방법에 있어 교과서를 보완하며 수업 내용을 풍부하게 한다.

지금까지 밝혀진 바에 의하면 사서와 교사들이 협업할 때 학생들은 수준 높은 문해력, 독서능력, 학습능력, 문제해결능력, 그리고 정보통신기술(ICT)능력을 갖추게 된다.

학교도서관서비스는 학교공동체의 모든 구성원들에게 연령, 종족, 성, 종교, 국적, 언어, 직업, 또는 사회적 신분에 관계없이 평등하게 제공해야 한다. 도서관의 주된 서비스와 자료를 이용할 수 없는 (장애를 가진) 사람들에게는 특수 자료와 서비스를 제공해야 한다.

도서관의 장서와 서비스 접근은 유엔인권자유선언에 기초하여, 어떠한 이념적, 정치적, 종교적 검열이나 상업적 압력에 영향을 받지 않는다.

재정, 법제, 네트워크

학교도서관은 문맹퇴치, 교육, 정보, 그리고 경제, 사회, 문화발전을 위한 모든 장기적 전략수립에 필수적인 요소이다. 지역, 광역, 중앙정부는 법적, 정책적으로 책임을 지고 학교도서관을 지원해야 한다. 학교도서관은 유능한 직원, 자료, 정보기술 및 제반 시설을 위한 적절하고도 지속적인 재정을 확보해야 한다. 학교도서관은 무료로 운영되어야 한다.

학교도서관은 지역, 광역, 국가도서관 정보네트워크에 있어 필수적인 파트너이다.

학교도서관은 공공도서관과 같은 다른 형태의 도서관들과 시설과 자원을 공유하면서도 학교도서관의 고유 목적을 알리고 지켜야 한다.

학교도서관의 목적

학교도서관은 교육과정에 통합적 기능을 수행한다.

다음은 문맹퇴치, 정보 리터러시, 교수, 학습, 문화 개발을 위한 학교도서관의 핵심 서비스이다.:

- 학교의 사명과 교육과정에 따른 교육 목적의 지원 및 강화
- 어린이에게 독서와 학습을 좋아하는 습관, 그리고 전 생애에 걸친

도서관 이용습관을 개발하고 유지하게 한다.

- 지식, 이해력, 상상력, 오락을 위해 정보를 이용하고 창조하는 경험의 기회 제공
- 학생들에게 지역사회의 정보소통 방법에 대한 감을 잡게 하고, 정보미디어의 형태나 형식에 상관없이 정보를 평가, 활용할 수 있는 능력을 배우고 익힐 수 있도록 지원함.
- 학생들에게 지역, 광역, 국가, 세계의 정보자원에 대한 접근점을 제공하고, 다양한 아이디어, 경험, 오피니언을 접할 수 있는 기회를 제공
- 문화적 사회적 인식 및 감각을 북돋는 여러 가지 활동 조성
- 학교의 사명을 달성할 수 있도록 학생, 교사, 교직원, 학부모들과 협력함.
- 민주주의에서는 정보에의 접근 및 지적자유가 책임 있는 참여 시민으로 살아가는데 필수적이라는 개념을 심어줄 것.
- 전체 학교공동체 및 학교를 넘어서는 지역사회에 대하여 학교도서관의 자원과 서비스를 제공하고, 독서능력 증진활동을 전개함.

학교도서관은 도서관의 정책 및 서비스개발, 정보자원의 선택 및 수서, 적정 정보원에 대한 물리적, 지적 접근 제공, 교육시설, 유능한 직원을 채용함으로써 이러한 기능을 충족시켜야 한다.

직원

학교도서관 사서는 학교도서관의 계획 및 경영책임자로서 인사관리에서 전문 능력과 자질을 갖춘 적임자를 배치함으로서 전문성을 확보해야 한다. 학교도서관 사서는 학교의 모든 구성원들과 협력하여 일하고, 공공도서관 및 기타 기관과도 유대관계를 가지고 업무를 수행해야 한다.

학교도서관 사서의 역할은 국가의 법적, 재정적 테두리 내에서 해당 학교의 예산, 교육과정, 교육방법에 따라 다양할 것이다. 그러한 특수한 맥락 속에서도 학교도서관 사서가 활발히 수행해야 할 공통부분은 효과적인 학교도서관 서비스를 개발, 운영하는 것이다.

네트워크 환경이 확대됨에 따라 학교도서관 사서들은 교사 및 학생들에게 각기 다른 정보처리 기술을 기획하고 가르치는 일에 심혈을 기울여야 한다. 그러므로 사서들은 지속적으로 전문성을 개발하고 계속 교육을 받아야 한다.

운영 및 관리

효과적이고 책임 있는 도서관 경영을 담보하기 위하여:

- 학교도서관 서비스 정책에는 교육과정과 관련한 학교도서관의 목적 우선순위, 서비스에 관한 사항을 규정해 두어야 한다.
- 학교도서관은 전문적 표준에 따라 설립 운영해야 한다.
- 서비스는 학교공동체의 전 구성원이 접근할 수 있어야 하며 지역사회와의 맥락에서 운영해야 한다.
- 교사, 학교의 중견간부, 행정가, 학부모, 기타 사서 및 정보전문가들과 협력하면서 지역사회 단체들의 협력을 이끌어내야 한다.

본 선언의 실행

정부는 교육행정을 담당하는 부처 장관을 통하여 본 선언의 원칙을 실행할 수 있는 전략, 정책, 계획을 수립하도록 해야 한다. 그 계획에는 본 선언의 배포와 사서와 교사를 위한 지속적인 훈련프로그램에 관한 사항을 포함해야 한다.

부록 B: 학교도서관 예산계획

학교사서는 학교도서관 예산계획의 개발과 관련하여 다음 사항을 이해할 필요가 있다.

- 학교의 예산책정 절차
- 예산 주기 및 일정표
- 예산 수립과정에 관련되는 핵심 직원
- 학교도서관의 필요성에 대한 인식
- 예산 회계처리 과정

예산계획의 요소는 다음 사항을 포함한다.

- 자료구입비(예: 도서, 정기간행물, 멀티미디어, 디지털자료)
- 행정관리 소모품비
- 이용 촉진을 위한 이벤트 및 재료비
- 기타 서비스(예: 복사, 수리)
- 학교의 일반예산에 포함되지 않는 ICT장비, 소프트웨어, 라이선싱 이용경비

일반적으로 학교도서관의 자료예산은 교직원 급여, 특수교육비, 운송비, 설비개선비를 포함하여 적어도 학교예산의 5%는 되어야 한다.

인건비는 도서관 예산에 포함할 수 있다. 그러나 어떤 학교에서는 일반 인건비예산에 포함하여 책정한다. 어떻게 책정하든 학교도서관 사서의 인건비 책정에는 학교도서관 사서가 참여해야 한다. 직원에 관련되는 예산은 학교도서관의 개방시간, 학교도서관이 제공하는 서비스의 질과 범위 등 주요 이슈들과 연관하여 책정한다. 새로운 서가 혹은 시설 개선과 같은 특수 프로젝트나 개발에 관한 예산은 특별 자금을 신청할 수 있다.

부록 C: 탐구기반 학습을 위한 교육 모델

잘 개발된 탐구기반 학습과정 모델로는 다음과 같은 것들이 있다.

Michael Marland's Nine Questions (United Kingdom)

Marland, M. (1981). *Information skills in the secondary curriculum.* Schools Council Methuen.

Stripling and Pitts' REACTS Model (USA)

Stripling, B., & Pitts, J. (1988). *Brainstorms and blueprints: Teaching research as a thinking process.* Westport, CT: Libraries Unlimited.

The Information Process (Australia)

Australian School Library Association and Australian Library and Information Association. (2001). *Learning for the future: Developing information services in schools* (2nd ed.). Carlton South, Australia: Curriculum Corporation.

Focus on Inquiry (Canada)

Alberta Learning. (2003). *Focus on inquiry: A teacher's guide to inquiry-based learning.* Edmonton, AB: Alberta Learning, Learning Resources Branch.

Guided Inquiry (USA)

Kuhlthau, C. C., Maniotes, L. K., & Caspari, A. K. (2007). *Guided inquiry: Learning in the 21st century.* Westport, CT: Libraries Unlimited.

Kuhlthau, C. C., Maniotes, L. K., & Caspari, A. K. (2012). *Guided inquiry design: A framework for inquiry in your school.* Westport, CT: Libraries Unlimited.

Schmidt, R. (2013). *A guided inquiry approach to high school research.* Westport, CT: Libraries Unlimited.

부록 D: 학교도서관 평가 체크리스트 사례(캐나다)

정보 리터러시 습득: 캐나다 학교도서관 프로그램 기준(pp. 74-77). 오타와, 캐나다: 캐나다 학교도서관협회 및 사서교사협회, 2003에서 인용.

1. 정보 리터러시 및 독서 증진 프로그램	그렇다	보통이다	그렇지 않다
a. 정보 리터러시 기술에 연관한 탐구기반 학습			
b. 교육과정을 통한 정보 리터러시 프로그램 통합			
c. 교사, 사서교사, 행정직, 학부모, 지역사회 구성원들과의 협업			
d. 학생의 성취 보고서 및 평가의 사서교사 참여			
e. 모든 학생의 도서관 프로그램에 대한 평등한 접근			
f. 독서 및 리터러시 프로그램 개발, 지원, 실행			

2. 기술 및 행정직원의 보조를 받는, 자질, 경쟁력, 높은 동기를 가진 사서 교사 인사관리 모델	그렇다	보통이다	그렇지 않다
a. 정보 자원 기반, 탐구학습을 통한 교과목적 및 정보 리터러시 목적에 부합하는 교과교사와의 협업 계획 및 수업			

b. 탐구학습 프로젝트 및 수요기반 학습 프로젝트에서 직원 및 학생들에 대한 사서 교사의 수업기술 및 정보 리터러시 기술			
c. 교육과정 및 지역의 관심에 기초한 다양한 정보자원 개발			
d. 인적자원의 효과적 관리(행정직, 기술직, 학생 봉사원, 자원 활동가)			
e. 장비(임차, 취득, 및 수선)의 효과적 관리			
f. 시설(등록, 전시, 가구, 유지보수)의 효과적 관리			
g. 행정 처리과정(대출, 수서, 예산, 주문, 추적, 목록, 서가배열, 보고서, 데이터 관리)			
h. 리더십(공동 프로젝트에서 얻은 새 학습이론 새 수업기법의 통합 적용)			
i. 학생 학습지도에 대한 개인적인 열정과 헌신			
j. 전문성 개발(예: 웹 기반 활동 및 기회 활용)			

3. 학교의 목적과 연관되는 장기 종합계획에 포함된 재정모델	그렇다	보통이다	그렇지 않다
a. 사서교사가 매년 교육과정 필요 및 모든 직원 및 프로그램에 기초여 준비하는 프로그램 예산			
b. 기본 예산 플러스 장기계획에 의한 학생 1인당 연간 예산			
c. 경상 및 신규 사업에 포함되는 예산			
d. 정보자원, 소모품, 수선, 장비, 서비스 계약, 전문성 개발, 자본적 지출			
e. 학교의 우선 요구를 대비한 예산			

f. 이해관계자들의 요구를 반영한 예산			
g. 특수 프로그램에 소요되는 예산 – 작가 방문, 독서 콘서트 등			

4. 학교도서관은 학습자들의 공식 비공식 요구를 충족하기 위해 전문적으로 선택된 광범위하고 적절한 학습자원을 구비한다.	그렇다	보통이다	그렇지 않다
a. 학교의 학습 요구를 반영한 선택정책이 있다.			
b. 다양한 자료 형태간의 균형(예: 인쇄, 연속간행물, 비디오, 오디오, 전자자료, 온라인 데이터베이스, 인터넷, 기타)			
c. 자료의 접근 수준에 있어서의 균형			
d. 충분한 컴퓨터 워크스테이션 및 프린터			
e. 충분한 시청각 장비			
f. 학생 1인당 충분한 자료의 수(량)			
g. 정보자원과 공동체의 학습 요구, 예를 들면 교육과정 및 관심(질) 간의 상관성 정도			
h. 장서의 최신성(폐기, 보완) 및 수선			
i. 중앙 종합 데이터베이스에의 접근성			
j. 디지털 도서관 자원에의 접근성			
k. 웹사이트 정보에의 접근성			
l. 접근, 자원공유 협력 절차			

5. 도서관은 교육과정을 지원하는 최신의 정보기술을 보유하고 있다.	그렇다	보통이다	그렇지 않다
a. 도서관 정보기술 이용을 위한 효과적이고 신뢰성 있는 프로그램을 제공한다.			
b. 학생들이 새롭고 유의미한 정보를 검색, 분석, 소통할 수 있는 충분한 워크스테이션 및 소프트웨어를 갖추고 있다.			
c. 학교에 소속된 전 학생과 교직원은 하루 24시간, 일주일에 7일 현행 정보자원에 접근할 수 있다.			
d. 도서관의 일상 업무를 자동시스템으로 조직하고 운영할 수 있다.			

6. 도서관 시설은 안전성, 융통성, 공간구성, 디자인이 다양한 학습활동을 하기에 적절하다.	그렇다	보통이다	그렇지 않다
a. 개별, 소집단학습, 학급단위학습을 위한 작업 공간			
b. 새로 등장하는 정보기술 및 애플리케이션에 적응할 수 있도록 디자인 되었는지			
c. 도서관을 새로운 기능과 전통적 기능의 조화, 효율성, 도서관 품질제고 및 확장 등에 알맞게 구조와 형태를 변경할 수 있는 융통성이 있는지			
d. 안락함 – 소음, 조명, 온도, 배선, 비품			
e. 수업 전날, 수업 당일, 수업 다음날 도서관 접근이 가능한지			
f. 시각적으로 매력이 있는지			
g. 안전성			

부록 E: 학교장을 위한 학교도서관 평가 체크리스트

학교장을 위한 도서관 프로그램의 12가지 체크리스트(미국)

도우그 존슨의 불로그

(http://doug-johnson.squarespace.com/blue-skunk-blog/2012/1/10)에서 검색

이 체크리스스크의 목적은 도서관 혹은 도서관 프로그램에 대한 공식적인 평가도구를 제공하는 데 있는 것이 아니라, 학교도서관의 전반적 프로그램을 북돋기 위하여 필요한 추가적 자료 및 도움이 필요한 영역이 무엇인지를 인식하게 하여 학교경영자로서의 능력을 쌓도록 도움을 주는 데 있다.

지난 20세기에 일어난 정보기술, 학습 연구, 도서관의 전문성에 대한 급격한 변화는 학교도서관 프로그램의 효과성이라는 측면에서 매우 큰 혼돈을 야기했다. 당신의 학교도서관은 어떤 일관된 흐름을 유지하고 있는가? 아래의 체크리스트는 당신의 도서관 프로그램을 신속히 평가하는데 활용할 수 있을 것이다.

1. 전문 직원 및 의무

- 당신의 도서관은 충분한 자격을 갖춘 학교도서관 사서가 근무하는지?
- 그 직원은 전문직 의무를 충실히 수행하는지? 사무직, 기술직, 전문직 등 전체 도서관 직원에 대한 문서화된 직무기술서가 갖추어져 있는지?
- 사서는 자치단체와 국가 도서관 조직에서 발행하는 현행 전문기준이 기술하는 사서의 역할 변화를 이해하고 있는지?
- 사서는 정보 리터러시, 정보기술, 이러한 기술을 내용적으로 통합 적용할 수 있도록 정규적인 직원개발기회를 제공하는지?
- 사서는 전문직 조직의 일원으로 능동적으로 활동하는지?
- 사서는 학교 전체 교사진의 일원으로 인정을 받는지?

2. 전문적인 지원

- 사서에게 사무업무를 도와줌으로써 사서가 사무적 잡일에 신경쓰지 않고 전문직 의무를 충분히 수행할 수 있는지?
- 사서에게 기술적 업무를 도와줌으로써 사서가 기술적인 일에 신경쓰지 않고 전문직 의무를 충분히 수행할 수 있는지?
- 학교도서관의 기획 및 지도를 담당하는 지역 교육청의 감독자, 지도지원팀 또는 담당부서장이 있는지?
- 분교장, 현장지도위원회, 인력개발팀은 사서직원에게 그들의 지식과

능력을 업데이트 할 수 있는 워크숍, 전문가회의, 컨퍼런스 등에 참석할 수 있게 해주는지?

- 사서는 지역의 전문적 학습공동체 및 비공식의 개인적 학습네트워크에 참여하는지?

3. 장서규모 및 장서개발

- 도서관의 책과 오디오 자료가 커리큘럼 수요를 충족하는지? 인쇄자료 장서의 기본 규모는 설정되어 있는지? 불필요 장서의 폐기는 잘 하고 있는지?
- 여러 다른 학습 스타일에 맞는 다양한 미디어를 이용할 수 있는지?
- 온라인 자료를 제때에 장서에 추가하는지? 온라인 자료 이용을 위한 충분한 컴퓨터 및 광역 인터넷 시설을 갖추고 있는지?
- 인쇄자료와 디지털자료의 균형유지를 위해 최근에 평가를 시행한 적이 있는지? 인쇄자료에 대한 온라인 자료 대체구독은 이루어지고 있는지? 인쇄자료 소장공간은 효과적으로 재배치하고 있는지?
- 전문 선택정보에 의한 최신자료 선택이 이루어지고 있는지? 장서 지도를 통한 커리큘럼 연계가 이루어지고 있는지?

4. 시설

- 도서관의 위치는 모든 교실로부터 접근하기 쉬운지? 야간이나 주

말에 외부 이용자들을 위한 지역사회 접근 기능을 갖추고 있는지?

- 도서관은 안락한 비품배치, 교육적인 레이아웃, 정보 친화적 전시 등 학습 분위기를 갖추고 있는지? 도서관은 소음을 줄이기 위해 정전 방지 및 전자 장비 보호를 위한 카펫을 설치했는지? 여름철에 도서관 자료와 장비가 높은 온습도로 인해 손상되지 않도록 적정 온습도를 유지할 수 있는지?
- 도서관은 일반적인 교육시설, 이야기 방(초등학교), 프레젠테이션 공간(중·고등학교), 그리고 개인, 소집단, 학급단위 수업을 할 수 있는 공간을 갖추고 있는지?
- 도서관은 학생들과 교사들이 수업 또는 단독으로 사용할 수 있고, 사서가 학생들을 가르치는데 사용할 수 있는 컴퓨터와 무선 랩톱컴퓨터를 보유하고 있는지? 도서관은 멀티미디어 워크스테이션 및 디지털 영상 제작 시설을 보유, 지원하는지?
- 도서관은 음성, 화면, 데이터를 위한 적정량의 네트워크를 잘 갖추고 있는지? 도서관은 라우터, 파일 서버, 비디오 헤드 등 정보네트워크의 허브로서 기술직원이 상주하며 서비스하는지?
- 도서관은 학생, 교직원 및 그 가족을 위한 유용한 최신의 웹정보자원을 링크하고 있는지?

5. 교과과정 및 통합과정

- 사서는 학년 수준별 또는 팀별 학습설계에 능동적으로 참여하는지?
- 사서는 교육과정내용 편성위원회에 능동적으로 참여하는지?
- 사서는 수준별 또는 내용 영역별 전문 학습공동체의 일원으로 참여하는지?
- 도서관 정보자원은 내용면에서 교육과정 검토 사이클에 따라 검토하는지?
- 도서관 및 정보기술을 따로 분리해서 가르치지 않고 내용의 일환으로 가르치는지? 정보접근검색기술과 동시에 정보를 평가, 처리, 소통할 수 있는 정보 리터러시 기술을 가르치는지?
- 정보기술 리터러시 교육과정에 온라인 정보의 적절하고 안전한 이용에 관한 것도 들어 있는지?

6. 자료기반 수업

- 사서는 도서관의 리더십을 구축하여 교과서를 넘어서는 교수활동을 도와주고 각 수준별로 차별화된 수업에 도움이 되는 자료를 제공하는지?
- 교사 및 직원들은 사서를 수업설계자 및 진정한 자료 평가자로 인정하는지? 도서관 프로그램은 모든 교육과정을 통하여 탐구기반 학습 및 학생 중심 학습활동을 지원하는지? 사서는 학생들 및 교사들과

더불어 창의적 사고능력 및 책임 있는 디지털 시민을 기를 수 있도록 광범위한 기회를 조성하는데 협력하는지?

- 사서가 단지 교사들의 수업 준비만 지원하는 것이 아니라 교과교사와 팀 티칭의 일원으로 참여할 수 있는 융통성 있는 교육스케줄을 운영하는지?
- 모든 수준의 학생들이 정보 리터러시 및 정보기술을 이용하고 벤치마킹할 수 있는 분명한 서면 자료를 갖추고 있는지? 이러한 벤치마킹 자료는 사서와 교사가 협력하여 평가하는지? 그 평가 결과는 전체 이해관계들과 공유하는지?

7. 정보기술

- 도서관은 다음과 같은 최신 정보기술을 이용자에게 접근할 수 있게 제공하는지?
- 장서구성에 대한 온라인 도서관 목록 및 대출 시스템
- 상호대차 협력관계에 있는 지역의 공공, 대학, 전문도서관 등 지역 장서에 접근할 수 있는 온라인 종합목록
- 인터넷을 통한 온라인 목록에의 접근
- 정기간행물 기사색인, 백과사전, 지도, 용어사전, 어학사전, 시소러스, 독자서평, 연감 등 광범위하고 다양한 온라인 참고 도구
- 워드프로세서, 멀티미디어, 프레젠테이션 프로그램, 스프레드시트,

데이터베이스, 데스크톱 출판프로그램, 그래픽 프로그램, 디지털 정지화상 및 동영상 편집 소프트웨어 등 학생들의 능력 수준에 맞는 광범위하고 다양한 컴퓨터 활용 자료생산 프로그램

- 위키스, 블로그, 기타 온라인 공유프로그램, 온라인 자료생산 도구 및 파일 저장소와 같은 클라우드 컴퓨터 등 협력학습/네트워크 도구에의 접근
- 데스크 톱, 회의 장비 및 소프트웨어 접근
- 교과과정을 지원하는 실습, 시뮬레이션, 개인교사 등 교육용 컴퓨터 프로그램
- 사서와 교사와 협력하여 이러한 제반 정보자원의 이용에 필요한 기술을 가르치는지?

8. 참고자료, 네트워크 구성 및 도서관간 상호대차

- 사서는 교내 학생들 및 교직원들에게 참고서비스를 제때에 효과적으로 제공할만한 전문성을 가지고 있는지?
- 귀교는 지역의 정보종합시스템 또는 컨소시엄의 회원인지?
- 사서는 학생들과 직원들의 요구 중 자관 장서에 없는 자료를 상호대차를 통하여 충족시켜 주는지?
- 사서는 지역 및 광역의 다른 학교들과 협력하여 장서구축 및 구입계획 수립에 동참하는지?

9. 계획 수립 및 연도별 목적

- 도서관 프로그램은 지역 전체의 장기적인 목적을 반영하고 있는지?
- 사서는 학교의 전체 리더십에 부합하는 교육과정 목적을 기반으로 직접적으로 연관되는 장기적 목적 위에서 연도별 목적을 설정하는지?
- 사서에 대한 평가의 일정 부분은 해당연도 목적의 달성에 기반을 두고 있는지?
- 도서관 프로그램은 학교운영위원회에 보고하는지? 그리고 지역사회 정보기술 기획회의에 보고하는지?

10. 예산

- 도서관 프로그램예산은 영기준예산 또는 목표예산인지? 예산은 프로그램의 목적과 잘 연계되는지?
- 사서는 소요되는 자료, 장비, 소모품에 대한 분명한 합리적 예산근거를 작성하는지?
- 예산에 프로그램의 유지 및 증가요소를 다 반영하는지?
- 사서는 지출에 대한 정확하고 분명한 기록을 유지하는지?
- 사서는 예산신청서를 적기에 작성하는지?

11. 도서관 정책/의사전달

- 현재 유효한 자료선택 및 재검토에 관한 전반적인 정책이 있는지?

직원은 지적 자유와 도서관 이용자의 프라이버시에 관한 정책을 인지하고 있는지? 이러한 정책은 디지털 자료에도 확대 적용되는지?

- 지역사회는 인터넷 및 정보기술에 대해서도 CIPA(역자 주: CIPA는 the Comité International de Photogrammétrie Architecturale의 약어로 영상자료 이용에 대한 국제기구로 사료됨)의 안전 규정 및 이용 접근정책(또는 정책 이행의 책임)을 준수하는지?
- 사서는 저작권법을 잘 이해하고 있는지? 사서는 다른 사람들이 지적 소유권을 설정하고자 할 때 의사결정에 도움을 줄 수 있는지?
- 사서는 학생, 직원, 행정가, 지역사회에 대하여 프로그램의 목적과 서비스에 대하여 의사를 전달할 수 있는 공식적 소통수단을 가지고 있는지? 도서관의 웹사이트는 전문성이 있고, 검색이 편리하며, 현재 유용한 것인지? 사서는 이해관계자들과의 의사소통을 위한 사회적 네트워크를 이용할 수 있는지?

12. 평가

- 사서는 프로그램의 목적과 목표의 달성 및 지역사회의 목적 충족 정도를 판단, 보고할 수 있는 보고방법을 가지고 있는지? 사서는 질적, 양적으로 측정한 도서관의 연차보고서를 작성하여 학교경영자, 직원, 학부모들에게 보고하는지?
- 도서관 정보기술에 관한 모든 새로운 우선순위 결정이 평가소요에

들어 있는지?

- 지역 교육청은 도서관에 대한 인정과정의 일환으로 외부 평가 팀을 이용하여 도서관의 프로그램을 정기적으로 평가하는지?
- 사서는 학술연구자로 요청을 받을 경우 공식 연구원으로 참여하는지?

International Federation of
Library Associations and Institutions

IFLA School Library Guidelines

Written by the IFLA School Libraries Section Standing Committee
Edited by: Barbara Schultz-Jones and Dianne Oberg, with contributions from the International Association of School Librarianship Executive Board

2nd revised edition

June 2015
Endorsed by the IFLA Professional Committee

IFLA
P.O. Box 95312
2509 CH Den Haag
Netherlands

www.ifla.org

Table of Contents

Preface

These guidelines constitute the second edition of the IFLA/UNESCO School Library Guidelines (IFLA Professional Reports 77). The first edition of the school library guidelines was developed in 2002 by the School Libraries Section, then called the School Libraries and Resource Centres Section. These guidelines have been developed to assist school library professionals and educational decision-makers in their efforts to ensure that all students and teachers have access to effective school library programs and services, delivered by qualified school library personnel.

The drafting of these revised guidelines involved discussion, debate, and consultation with many people from many countries at workshops during IFLA conferences and mid-year meetings, also through ongoing writing and review in person and online. The editors are indebted to the contributions of members of the Standing Committee of the IFLA Section of School Libraries and the executive board of the International Association of School Librarianship (IASL), as well as the other members of the international school library community who shared their expertise and their passion for the project. We appreciate the review and comments, duly incorporated in these guidelines, by the IFLA Indigenous Matters SIG.

Our thanks to members and officers of the IFLA School Libraries Standing Committee: Nancy Achebe (Nigeria), Tricia Adams (UK, Information Coordinator/Web Editor), Lisa Åström (Sweden), Lesley Farmer (USA, Blog/Newsletter Editor), Karen Gavigan (USA), Rei Iwasaki (Japan), Mireille Lamouroux (France), Randi Lundvall (Norway), Danielle Martinod (France), Luisa Marquardt (Italy), Dianne Oberg (Canada, Secretary), Barbara Schultz-Jones (USA, Chair), and Annike Selmer (Norway). Corresponding Members: Lourense Das (Netherlands), Patience Kersha (Nigeria), B. N. Singh (India), Diljit Singh (Malaysia). Officers and directors of IASL: Lourdes T. David (Philippines), Busi Diamini (South Africa), Nancy Everhart (USA), Elizabeth Greef (Australia, Vice-President), Madhu Bhargava (India), Kay Hones (USA, Vice-President), Geraldine Howell (New Zealand), Katy Manck (USA, Treasurer), Luisa Marquardt (Italy), Dianne Oberg (Canada), Diljit Singh (Malaysia, President), Ingrid Skirrow (Austria), Paulette Stewart (Jamaica), and Ayse Yuksel-Durukan (Turkey). Other colleagues who also made significant contributions at various stages of the writing and review process include Ingrid Bon (Netherlands), Foo Soo Chin (Singapore), Veronika Kámán (Hungary), Susan Tapulado (Philippines), Ross Todd (USA), and Gloria Trinidad (Philippines).

Barbara Schultz-Jones, Chair
Dianne Oberg, Secretary
IFLA Section of School Libraries

June 2015

Executive Summary

School Library Manifesto. School libraries around the world share a common purpose, expressed in the 1999 *IFLA/UNESCO School Library Manifesto: The school library in teaching and learning for all.* School library personnel uphold the values of the *United Nations Declaration of the Rights of the Child* (1959), the *United Nations Convention on the Rights of the Child* (1989), the *United Nations Declaration on the Rights of Indigenous People* (2007), and of the Core Values of IFLA. School libraries are envisioned in the *Manifesto* as a force for the enhancement and improvement of teaching and learning throughout the school community—for educators as well as for students.

School library guidelines. All guidelines represent a compromise between what we aspire to achieve and what we can reasonably expect to achieve. The contributors to this document were inspired by the mission and values embodied in school libraries, and they recognized that school library personnel and educational decision-makers, even in countries with well-resourced and well-supported school libraries, must struggle to be relevant to the learning needs of the whole school community and to respond thoughtfully to the changing information environment within which they work.

The goal of school libraries. The goal of all school libraries is to develop information literate students who are responsible and ethical participants in society. Information literate students are competent self-directed learners who are aware of their information needs and actively engage in the world of ideas. They display confidence in their ability to solve problems and know how to locate relevant and reliable information. They are able to manage technology tools to access information and to communicate what they have learned. They are able to operate comfortably in situations where there are multiple answers or no answers. They hold high standards for their work and create quality products. Information literate students are flexible, able to adapt to change, and able to function both individually and in groups.

Frameworks for school libraries. School libraries exist within a framework of local, regional, and national authority to provide equity of opportunity for learning and for developing the abilities needed to participate in the knowledge society. In order to maintain and continuously respond to an evolving educational and cultural environment, school libraries need to be supported by legislation and sustained funding.

School libraries also exist within an ethical framework that considers the rights and responsibilities of students and other members of the learning community. Everyone who works in school libraries, including volunteers, have a responsibility to observe high ethical standards in their dealings with each other and with all members of the school community. They endeavour to put the rights of library users before their own comfort and convenience and to avoid being biased by their personal attitudes and beliefs in providing library service. They deal with all children, youth, and adults on an equal basis regardless of their abilities and background, maintaining their right to privacy and their right to know.

Staffing school libraries. Because the role of school libraries is to facilitate teaching and learning, the services and activities of school libraries need to be under the direction of professional staff with the same level of education and preparation as classroom teachers. Where school librarians are expected to take a leadership role in the school, they need to have the same level of education and preparation as other leaders in the school, such as school administrators and learning specialists. The operational aspects of school libraries are best handled by trained clerical and technical support staff in order to ensure that school librarians have the time needed for the professional roles of instruction, management, collaboration, and leadership.

Staffing patterns for school libraries vary depending on the local context, influenced by legislation, economic development, and educational infrastructure. However, more than 50 years of international research indicates that school librarians require formal education in school librarianship and classroom teaching in order to develop the professional expertise required for the complex roles of instruction, reading and literacy development, school library management, collaboration with teaching staff, and engagement with the educational community.

School library collections. School librarians work with administrators and teachers to develop policies that guide the creation and maintenance of the library's collection of educational materials. The collection management policy must be based upon the curriculum and the particular needs and interests of the school community and reflects the diversity of society outside the school. The policy makes it clear that collection building is a collaborative endeavour and that teachers, as subject experts with valuable knowledge about the needs of their students, have an important role to play in helping to build library collections. Also vital is ensuring that school libraries acquire resources that have been created both locally and internationally and that reflect the national, ethnic, cultural, linguistic, indigenous, and other unique population identities of members of the school community.

Instructional programs of school libraries: School librarians should focus on the core pedagogical activities of:

- literacy and reading promotion;
- media and information literacy (e.g., information literacy, information skills, information competences, information fluency, media literacy, transliteracy);
- inquiry-based learning (e.g., problem-based learning, critical thinking);
- technology integration;
- professional development for teachers; and
- appreciation of literature and culture.

School librarians recognize the importance of having a systematic framework for the teaching of media and information skills, and they contribute to the enhancement of students' skills through collaborative work with teachers.

School library evaluation: Evaluation is a critical aspect of an ongoing cycle of continuous improvement. Evaluation helps to align the library's programs and services with the goals of the school. Evaluation demonstrates to students and teachers, to library staff, and to the wider educational community the benefits derived from school library programs and services. Evaluation gives the evidence needed to improve programs and services and also helps both library staff and library users understand and value those programs and services. Successful evaluation leads to renewal of programs and services, as well as development of new programs and services.

Maintaining support for the school library: Evaluation also is essential to guide initiatives related to public relations and advocacy. Because the role of school libraries in teaching and learning is not always well understood, supportive relationships need to be built with the school library's stakeholder groups and supporters to ensure that library funding and other kinds of support are maintained.

About this document: This is the second edition of school library guidelines published by the IFLA Section of School Libraries. These guidelines have been developed to assist school library professionals and educational decision-makers in their efforts to ensure that all students and teachers have access to effective school library programs and services, delivered by qualified school library personnel. The drafting of these guidelines involved discussion, debate, and consultation with many people from many countries at workshops during IFLA conferences and mid-year meetings, also through ongoing writing and review in person and online. The editors are indebted to the contributions of members of the Standing Committee of the IFLA Section of School Libraries and the Executive Board of the International Association of School Librarianship (IASL), as well as the other members of the international school library community who shared their expertise and their passion for the project.

Barbara Schultz-Jones, Chair
Dianne Oberg, Secretary
IFLA Section of School Libraries

June 2015

Recommendations

The following recommendations have been developed for use by school library professionals and educational decision-makers in their efforts to ensure that all students and teachers have access to effective school library services and programs that are delivered by qualified school library personnel. The recommendations are presented in alignment with the text of the guidelines; the supporting sections of the text are noted at the end of each recommendation.

Those wishing to use the recommendations as one aspect of planning, developing, promoting, or evaluating a school library may want to utilize a scale to assess the status of each recommendation in relation to a particular school library or school library system (e.g., "Yes, Somewhat, No" (see Appendix D: Sample Evaluation Checklist) or "Exploring, Emerging, Evolving, Established, Leading into the Future" (see *Leading Learning: Standards of Practice for School Library Learning Commons in Canada*, 2014, p. 9)).

Recommendation 1. The mission and purposes of the school library should be stated clearly in terms that are consistent with the principles of the *IFLA/UNESCO School Library Manifesto* and the values expressed in the *United Nations Declaration of the Rights of the Child*, the *United Nations Declaration on the Rights of Indigenous People*, and in the Core Values of IFLA. [Introduction, 1.7]

Recommendation 2. The mission and purposes of the school library should be defined in terms that are consistent with the expectations of national, regional, and local educational authorities, also the outcomes of the school's curricula. [Introduction, 1.1-1.8]

Recommendation 3. A plan should be in place for the development of the three features necessary for the success of a school library: a qualified school librarian; a collection that supports the curriculum of the school; and an explicit plan for ongoing growth and development of the school library. [1.1–1.8]

Recommendation 4. Monitoring and evaluating school library services and programs, as well as the work of the school library staff, should be conducted on a regular basis to ensure that the school library is meeting the changing needs of the school community. [1.9, 6.1–6.4]

Recommendation 5. School library legislation should be in place, at an appropriate governmental level or levels, to ensure that legal responsibilities are clearly defined for the establishment, support, and continuous improvement of school libraries accessible to all students. [2.1-2.2, 2.4-2.7]

Recommendation 6. School library legislation should be in place, at an appropriate governmental level or levels, to ensure that ethical responsibilities of all members of the school community are clearly defined, including such rights as equity of access, freedom of information and privacy, copyright and intellectual property, and children's right to know. [2.3, 3.6-3.8]

Recommendation 7. School library services and programs should be under the direction of a professional school librarian with formal education in school librarianship and classroom teaching. [3.1-3.4]

Recommendation 8. The roles of a professional school librarian should be clearly defined to include instruction (i.e., literacy and reading promotion, inquiry-centred and resource-based), library management, school-wide leadership and collaboration, community engagement, and promotion of library services. [3.5, 3.5.4]

Recommendation 9. All school library staff—professional, paraprofessional, and volunteer—should clearly understand their roles and responsibilities to work in accordance with library policies, including those related to equity of access, right to privacy, and right to know for all library users. [3.1, 3.2, 3.6, 3.7]

Recommendation 10. All school library staff should endeavour to develop collections of physical and digital resources consistent with the school's curriculum and with the national, ethnic, and cultural identities of members of the school community; they also should endeavour to increase access to resources through practices such as cataloguing, curation, and resource sharing. [4.2.3, 4.3, 4.3.1-4.3.4]

Recommendation 11. The facilities, equipment, collections, and services of the school library should support the teaching and learning needs of the students and the teachers; these facilities, equipment, collections, and services should evolve as teaching and learning needs change. [4.1-4.3]

Recommendation 12. The connections among school libraries and with public libraries and academic libraries should be developed to strengthen access to resources and services and to foster their shared responsibilities for the lifelong learning of all community members. [4.2, 5.4]

Recommendation 13. The core instructional activities of a school librarian should be focused on: literacy and reading promotion; media and information literacy instruction; inquiry-based teaching; technology integration; and professional development of teachers. [5.2-5.7]

Recommendation 14. The services and programs provided through the school library should be developed collaboratively by a professional school librarian working in concert with the principal, with curriculum leaders, with teaching colleagues, with members of other library groups, and with members of cultural, linguistic, indigenous, and other unique populations to contribute to the achievement of the academic, cultural, and social goals of the school. [3.5, 3.5.4, 5.1-5.8]

Recommendation 15. Evidence-based practice should guide the services and programs of a school library and provide the data needed for improvement of professional practice and for ensuring that the services and programs of a school library make a positive contribution to teaching and learning in the school. [5.1, 5.2]

Recommendation 16. The use and support of the services and programs of a school library should be enhanced by planned and systematic communication with school library users—current and potential—and with the library's stakeholders and decision-makers. [6.4, 6.5]

Introduction

School libraries around the world, in their many forms, share a common purpose: the enhancement of "teaching and learning for all." For that reason, school library personnel advocate for equity of opportunity for all. School library personnel uphold the values of the *United Nations Declaration of the Rights of the Child* (1959), the *United Nations Convention on the Rights of the Child* (CRC, 1989), the *United Nations Declaration on the Rights of Indigenous People* (2007), and of the Core Values of IFLA:

- The endorsement of the principles of freedom of access to information, ideas and works of imagination and freedom of expression embodied in Article 19 of the *Universal Declaration of Human Rights*
- The belief that people, communities, and organizations need universal and equitable access to information, ideas and works of imagination for their social, educational, cultural, democratic, and economic well-being
- The conviction that delivery of high quality library and information services helps guarantee that access.
- The commitment to enable all Members of the Federation to engage in and to benefit from its activities without regard to citizenship, disability, ethnic origin, gender, geographical location, language, political philosophy, race, or religion (www.ifla.org/about/more).

The guidelines are based on the foundational principles of school library development expressed in the *IFLA/UNESCO School Library Manifesto: The school library in teaching and learning for all* (see Appendix A). The *School Library Manifesto*, first published in 1999, has been translated into many languages, and it continues to be used by school library advocates to raise the profile of school libraries in their schools and in their regions and countries.

The manifesto states: "*Governments, through their ministries responsible for education, are urged to develop strategies, policies, and plans that implement the principles of this Manifesto.*" The guidelines in this document have been produced to inform decision makers at national and local levels around the world, and to give support and guidance to the library community. They have been written to help school leaders implement the principles expressed in the *Manifesto*. Because schools and school libraries vary a great deal from country to country, the guidelines will need to be read and used with awareness of and sensitivity to the local context.

This document is intended to be both inspirational and aspirational. The many contributors to this document were inspired by the mission and values of the school library, and they recognised that school library personnel and educational decision-makers, even in countries with well-resourced and well-supported school libraries, must struggle to be relevant to the learning needs of the whole school community and to respond thoughtfully to the changing information environment within which they work.

All guidelines represent a compromise between what we aspire to achieve and what we can reasonably expect to achieve. It is important that the standards and guidelines that school librarians might use to guide their practice and that might be used in advocating for future improvements in school library services and programs are applicable to the local situation. Standards and guidelines should "resonate" with the people who best know that local situation. When increases in funding and staffing or for renovations of a facility are proposed, the evidence related to the contributions such changes will make in terms of student learning and teacher success provide more compelling arguments than arguments related to achieving a set of standards.

Meeting all the standards for funding, for technology, for collections, for staffing, and for facilities does not necessarily guarantee the best teaching and learning environment. What is more important is the way that the members of the school community think about school libraries: working in service of the *moral purpose* of school libraries (i.e., making a difference in the lives of young people) and of the *educational purpose* of school libraries (i.e., improving teaching and learning for all). Facilities, collections, staff, and technology are only means to that end.

Principals and other stakeholders, including school library personnel, need to keep in mind an important question—what value can and do students and teachers get from having access to school library services and programs? Research over the past four decades has shown that school libraries, properly staffed and resourced, can have a significant impact on student achievement. The most critical resource of a school library is a qualified professional school librarian who collaborates with other teachers to create the best possible knowledge-building and meaning-making learning experiences for students.

The *IFLA School Library Guidelines* can be used to support the development and improvement of school libraries in different ways in different regions. It can be challenging to see the possibilities for school libraries in developing and emerging countries, but the *moral purpose* and the *educational purpose* of school libraries can be addressed in these environments, in diverse and creative ways, sometimes through providing the basic-building blocks of literacy that are fundamental to school library development. Examples of innovative literacy projects can be found in a recent IFLA-sponsored book, *Global Perspectives on School Libraries: Projects and Practices* (Marquardt & Oberg, 2011). Examples of innovative initiatives for developing, implementing, and promoting school library guidelines can be found in the recently published IFLA-sponsored book, *Global Action on School Library Guidelines* (Schultz-Jones & Oberg, 2015).

The *IFLA/UNESCO School Library Manifesto* articulates the foundational principles of school library development; *School Library Guidelines* give direction as to the practical implementation of those foundational principles. *School Library Guidelines* challenge us to think globally and act locally in our efforts to provide the best possible school library services in the support of "teaching and learning for all."

Thinking Globally

These school library guidelines envision a world of inclusion, equity of opportunity, and social justice. They will be implemented in the context of the 21st century and characterised by change, mobility, and interconnection across different levels and sectors. Worldwide, people's lives are being affected by trends, such as globalisation; economic and social instability and change; evolving digital and mobile technologies; and sustainability or "greening" of the environment.

Education is changing through changes in curricula and through enhanced technology (e.g., cloud computing, gaming, smartphones, 1to1 computing). New funding models for education are needed in financial and legislative contexts in many countries that emphasize reducing costs and public expenditure on schools and universities. The number of high school graduates is increasing worldwide but the number of tertiary graduates is still lagging in many countries. Economic and social changes are increasing the number of foreign students and second language learners in schools and universities. The ubiquity of technology has changed the way learners access information and interact with others (OECD, 2014).

Libraries are being affected by the digital agenda and by trends such as "open" access data, learning initiatives, and convergence. Governments in many parts of the world have developed planning documents similar to the European Union's *The Digital Agenda* (http://ec.europa.eu/digital-agenda/en), which is based on seven pillars:

1) Digital Single Market – breaking down barriers to the free flow of online services and content across national borders
2) Interoperability and Standards – new standards for IT devices, applications, data repositories, and services will ensure seamless interaction anywhere, just like the Internet
3) Trust and Security – reinforced rules on personal data security and coordinated responses to cyber-hacking
4) Fast and Ultra-fast Internet – increased investment to provide faster access and faster downloads
5) Research and Innovation – increased investment in ICT in order to commercialize innovations
6) Enhancing Digital Literacy, Skills, and Inclusion – education and training to address the digital divide, especially for the disadvantaged
7) ICT-enabled Benefits – to reduce energy consumption, streamline public services, and provide access to cultural heritage

The digital agenda increases the need for school library personnel to develop and enhance their digital skills and to be prepared to work with others in the school community to develop and enhance the digital skills and knowledge of students and teachers. Worldwide, school library services and programs have been or soon will be affected by the changes in digital and mobile technology, and these changes increase the need for teaching the principles of digital citizenship.

Acting Locally

The *School Library Guidelines* are intended to be adapted and implemented in ways that suit local contexts, especially legislative and curriculum contexts. The legislation governing school library development may be included in an Education Act or a Library Act, in both Acts, or in neither. School curriculum documents may be developed nationally or locally; these documents may define specifically the mission, role, and purposes of the school library, or they may be entirely silent on these matters.

The *School Library Guidelines* are intended to guide governments, library associations, schools, school leaders and local communities in the process of aligning school libraries to local educational outcomes, to the informational needs of the school community, to the social, ethnic, cultural, linguistic, indigenous and other unique population dimensions of the community within and beyond the school.

The *School Library Guidelines* call on educational decision-makers, including government legislators and school administrators, to consider the research evidence that shows the contributions quality school library services can make to the educational success of its youth. The guidelines also call on school library personnel to develop and enhance the competences they need to keep pace with the ongoing changes in education and society and to become agents of and catalysts for change.

References

Marquardt, L., & Oberg, D. (2011). *Global perspectives on school libraries: Projects and practices.* The Hague, Netherlands: De Gruyter Saur.

Schultz-Jones, B. & Oberg, D. (2015). *Global action on school library guidelines.* The Hague, Netherlands: De Gruyter Saur.

OECD (Organization for Economic Co-operation and Development). (2014). *Education at a glance 2014: OECD indicators.* Paris: OECD Publishing. Retrieved from dx.doi.org/10.1787/eag-2014-en

Chapter 1
Mission and Purposes of a School Library

"The school library provides information and ideas that are fundamental to functioning successfully in today's information and knowledge-based society. The school library equips students with life-long learning skills and develops the imagination, enabling them to live as responsible citizens." School Library Manifesto

1.1 Introduction

This chapter is a general statement on the mission and purpose of a school library, as defined by the *IFLA/UNESCO School Library Manifesto* (1999). A school library is envisioned in the *Manifesto* as a force for enhancement and improvement of teaching and learning throughout the school community—for educators as well as for students. The key issues identified in the *Manifesto* are developed in greater detail in subsequent chapters.

1.2 Context

School libraries exist throughout the world as learning environments that provide space (physical and digital), access to resources, and access to activities and services to encourage and support student, teacher, and community learning. The growth of school libraries parallels the growth in education that seeks to equip students with knowledge to operate within and contribute to the betterment of society. While the range of school library facilities and operations varies throughout the world, school libraries everywhere are focused on supporting and advancing student learning. A school library provides a range of learning opportunities for individuals, small groups, and large groups with a focus on intellectual content, information literacy, and cultural and social development. The learner-oriented focus of a school library supports, extends, and individualises a school's curriculum.

> *Example*
> The Lubuto Library Project provides culturally relevant resources and educational experiences to orphans and other vulnerable children and youth in Zambia.

1.3 Definition of a school library

A school library is a school's physical and digital learning space where reading, inquiry, research, thinking, imagination, and creativity are central to students' information-to-knowledge journey and to their personal, social, and cultural growth. This physical and digital place is known by several terms (e.g., school media centre, centre for documentation and information, library resource centre, library learning commons) but *school library* is the term most commonly used and applied to the facility and functions.

More than 50 years of international research, collectively, (see, for example, Haycock, 1992, in LRS (2015) *School Libraries Impact Studies* in the USA www.lrs.org/data-tools/school-libraries/impact-studies/ and Williams, Wavell, C., and Morrison (2013) in the United Kingdom www.scottishlibraries.org/storage/sectors/schools/SLIC_RGU_Impact_of_School_Libraries_2013.pdf) identifies the following features that distinguish a school library:

- It has a qualified school librarian with formal education in school librarianship and classroom teaching that enables the professional expertise required for the complex roles of instruction, reading and literacy development, school library management, collaboration with teaching staff, and engagement with the educational community.
- It provides targeted high-quality diverse collections (print, multimedia, digital) that support the school's formal and informal curriculum, including individual projects and personal development.
- It has an explicit policy and plan for ongoing growth and development.

School libraries, like other aspects of the educational system, go through phases of growth and development. However, these three features of a school library are necessary for the fulfilment of the mission and purpose of a school library. Research shows that the potential of a school library for having an impact on student learning is dependent on the extent to which these features are present in a school.

A school library operates as a:

- dedicated physical and digital space in a school that is open and accessible to all;
- information space providing equitable and open access to quality information sources across all media, including print, multimedia, and curated digital collections;
- safe space where individual curiosity, creativity, and an orientation toward learning are encouraged and supported and where students can explore diverse topics, even controversial topics, in privacy and safety;
- instructional space where students learn the capabilities and dispositions for engaging with information and for creating knowledge;
- technological space providing a diverse range of technology tools, software, and expertise for the creation, representation, and sharing of knowledge;
- literacy centre where the school community nurtures reading and literacy development in all its forms;
- centre for digital citizenship where the learning community learns to use digital tools appropriately, ethically, and safely, and learns strategies to protect identity and personal information;
- information environment for all in the community through equitable access to resources, technology, and information skills development that are not always available in homes; and
- social space open for cultural, professional, and educational events (e.g., events, meetings, exhibits, resources) for the general community.

1.4 Role of a school library within a school

A school library operates within a school as a teaching and learning centre that provides an active instructional program integrated into curriculum content, with emphasis on the following:

- Resource-based capabilities – abilities and dispositions related to seeking, accessing, and evaluating resources in a variety of formats, including people and cultural artefacts as sources. These capabilities also include using information technology tools to seek out, access, and evaluate these sources, and the development of digital and print-based literacies.
- Thinking-based capabilities – abilities and dispositions that focus on substantive engagement with data and information through research and inquiry processes, the

processes of higher order thinking, and critical analysis that lead to the creation of representations/products that demonstrate deep knowledge and deep understanding.
- Knowledge-based capabilities – research and inquiry abilities and dispositions that focus on the creation, construction, and shared use of the products of knowledge that demonstrate deep knowledge and understanding.
- Reading and literacy capabilities – abilities and dispositions related to the enjoyment of reading, reading for pleasure, reading for learning across multiple platforms, and the transformation, communication, and dissemination of text in its multiple forms and modes to enable the development of meaning and understanding.
- Personal and interpersonal capabilities – the abilities and dispositions related to social and cultural participation in resource-based inquiry and learning about oneself and others as researchers, information users, knowledge creators, and responsible citizens.
- Learning management capabilities – abilities and dispositions that enable students to prepare for, plan, and successfully undertake a curriculum-based inquiry unit.

A school librarian plays a leadership role in developing these capabilities through individual and collaborative instruction and facilitation explicitly connected to curriculum content and outcomes.

1.5 Conditions for an effective school library program

Research has shown that the most critical condition for an effective school library program is access to a qualified school library professional. A school library without a pedagogical program (i.e., planned comprehensive offering of teaching and learning activities) will not be able to have the kind of impact on teaching and learning that the research demonstrates is possible with a qualified school library professional who carries out the roles outlined in Section 3.4.

A school library should be managed within a clearly structured policy framework that recognises the library as a centre of reading, inquiry, and collaborative productions. The library policy should be devised bearing in mind the overarching policies and needs of the school and should reflect its ethos, mission, aims, and objectives, as well as its reality. Administrative support for the role of a school library through the library policy is essential to realize the full benefit of a school library program. The facilities, the physical and digital resources, and the human resources required to activate an effective school library program are discussed in later chapters.

1.6 Vision statement for a school library

The vision statement projects the future state desired for a school library. The vision could vary worldwide, depending on the starting position of the school library. Ultimately, constructing a vision for the school library to play a central role in education that transcends current constraints creates a future oriented ambition to provide a multi-functional learning space.

The vision incorporates the five key trends identified in the *IFLA Trend Report 2013* (trends.ifla.org):
1) New technologies will both expand and limit who has access to information.
2) Online education will democratise and disrupt global learning.
3) The boundaries of privacy and data protection will be redefined.
4) Hyper-connected societies will listen to and empower new voices and groups.
5) The global information economy will be transformed by new technologies.

1.7 Mission statement for a school library

The mission is a definition of the nature, purpose, and role of the school library as part of the school's shared purpose and commitment. The mission for school libraries worldwide is articulated by the 1999 *IFLA/UNESCO School Library Manifesto* (Appendix A). The mission statement for an individual school library should reflect the components of the *Manifesto's* mission to align with the educational context within which the school and school library resides. It should provide direction to focus resources and guide planning and to communicate the intent to serve the community by defining an understanding of the needs of its members; the skills, resources, and capacity needed to fulfil those needs; and an expected outcome that will benefit the community—align with the educational purpose of preparing students for their future work and as citizens.

1.8 School library services

To meet the needs of the learning community the school library provides a range of services. These services may be delivered within or from a school library facility. The provision of services using information and communication technology (ICT) also presents opportunities to extend the reach of the library to all areas of the school and to the home. A strong networked information technology infrastructure provides access to collections, community resources, and curated digital collections, as well as the tools for undertaking research-based inquiry and the construction, presentation, and sharing of knowledge.

School library services include:

- professional development for the teaching faculty (e.g., reading and literacy, technology, inquiry and research processes);
- vibrant literature/reading program for academic achievement and personal enjoyment and enrichment;
- inquiry-based learning and information literacy development; and
- collaboration with other libraries (public, government, community resources).

School libraries provide significant value to the educational community. The value added extends beyond the materials in a school library collection to the services provided through a vibrant school library program and a qualified school librarian.

1.9 Evaluation of school library services and programs

Evaluation of school library services and programs is an essential aspect of school library development. Evaluation serves accountability purposes: It helps to determine if the school library services and programs are meeting the needs of the school community. Evaluation also should contribute to the ongoing transformation of school library services and programs by influencing stakeholders' thinking about the school library and developing their support for the school library. Selecting an evaluation method or approach will depend on the needs of the school community and the developmental stage of the library (e.g., program quality, stakeholder perceptions, program content, and program impact).

An evaluation focusing on overall program quality might utilise international, national, or local standards to examine and to rate the many aspects of a school library (e.g., staffing, facilities, technology, and collections, as well as instructional programs). An evaluation focusing on improvement of school library practices, often called evidence-based practice, might utilise data such as student learning products; instructional patterns (by class, grade, or subject); surveys of students, teachers and/or parents; or records from the library's circulation and cataloguing system. Chapter 6 of this document will explore in more depth the need for evaluation and its usefulness in management and in public relations (promotion, marketing, advocacy).

Useful Resources

American Association of School Librarians. (2014). *Governing documents.* Retrieved from www.ala.org/aasl/about/governing-docs

American Association of School Librarians. (2011). *Standards for the 21st century learner.* Retrieved from www.ala.org/aasl/standards-guidelines/learning-standards

Hay, L., & Todd, R. J. (2010). *School libraries 21C.* NSW Department of Education and Training. Retrieved from www.curriculumsupport.education.nsw.gov.au/schoollibraries/assets/pdf/21c_report.pdf

Haycock, K. (1992). *What works: Research about teaching and learning through the school's library resource center.* Seattle, WA: Rockland Press.

IFLA/UNESCO School Library Manifesto. (1999). Retrieved from www.ifla.org/publications/iflaunesco-school-library-manifesto-1999

Library Research Service [Colorado State Library, Colorado Department of Education]. *School libraries impact studies.* Retrieved from www.lrs.org/data-tools/school-libraries/impact-studies/

Groupe de Recherche sur la Culture et la Didactique de l'information. (2010). *Parcours de formation à la culture de l'information* [The learning path to an information culture]. Retrieved from http://culturedel.info/grcdi/?page_id=236

Williams, D., Wavell, C., & Morrison, K. (2013). *Impact of school libraries on learning: Critical review of published evidence to inform the Scottish education community.* Aberdeen, Scotland: Robert Gordon University, Institute for Management, Governance & Society (IMaGeS). Retrieved from www.scottishlibraries.org/storage/sectors/schools/SLIC_RGU_Impact_of_School_Libraries_2013.pdf).

Chapter 2
Legal and Financial Framework for a School Library

"As the responsibility of local, regional, and national authorities, [school libraries] must be supported by specific legislation and policies. School libraries must have adequate and sustained funding for trained staff, materials, technologies, and facilities. They must be free of charge." School Library Manifesto

2.1 Introduction

A school library responds to the needs of the educational community within which it is located and works for the benefit of all members of that community. A school library exists within a framework of local, regional, and national authority to provide equity of opportunity for learning and for developing the abilities needed to participate in the knowledge society. In order to maintain and continuously respond to an evolving educational and cultural environment, school libraries need to be supported by legislation and sustained funding.

2.2 Legal bases and issues

Around the world, there are many different models of the relationship between school libraries and government. Additionally, the laws that govern their activities and funding arrangements can be varied and complex. For example, school library legislation, policies, and standards might be the responsibility of a country's Ministry of Education or Ministry of Culture, or the responsibility might be shared between the two ministries. Some countries throughout the world give responsibility for school libraries, either in whole or in part, to various provinces, states or municipalities.

As a principle of practice, school libraries adapt over time to their legal and political setting, to provide a learning environment that positions and maintains the school library as a centre of inquiry, discovery, creativity, critical engagement, and innovative pedagogy. The continual evolution of a sustaining level of resources that enables a school library to fulfil a standard of student support for intellectual development and skill advancement requires that systemic guidelines exist within a school system and beyond.

2.3 Ethical bases and issues

A school library exists within an ethical framework that considers the rights and responsibilities of students and other members of the learning community. A school library employs a holistic approach to ensure that all cultural, linguistic, indigenous, and other unique populations are welcome. The core values of equity of access to recorded knowledge and information and of intellectual freedom are embodied in Article 19 of the *Universal Declaration of Human Rights* and in the values of IFLA (www.ifla.org/about/more).

Other considerations include, but are not limited to:

- Library Bill of Rights
- Freedom of information and privacy
- Statements of copyright, intellectual property and plagiarism
- *Rights of the Child* (www.un.org/cyberschoolbus/humanrights/resources/child.asp)
- *Rights of Indigenous People* (http://undesadspd.org/indigenouspeoples/declarationontherightsofindigenouspeoples.aspx)

A school library develops the skills and understandings required of responsible citizenship through programs that educate students and the learning community on ethical issues such as freedom of information, intellectual property, and plagiarism.

2.4 Infrastructure Support for School Library Development

A system of support for school library implementation and development needs to be established within the administrative unit responsible for education at the national and/or regional/local level. Efforts should be made to define and implement a basic level of school library services and activities so that students and teachers are able to understand and access a school library as a resource for teaching and learning. The work of such education service centers can include attention to issues such as: initial and continuing education of school librarians, professional consultations, research studies, collaboration with groups of school librarians and their professional associations, and development of standards and guidelines.

The nature and extent of school library services and activities varies from country to country and from school to school. However, the increasing mobility of students and their families means that consistency across schools and access to school libraries enhances the capacity of educational systems to meet the needs of members of the school community.

> *Example*
> The Texas Legislature in the USA created a system of 20 regional education service centers in 1967 to assist school districts across the state. The role of the education service center is to work alongside school districts to carry out three main objectives: assist school districts in improving student performance in each region of the system; enable school districts to operate more efficiently and economically; and implement initiatives assigned by the legislature or commissioner. Education service centers provide professional development, technical assistance, and management of educational programs to aid administrators, school librarians, and teachers.

2.5 Policies

A school library should be managed within a clearly structured policy framework that recognises the library as a core resource and centre for reading and inquiry. A school library policy should be devised bearing in mind the overarching policies and needs of the school and should reflect the ethos, mission, aims, and objectives, as well as the reality of the school.

The policy should make it clear that the library is for all. It should be developed by the school librarian, working together with the teachers and administrators (i.e., principals, heads of schools, educational staff). The draft policy should be shared widely, throughout the school community, and supported by open discussion. The resulting policy should be widely shared in order that the philosophy, concepts, and intentions for practice and development are understood, endorsed, and ready to be put into practice. The policy document and the plans developed based on the policy should specify the role of the library in relation to the following components:

- Formal and informal curriculum in the school
- Learning methods in the school
- National and local standards and criteria
- Learning and personal development needs of students
- Needs of teachers
- Raising levels of academic achievement
- Developing inquiry skills
- Promoting and motivating reading
- Open-mindedness and civic engagement

All are essential in creating a realistic policy framework and subsequent action plans. The action plan should be made up of goals, tasks, and strategies, as well as monitoring and evaluation routines. The policy and action plans should be active documents, subject to regular review.

2.6 Planning

Planning a school library requires the active involvement of the school librarian in consultation with administrators, faculty, and students to determine the relationship of the school library to the rest of the school learning community. Important dimensions to consider within the planning process include:

- sustainable development goals identified by future-oriented studies by national and international groups;
- a national and school-level educational mission, philosophy, goals, and objectives;
- a vision statement that describes the value of the school library to the school and the role of stakeholders, cultural partners and funders in the educational process;
- a needs assessment that identifies the role of the school library now and envisions where it should be in the future as a learning centre;
- a plan to connect the school community with access to quality resources, facilities, and physical and digital learning environments;
- a technology plan with future projections of technology and potential changes in delivery of information and services;
- a dynamic action plan of student-centred and community-centred activities;
- a plan for the development of professional skills for school library personnel; and
- an evaluation plan that provides for continuous improvement through evidence-based research, demonstrating the impact of library services on student success.

Example
In a rural area of Indonesia, school staff works with library school faculty, a government ministry, and an international development agency to develop a model school library.

2.7 Funding

To ensure the currency and vitality of a school library's instructional and information base, the library needs an appropriate budget allocation, taking into account local reality. Budget expenditures should relate to the school's policy framework for the school library and reflect an investment in student, teacher, and staff development.

A school librarian works with senior management to develop the budget and explore responsible options for the delivery of quality resources and services to the entire school community. Financial support for a school library reflects the research indicating that:

- Size and quality of a school library's teaching/support staff and its collections are the best school predictors of academic achievement.
- Students who score higher on standardised tests tend to come from schools with more school library staff and more access to services and resources such as books, periodicals, and online material, regardless of other factors such as economic ones. (See, for example, IASL Research Abstracts www.iasl-online.org/research/abstracts; Kachel & Lance, 2013.)

Budget spending is carefully planned for the whole year and is related to the policy framework. The components of a budget plan are presented in Appendix B. Annual reports illuminate how the library budget has been used and clarify whether the amount of money spent on the library program and its resources has been enough to cover its tasks and attain the policy targets. Annual reports should include evidence of the quality of school library services and programs and their impact on teaching and learning in the school. Chapter 6 of this document explores in more depth the need for evaluation and its usefulness in school library management.

Useful Resources

American Association of School Librarians. (2011). *Standards for the 21st century learner.* Retrieved from www.ala.org/aasl/standards-guidelines/learning-standards

American Library Association. (2010). *Intellectual Freedom Manual* (8th ed.). Retrieved from www.ala.org/advocacy/intfreedom/iftoolkits/ifmanual/intellectual

American Library Association. (1996). *Library Bill of Rights.* Retrieved from www.ala.org/advocacy/intfreedom/librarybill

Australian School Library Association. (2000). *School Library Bill of Rights.* Retrieved from www.asla.org.au/policy/bill-of-rights.aspx

Hay, L. & Todd, R. J. (2010). *School libraries 21C.* NSW Department of Education and Training. Retrieved from www.curriculumsupport.education.nsw.gov.au/schoollibraries/assets/pdf/21c_report.pdf

International Federation of Library Associations. (2015). *Indigenous Matters Special Interest Group.* Retrieved from www.ifla.org/indigenous-matters

International Federation of Library Associations. (2015). *Lesbian, Gay, Bisexual, Transgender and Queer/Questioning Users Special Interest Group.* Retrieved from www.ifla.org/lgbtq

International Federation of Library Associations. (2015). *IFLA/UNESCO Multicultural Library Manifesto.* Retrieved from www.ifla.org/node/8976

Kachel, D. E., & Lance, K. C. (2013). Latest study: A full-time school librarian makes a critical difference in boosting student achievement. *School Library Journal, 59*(3), 28.

Chapter 3
Human Resources for a School Library

"The school librarian is the professionally qualified staff member responsible for planning and managing the school library, supported by staffing as adequate as possible, working together with all members of the school community, and liaising with the public library and others." School Library Manifesto

3.1 Introduction

The core function of a school library is to provide physical and intellectual access to information and ideas. The richness and quality of a school library program primarily depends upon the human resources available within and beyond a school library. In order to meet the teaching and learning needs of a school community, it is essential to have a well-trained and highly motivated staff, in sufficient numbers according to the size of the school and its unique needs. Everyone working in a school library should have a clear understanding of library services and policies, well defined duties and responsibilities, and properly regulated conditions of employment and compensation that reflect the role expectations of their positions.

3.2 Staffing roles and rationale

Because a school library facilitates teaching and learning, the program of a school library needs to be under the direction of professional staff with the same level of education and preparation as classroom teachers. Where a school librarian is expected to take a leadership role in the school, the school librarian needs to have the same level of education and preparation as other leaders in the school, such as school administrators and learning specialists. The operational aspects of a school library are best handled by trained clerical and technical support staff in order to ensure that a school librarian has the time needed for the professional roles of instruction, management, collaboration, and leadership.

3.3 Definition of a school librarian

A school librarian is responsible for the school's physical and digital learning space where reading, inquiry, research, thinking, imagination, and creativity are central to teaching and learning. This role is known by several terms (e.g., school librarian, school library media specialist, teacher librarian, *professeurs documentalistes*) but *school librarian* is the term most commonly used. The qualifications of school librarians vary across the world and may include librarians with or without teacher training and librarians with training in other library specialties.

How school libraries are defined varies across the world and may include being served through the public library. Staffing patterns for school libraries also change depending on the local context, which is influenced by legislation, economic development, and educational infrastructure. However, more than 50 years of international research, collectively, (see, for example, Haycock, 1992, in LRS (2015) *School Libraries Impact Studies* www.lrs.org/data-tools/school-libraries/impact-studies) indicates that a school librarian requires formal education in school librarianship and classroom teaching that provides the professional expertise required for the complex roles of instruction, reading and literacy development, school library management, collaboration with teaching staff, and engagement with the educational community.

Example
In France, school librarians (*professeurs documentalistes)* who work in junior high schools and high schools are recruited and trained at the same education level and have the same status as other teachers.

Example
In South Tyrol, Italy, school librarian staff are recruited by the Province of Bozen to work in K-13 level schools according to their qualifications and training in librarianship (Province of Bozen Law n. 17/1990; Province of Bozen Collective Labour Agreement, March 4, 2006). A school library assistant must have completed secondary education (K-13) and a course of librarianship (at least one year of theory and practice). A qualified school librarian must have completed higher education (at least a three-year degree). See: Berufsbilder "BibliothekarIn" und "DiplombibliothekarIn" (i.e., Librarian and Qualified Librarian Job Profiles, at www.provinz.bz.it/kulturabteilung/bibliotheken/1459.asp)

Example
In Portugal, since 2009, the school librarian (*professor bibliotecário*) has been a school teacher who has specialized in librarianship. See "Formação" (Education) at: www.rbe.mec.pt/np4/programa.html

3.4 Competencies needed to provide school library programs

The qualifications of a professional school librarian include:

- teaching and learning, curriculum, instructional design and delivery;
- program management – planning, development/design, implementation, evaluation/improvement;
- collection development, storage, organization, retrieval;
- information processes and behaviours – literacy, information literacy, digital literacies;
- reading engagement;
- knowledge about children's and young adult literature;
- knowledge of disabilities that affect reading;
- communication and collaboration skills;
- digital and media skills;
- ethics and social responsibility;
- service for the public good – accountability to the public/society;
- commitment to lifelong learning through continuing professional development; and
- socialisation to the field of school librarianship and to its history and values.

The development of a school librarian's professional competencies and dispositions can be achieved in a variety of ways—usually through a diploma or degree program or continuing professional development completed after initial certification in teaching or in librarianship. The goal of school librarian education is actualization of teaching and librarianship skills.

In countries where there are specific school librarian education programs, the curriculum should include, in addition to the core competencies of librarianship, an understanding of education (learning, curriculum, teaching), of digital technology and social media, and of youth, culture, and literacies. Together, these areas of study should result in a deep and comprehensive understanding of information literacy from a creative thinking and problem-solving perspective. School library education should also address the role of a professional school librarian as a leader from the side, as a change agent or catalyst, and as a member of the school library community.

> *Example*
> In France, the competency framework for teachers, *Référentiel de compétences des enseignants,* presents a list of educational skills whose mastery must be accomplished by any teacher, including the school librarian. This list includes specific library and information sciences skills for school librarians. Information literacy skills must be recognized as essential for every member of the education community: This common knowledge is a prerequisite for any efficient pedagogical collaboration.

3.5 Roles of a professional school librarian

The key roles of a professional school librarian are: instruction, management, leadership and collaboration, and community engagement. Each one is discussed in more detail below.

3.5.1 Instruction

The instructional role of a professional school librarian encompasses a wide diversity of teaching situations with individual students, small groups of students, and classes of students, and also includes informal and formal professional development of teaching colleagues. The core activities of the instructional work of a school librarian, detailed in Chapter 5, include:

- literacy and reading promotion;
- information literacy (information skills, information competences, information fluency, media literacy, transliteracy);
- inquiry-based learning (problem-based learning, critical thinking);
- technology integration; and
- professional development for teachers.

> *Example*
> Various pedagogical frameworks have been produced and used as guidelines for teachers: from France, *Benchmarks for the implementation of the learning path to an information culture [Repères pour la mise en œuvre du Parcours de formation à la culture de l'information];* from Belgium, *Media literacy skills: A major educational challenge [Les compétences en éducation aux medias: un enjeu éducatif majeur];* and from *UNESCO Media and information literacy: A training program for teachers* [*Education aux medias et à l'information: programme de formation pour les enseignants].*

3.5.2 Management

The management role of a professional school librarian involves organizing the documentation systems and processes of a school library for optimum use. This includes the library facilities (both physical and digital environments), the material resources (both physical and digital), and the pedagogical programs and services (both physical and digital). The management of human resources may also be part of this role—recruiting, selecting, training, supervising, and evaluating library staff.

3.5.3 Leadership and collaboration

A school librarian's main role is to contribute to the mission and goals of the school. In collaboration with the school's administrators and teachers, the librarian develops and implements curriculum-based library services and programs that support teaching and learning for all. The librarian contributes knowledge and skills related to the provision of information and the use of resources to such teaching and learning activities as inquiry and project work, problem-solving activities, literacy activities, reading engagement, and cultural activities. A school librarian may take a role, alone or in collaboration with other specialists in the school, in the integration of technology and in the provision of professional development for teachers and for administrators.

Collaboration is an essential part of a school librarian's work. A school librarian works with the school's administrators to develop understanding and support of the library's contribution to the mission and goals of the school. A school librarian should report directly to the principal, head teacher, or deputy head of the school and should be expected to participate in the school-wide planning and other leadership teamwork. Within the school community, a school librarian should work to facilitate school-wide continuity and cohesiveness through activities such as cross-curriculum inquiry projects and interdisciplinary learning units. A school librarian should collaborate with other school librarians to extend and continue their professional development and learning.

> *Example*
> In north Texas, USA, the school library directors for many school libraries meet monthly to exchange ideas and present new approaches to programs and services.

> *Example*
> In the United Kingdom, there are well-established regional groups of school librarians that meet each school term for training and networking opportunities.

3.5.4 Community engagement

Community engagement encompasses programming, collection development, and outreach efforts that welcome diverse cultural, linguistic, indigenous, and other unique populations into our libraries. School libraries should recognize the importance of families in the education of their children and the value of intergenerational transfer of knowledge.

Children are supported by families and communities. There needs to be a holistic approach that enables people from diverse backgrounds to be employed in school libraries, to participate and contribute at governance levels, and to support equitable access to information, ideas, and works of imagination for their social, educational, cultural, democratic, and economic well-being. One of the core values of many communities is the intergenerational transfer of wealth and knowledge. The transfer of knowledge in a manner that is effective and meaningful to children from these communities may differ significantly from the dominant culture within which the school library operates. For all children 'identity' and 'belonging' are essential components to literacy and learning achievement.

A school librarian should, if possible, also liaise, with other library groups within the broader community, including public libraries and library associations. In order to improve library services for children and young persons in a given community, school libraries and public libraries should endeavour to cooperate. A written cooperation agreement should include: common measures for the cooperation; specification and definition of cooperation areas; clarification of economic implications and how to share costs; and a scheduled time period for the cooperation. Examples of cooperation areas include shared staff training; cooperative collection development and programming; coordination of electronic services and networks; class visits to the public library; joint reading and literacy promotion; and joint marketing of library services to children and young persons.

> *Example*
> In Oslo, Norway, the school administration and the public library have made a collaborative agreement and meet on a regular basis to discuss topics related to the 120 school libraries in the city. The public library's school service is staffed to advise and to provide loans of additional material to the schools. Advice is given in areas such as reading and literacy, collection development, and organizing the school library space. All school librarians and school teachers can seek help from this school service by e-mail or telephone. Materials that the schools cannot afford to buy or that they do not use regularly can be sent to the school library or directly to the classrooms.

3.5.5 Promoting library programs and services

Promoting library programs and services includes communicating to users about what the library has to offer and matching those programs and services to the needs and preferences of users. The programs, services, and facilities provided by the school library must be actively promoted so that target groups are aware of the library's role as a partner in learning and as a provider of programs, services, and resources. The target groups for promoting library services are the principal and the other members of the school administration, heads of departments, teachers, students, and parents. It is important to adjust communication to the nature of the school and to the different target groups.

A school library should have a written promotion plan, worked out in cooperation with the school administration and teaching staff. The plan should include the following elements: objectives; an action plan that indicates how the objectives will be attained; and the evaluation methods by which the success of the action plan will be assessed.

3.6 Roles and competencies of paraprofessional school library staff

Paraprofessional school library staff (i.e., library assistants, library technicians) report to the librarian and support the work of the librarian through their clerical and technological functions. Paraprofessional school library staff should have the training and development required for the operational routines of the school library such as shelving, lending, returning and processing library material, and providing technical services related to managing online circulation and cataloguing services also providing access to digital resources.

3.7 Roles and competencies of a school library volunteer

Volunteers should not work as substitutes for paid library staff, but may work in support roles based upon agreements that give a formal framework for their involvement in school library activities, including supervision by the school librarian. Students may also work as school library volunteers, within well-defined roles and under supervision. Student volunteers should be senior students, selected through a formal application process and trained to carry out tasks such as helping to create displays, re-shelving library materials, reading with younger children, and recommending books to fellow students.

> *Example*
> In Michigan, USA, an elementary school's Library Squad contributes to the behind-the-scenes work that keeps the library running smoothly. Once a week, these students shelve materials, collect books from kindergarten classrooms, and sometimes assist with labelling and barcoding new items.

> *Example*
> In Rome, Italy, high school students enrolled in a special needs programme help to keep the library running smoothly, which contributes to library management and to the students' personal development. The students also helped during the library renovation phase: This has stimulated improved coordination skills and wider interests, and increased their self-esteem.

> *Example*
> In Hungary, it has been obligatory since 2012 for secondary school students to do voluntary work that benefits local communities. This voluntary work can also be done in both school and public libraries.

3.8 Ethical standards

Everyone who works in the school library, including volunteers, have the responsibility to observe high ethical standards in their dealings with each other and with all members of the school community. They must endeavour to put the rights of the library users before their own comfort and convenience and avoid being biased by their personal attitudes and beliefs in providing library service. All children, youth, and adults should be dealt with on an equal basis regardless of their abilities and background: Their rights to privacy and their right to know must be maintained.

Everyone who works in the school library, including volunteers, should endeavour to embody the core values of librarianship: stewardship, service, intellectual freedom, rationalism, literacy and learning, equity of access to recorded knowledge and information, privacy, and democracy. The core values of equity of access to recorded knowledge and information and intellectual freedom are embodied in Article 19 of the *Universal Declaration of Human Rights* and in the values of IFLA (www.ifla.org/about/more).

Useful Resources

American Library Association. (2010). *ALA/AASL Standards for initial preparation of school librarians.* Retrieved from www.ala.org/aasl/education/ncate

CLEMI: Centre de liaison de l'enseignement et des médias d'information. (2013). *Proposition pour un référentiel enseignant en éducation aux médias* [Proposal for a repository in teaching media literacy] [pdf en ligne]. Retrieved from www.clemi.org/fichier/plug_download/29480/download_fichier_fr_referentiel_clemi_version2.pdf

Conseil supérieur de l'éducation aux médias. (2013). *Les compétences en éducation aux medias: Un enjeu éducatif majeur* [Media literacy skills: A major educational challenge]. Belgique: CSEM.

Gorman, M. (2000). *Our enduring values: Librarianship in the 21st century*. Chicago: American Library Association.

International Federation of Library Associations. (2012). *Professional Codes of Ethics for Librarians.* Retrieved from www.ifla.org/faife/professional-codes-of-ethics-for-librarians

International Federation of Library Associations. (2015). *Indigenous Matters Special Interest Group.* www.ifla.org/indigenous-matters

International Federation of Library Associations. (2015). *Lesbian, Gay, Bisexual, Transgender and Queer/Questioning Users Special Interest Group.* Retrieved from www.ifla.org/lgbtq

International Federation of Library Associations. (2015). *IFLA/UNESCO Multicultural Library Manifesto.* Retrieved from www.ifla.org/node/8976

Markless, S. (Ed.). (2009). *The innovative school librarian: Thinking outside the box.* London: Facet Publishing. [See Chapters 1 & 2, pp. 1-46.]

Ministère de l'éducation nationale. (2013). Référentiel de compétences des enseignants [Competency framework for teachers]. *Bulletin officiel de l'éducation nationale,* n°30, 25/07/2013.

National Forum on Information Literacy. (2014). *Policy statement on the importance of certified school librarians.* Retrieved from http://infolit.org/nfil-policy-statement-school-librarians

Simpson, C. (2003). *Ethics in school librarianship: A reader.* Worthington, OH: Linworth.

Wilson, C., Grizzle, A., Tuazon, R., Akyempong, K., & Cheung, C.K. (2012). *Education aux médias et à l'information: programme de formation pour les enseignants* [Media education and information: A training program for teachers]. Paris: UNESCO.

Chapter 4
Physical and Digital Resources of a School Library

"The library staff support the use of books and other information sources, ranging from the fictional to the documentary, from print to electronic, both on-site and remote. The materials complement and enrich textbooks, teaching materials, and methodologies." School Library Manifesto

4.1 Introduction

The physical and digital resources of a school library include facilities, equipment, and collections of resources for teaching and learning. Increasingly, technology extends the reach of a school library into the school as a whole and into the community. Technology also facilitates 24/7 access to school library resources and to resources beyond the school day and beyond the school calendar. The facilities, equipment, and collections of a school library need to evolve in response to changes in the teaching and learning needs of the students and the teachers.

4.2 Facilities

The functions and uses of a school library are of primary importance when planning new school buildings and renovating existing ones. The educational role of a school library should be reflected in its facilities. Today, many school libraries are being designed as "learning commons" in response to users' involvement in 'participatory culture,' which extends the users' roles from consumers of information to creators of information. Library learning commons provide facilities and equipment needed for creating information products as well as traditional learning and study spaces.

4.2.1 Location and space

There are no universal standards for the size and design of school library facilities, but it is useful to have criteria on which to base planning estimates. In general, libraries are moving from a resource-centred model to a learner-centred model: School and academic libraries are often designed as learning commons. The following considerations need to be included in planning school library facilities:

- Central location, on the ground floor if possible.
- Accessibility and proximity to teaching areas.
- Noise factors, with at least some parts of the library free from external noise.
- Appropriate and sufficient light, natural and/or artificial.
- Appropriate room temperature (e.g., air-conditioning, heating) to ensure good working conditions year round as well as the preservation of the collections.
- Appropriate design for library users with special needs.
- Adequate size to give space for the collection of books, fiction, non-fiction, hardback and paperback, newspapers and magazines, non-print resources and storage, study spaces, reading areas, computer workstations, display areas, and work areas for library staff.
- Flexibility to allow multiplicity of activities and future changes in curriculum and technology.

4.2.2 Organization of space

The following functional areas need to be provided:

- Study and research area – space for information desk, catalogues, on-line stations, study and research tables, reference materials and basic collections.
- Informal reading area – space for books and periodicals that encourage literacy, lifelong learning, and reading for pleasure.
- Instructional area – space with seats catering for small groups, large groups and whole classroom formal instruction, with appropriate instructional technology and display space (seating for 10% of the student population is often recommended).
- Media production and group project area – space for individuals, teams and classes (often called 'labs' or 'makerspaces').
- Administrative area – space for circulation desk, office area, space for processing of library media materials, and storage space for equipment, supplies, and materials.

4.2.3 Physical and digital access

Physical and digital access to the library should be maximized. With technology, digital access to the information resources of the school library can be provided throughout the school and beyond, 24/7. Where staff resources are limited, supervisory systems that include the use of trained student and adult volunteers should be considered.

4.3 Collection development and management

The school library needs to provide access to a wide range of physical and digital resources to meet the needs of the users and reflects their age, language, and demographics. Collections need to be developed on an ongoing basis to ensure that users have access to new and relevant materials. The collection management policy defines the purpose, scope, and contents of the collection as well as access to external resources and helps to ensure a wide range of high quality resources. Increasingly, digital resources such as ebooks (reference, fiction, non-fiction), online databases, online newspapers and magazines, video games, and multimedia learning materials are becoming a substantial part of the library's resources.

In addition to collections that meet student learning needs, a school library should include a collection of professional resources, both for the school library staff and for the teachers (i.e., materials on education, subjects taught, new teaching/learning styles and methods) and a collection of resources addressed to parents and caregivers.

> *Example*
> In Rome, Italy, the library in a primary school has developed a "Parents' Shelf" where resources on child psychology, education, and specific topics such as children's fears and self-esteem are made available.

4.3.1 Collection management policies and procedures

A school librarian works with school administrators and teachers in order to develop a collection management policy. Such a policy statement must be based upon the curriculum and the particular needs and interests of the school community and must reflect the diversity of society outside the school.

The following elements should be included in the collection management policy statement:

- The mission of a school library, consistent with the *IFLA/UNESCO School Library Manifesto.*
- Statements of intellectual freedom and of freedom of information.
- The purpose of the collection management policy and its relation to the curriculum and to the national, ethnic, cultural, linguistic and indigenous identities of its users.
- Long and short term objectives of the provision of resources.
- Responsibilities for collection management decisions.

The policy should make it clear that collection building is a collaborative endeavour and that teachers, as subject experts with valuable knowledge of the needs of their students, have an important role to play in helping to build the library collections. The policy should establish the method for reconsideration of resources consistent that is with the principles of intellectual freedom and of children's right to know. The policy should also identify the responsibility of school librarians for resisting efforts to censor materials, no matter the source of calls for limiting resources or access to resources.

Procedures for developing and managing the school library collection should be clearly laid out, in a separate document or as an appendix to the collection management policy document. The procedures manual should guide the selection and acquisition of resources and provide standards for the processing and organization (cataloguing, classification, shelving) of resources and for the maintenance, repair, and de-selection (weeding) of resources. The manual should include guidance in obtaining resources that have been created both locally and internationally and that reflect the national, ethnic, cultural, linguistic, and indigenous identities of members of the school community. The manual should also provide clear guidelines for the reconsideration of controversial materials.

> *Example*
> In France, the school librarian develops an acquisition policy in consultation with the school community that is linked to the policies articulated through the school's curriculum and instructional activities, as outlined in the 10 commandments of the acquisition policy.
> www.cndp.fr/savoirscdi/centre-de-ressources/fonds-documentaire-acquisition-traitement/les-10-commandements-dune-politique-dacquisition.html

4.3.2 Issues related to digital resources

The school library serves an important function as a significant access point to our information-based society. It must provide access to digital information resources that reflect the curriculum as well as the users' interests and culture. The emerging participatory culture enabled by social media has contributed to expansion of the role of library user, from information consumer to information creator. As a result, school librarians need to consider providing "makerspaces" with the computers and other production equipment needed for hands-on learning activities, including creating information products (e.g., videos, blogs, podcasts, 3D projects, posters, infographics).

The increasing availability of digital resources and of Internet access means that a school library's cataloguing system needs to be appropriate for classifying and cataloguing the resources according to accepted international or national bibliographic standards in order to facilitate the school library's inclusion in wider networks. In many places around the world, school libraries benefit from being linked together within a local or regional community through a union or shared cataloguing system. Such collaborations can increase the efficiency and quality of resources selection, cataloguing, and processing, making it easier to combine resources for maximum effect. In other places, school libraries benefit from coalitions or from government efforts that facilitate resource sharing of expensive commercial databases and online reference materials.

Example
In Alberta, Canada, the Ministry of Education fully funds the provision of quality online information resources in English and French to all students and teachers in the province through the Online Reference Centre.
www.learnalberta.ca/OnlineReferenceCentre.aspx.

Example
In France, easy access and use of digital resources by students is provided by *Correlyce platform* with over 300 editorial and indexed resources. www.correlyce.fr

The criteria for managing digital collections are similar to those for managing print collections. There are, however, some special considerations:

- Access – will access be improved or diminished by choosing a digital item over print?
- Financial and technical issues – will the cost of the digital item be higher in the long run because of on-going licensing fees or costs of changing to new formats?
- Legal and licensing issues – will the copyright laws or the licensing terms for digital materials limit the number of users, off-site access, or user privacy?
- Security – how will access to resources be protected?

4.3.3 Collection standards

Today, when a school library collection includes many digital resources available onsite or through external commercial databases and licensed reference materials, conventional school library collection standards are difficult to develop and apply. With or without access to national or local collection standards, collection development decisions should be based on curriculum requirements and instructional approaches.

A balanced collection of current and relevant items is needed to ensure access to resources for users of different ages, abilities, learning styles, and backgrounds. The collection should support the curriculum through information resources, whether in physical or digital formats. In addition, a school library should acquire materials for leisure purposes such as popular or graphic novels, music, computer games, films, magazines, comics, and posters. These resources should be selected in cooperation with students to ensure the materials reflect their interests and culture.

Example
The South Carolina Department of Education in the USA released collection development standards in 2012. According to the numbers of volumes per pupil, a collection is considered "at risk" (11 volumes), "basic" (13), or "Exemplary" (15). The percentage of fiction and non-fiction items in a collection should vary according to grade ranges and according to specific literacy projects or needs.

4.3.4 Resource sharing

School libraries should enhance access to library materials for their users through inter-library loans and resource sharing. However, because this is not a traditional function of many school libraries, there are rarely well-established systems to facilitate this. Inter-library loans and resource sharing are easier to arrange where school libraries are linked together by a union catalogue or by shared access to online databases and digital reference materials.

> *Example*
> In Vicenza, Italy, the libraries of 26 senior high schools, 15 comprehensive (primary and junior schools), and two private members (a foundation and a firm) have formed a network where resources and library software are shared and interlibrary loan services are provided.
> www.rbsvicenza.org/index.php?screen=news&loc=S&osc=news&orderby=Autore

> *Example*
> In Portugal, school and public libraries have a network and share the same library cataloguing and automated system. www.rbe.mec.pt/np4/home

> *Example*
> In the Netherlands and Flanders, the library is at the heart of the "Brede School" [Broad/Community School]. The school library is an integral, compact, and inclusive knowledge centre, which also provides the crossroads for a range of community educational services (e.g., infant and primary school, gym). www.bredeschool.nl/home.html

Useful Resources

Bon, I., Cranfield, A., & Latimer, K. (Eds.). (2011). *Designing library space for children.* Berlin/Munich: De Gruyter Saur. (IFLA Publications; Nr 154.)

Dewe, M. (2007). *Ideas and designs: Creating the environment for the primary school library.* Swindon, UK: School Library Association [UK].

Dubber, G., & Lemaire, K. (2007). *Visionary spaces: Designing and planning a secondary school library.* Swindon, UK: School Library Association [UK].

Durpaire, J-L. (2004). *Politique d'acquisition in Les politiques documentaires des Etablissements scolaires* [The acquisition policy within a school's policy] (pp. 34-36). Paris: Inspection Generale de l'Education Nationale.

La Marca, S. (Ed). (2007). *Rethink! Ideas for inspiring school library design.* Carlton, Victoria, Australia: School Library Association of Victoria.

Landelijk Steunpunt Brede Scholen. (2013). *Verschijningsvormen Brede Scholen 2013.* [Examples of Community Schools 2013] (2nd ed.). Den Haag, Netherland: bredeschool.nl. Retrieved from www.bredeschool.nl/fileadmin/PDF/2013/2013-05-28__13_170_LSBS_gew_herdruk_brochure_Verschijningvormen_4.pdf

Latimer, K., & Niegaard, H. (2007). *IFLA library building guidelines: Developments and reflections.* Munich: K.G. Saur.

Loertscher, D., Koechlin, C., Zwann, S., & Rosenfield, E. (2011). *The new learning commons: Where the learners win!* (2nd ed.) Clearfield, UT: Learning Commons Press.

Marquardt, L. (2013). La biblioteca scolastica, ambiente e bene comune per l'apprendimento [school libraries, learning environments and commons]. In M. Vivarelli (Ed.). *Lo spazio della biblioteca …* [The Library Space …]. Milano: Editrice Bibliografica. [See Chapter 4.6, pp. 299-334, and case study pp. 400-401.]

Molina, J. & Ducournau, J. (2006). Les 10 commandements d'une politique d'acquisition. [The 10 Commandments of an acquisition policy]. Retrieved from www.cndp.fr/savoirscdi/metier.html

OSLA (Ontario School Library Association). (2010). *Together for learning: School libraries and the emergence of the learning commons. A vision for the 21st Century.* Toronto, Canada: OSLA, 2010. Retrieved from www.accessola.com/data/6/rec_docs/677_olatogetherforlearning.pdf

Pavey, S. (2014). *Mobile technology and the school library.* Swindon, UK: School Library Association [UK]

Preddy, L. B. (2013). *School library makerspaces: Grades 6-12.* Westport, CT: Libraries Unlimited.

South Carolina Department of Education. (2012). *South Carolina standards for school library resource collections.* Columbia: SCDE. Retrieved from http://ed.sc.gov/agency/programs-services/36/documents/Standards_School_Library_Resource_Collections.pdf

Chapter 5
Programs and Activities of a School Library

"The school library is integral to the educational process." School Library Manifesto

5.1 Introduction

To be successful in fulfilling its educational mission, a school library must actively engage the educational community through well-researched programs of instructional and service activities. Programs and activities provided by a school library vary around the world because they need to align with the goals of the school and the broader community (see Section 3.5.4 Community engagement).

The terminology used to describe the programs and activities of a school library also varies around the world. For example, developing enthusiastic and skilled readers is variously described as 'reading promotion,' 'reading widely,' 'free voluntary reading,' 'leisure or recreational reading,' or 'reading for pleasure.' Whatever it is called, however, developing fluent readers who are motivated to read is an important aspect of school library programs and activities around the world.

> *Example*
> The annual Readathon in Namibia promotes a reading culture by providing children with stories in their home languages (Namibia has 13 written languages) and has been the impetus for publishing children's books in the home languages for schools and libraries.

Another area of contested terminology is that related to the use of information. Those activities once called 'bibliographic instruction' (instruction on how to use the library's texts and systems) and 'user education' (any means used to help users to understand the library and its services) are now more often referred to as 'information literacy' and 'inquiry.' What is regarded as exemplary library-related instruction in the use of information has changed over the years: a sources approach, during the 1960s and 1970s; a pathfinder approach, through the 1980s; and a process approach, beginning in the 1990s (Kuhlthau, 2004). The process approach emphasizes thinking about information and using information within a problem-solving perspective. It does not discard the knowledge from earlier approaches, such as the knowledge of tools, sources, and search strategies but does emphasize that this knowledge is best developed through inquiry within the teaching of thinking and problem solving.

5.2 Program and activities

A school library is an essential component of teaching and learning in the school; it also contributes to the social goals of a school such as student engagement, inclusion of diverse learners, and relationships with the broader community. The goals of a school library should be aligned with the goals of the school such as literacy, curriculum-based learning, and citizenship. The extent to which a school library can contribute to the achievement of school goals is dependent upon the resources and staffing allocated to the school library.

Example

In Hungary, many students study in the cities, but live in the villages near the cities, so they are "shuttling" between their schools and homes. Public transport limitations mean that many students have to wait before and after school lessons. Many school libraries respond to this situation by extending hours before classes begin and after the end of school time. As a result, students can spend their time in a safe, cultural, and community place. This also provides an opportunity to deepen the relationship between teacher librarians and students.

Services and activities must be designed by a qualified school librarian, working in close cooperation with the principal or head teacher, with heads of departments and other learning specialists in the school, with classroom teachers, with support staff, and with students. Without access to the expertise of a qualified school librarian who selects appropriate educational resources and collaborates with classroom teachers to design instruction based on those resources, the improvements in student achievement reported in the research literature are not attainable.

The instructional work of a qualified school librarian should focus on core activities, including:

- literacy and reading promotion;
- media and information literacy (e.g., information literacy, information skills, information competences, information fluency, media literacy, transliteracy, transmedia literacy);
- inquiry-based learning (e.g., problem-based learning, critical thinking);
- technology integration;
- professional development for teachers; and
- appreciation of literature and culture.

School library research related to the core activities provides a framework for action. The focus of core activities of a school library will depend on the programs and priorities of a school and should reflect the progression of curriculum expectations from grade to grade.

5.3 Literacy and reading promotion

A school library supports student literacy and promotes reading. Research shows that there is a direct link between reading level and learning results, and that access to reading materials is a key factor in developing enthusiastic and skilled readers (Krashen, 2004). School librarians should be pragmatic and flexible in their approach when providing reading material to users, supporting the individual preferences of readers, and acknowledging their individual rights to choose what they want to read. Students who are given the opportunity to select their own reading show improved test scores over time. Self-selection of reading material improves vocabulary development, grammar test performance, writing, and oral language ability. Students learning a second language improve fluency and comprehension when they have access to quality books in their second language. Struggling readers who are given access to alternate reading materials, such as audiobooks, show improved reading skills and improved attitudes toward reading.

Students with reading disabilities require alternate reading materials and, in some cases, may require special reading devices. A school librarian should be able to cooperate with specialized teachers for these students to support their reading needs. A school librarian should also support teachers in their work with classroom reading to meet local and national standards (e.g., helping out with recommendation of books appropriate for reading projects and of books that support the country's language standards).

A school library should provide an aesthetic and stimulating environment containing a variety of print and digital materials and offer opportunities for a wide range of activities from quiet reading to group discussions and creative work. A school librarian should ensure the most liberal borrowing policies possible and avoid, as much as possible, fines and other penalties for late returns and lost materials.

Literacy-based activities to encourage reading and enjoyment of media involve socio-cultural as well as cognitive learning aspects. Efforts should be made to ensure that a school library collection includes materials written and created both locally and internationally and that reflect the national, cultural, and ethnic identities of members of the school community. A school librarian should take the lead in ensuring that students have opportunities, in the classroom as well as in the library, for reading self-selected materials and for discussing and sharing what they are reading with others. New fiction and non-fiction materials should be promoted to both teachers and students through book talks, library displays, and information on the library's webpage. Special events to raise the profile of literacy and reading can be organized in the library or throughout the school such as exhibitions, author visits, and international literacy days. These special events can provide an opportunity for the parental involvement in the school. Parents may also participate in their children's literacy development through home reading programs and through read-aloud programs.

> *Example*
> In France, the *Babelio Challenge* stimulates reading and promotes children's literature through a social literary network: www.babelio.com

> *Example*
> In the United Kingdom, the Chartered Institute of Library and Information Professionals (CILIP) Carnegie and Kate Greenaway Medals have a well-established shadowing scheme, which stimulates reading activities across the UK related to the books nominated each year for the prizes.
> www.carnegiegreenaway.org.uk/shadowingsite/index.php

> *Example*
> In Italy, the Xanadu Project, established in 2004 by Hamelin Cultural Association and coordinated by the "Sala Borsa" Library in Bologna, is addressed to high school students (13-16 year-olds), and more recently to eighth graders, in different Italian regions. The scope of the project includes stimulating reflective and critical thinking, networking, and the appreciation of books, comics, movies, and music.
> www.bibliotecasalaborsa.it/ragazzi/xanadu2014/biblio.php

5.4 Media and information literacy instruction

A second mandate of a school library is developing students who can locate and use information responsibly and ethically for their lives as learners and citizens in an ever-changing world. The 2007 UNESCO document, *Understanding Information Literacy: A Primer*, written for policy-makers by Forest Woody Horton, Jr., is a useful overview of concepts and definitions related to information literacy and of the role that information literacy plays in formal and informal learning. UNESCO also promotes the concept of media and information literacy (MIL), recognizing the importance of media and information sources in our personal lives and in democratic societies. The 2011 UNESCO document, *Media and Information Literacy Curriculum for Teachers [MIL]*, explains why media literacy and information literacy should be considered together. The MIL curriculum framework for teachers addresses three areas of teaching and learning:

1) knowledge and understanding of media and information for democratic and social participation;
2) evaluation of media texts and information sources (focusing on who created it, for whom was it created, what is the message); and
3) production and use of media and information.

School librarians agree with the importance of having a systematic framework for teaching media and information skills, and they contribute to the enhancement of students' skills through collaborative work with teachers. The goal of an instructional program based on a media and information literacy curriculum is to develop students who are responsible and ethical participants in society. Information literate students should be competent self-directed learners. They should be aware of their information needs and actively engage in the world of ideas. They should display confidence in their ability to solve problems and know how to locate relevant and reliable information. They should be able to manage technology tools to access information and to communicate what they have learned. They should be able to operate comfortably in situations where there are multiple answers, as well as those with no answers. They should hold high standards for their work and create quality products. Information literate students should be flexible, able to adapt to change, and able to function both individually and in groups.

Example
In France, pupils are trained in the responsible use of the Internet. http://eduscol.education.fr/internet-responsable

Example
In France, training courses for school librarians are related to benchmarks for implementing Media and Information Literacy-Oriented Training courses. http://media.eduscol.education.fr/file/Pacifi/85/4/Reperes_Pacifi_157854.pdf

5.5 Inquiry-based learning models

Many countries, local authorities, and school libraries have worked out very successful models for designing instruction that develops media and information literacy skills within the context of inquiry projects. Creating models for inquiry-based learning involves years of research, development, and practical experimentation. Schools without a model recommended by their education authority should select a model that aligns most closely with the goals and learning outcomes of their curricula, rather than attempting to develop their own models. Examples of instructional models for inquiry-based learning are provided in Appendix C.

Instructional models for inquiry-based learning generally use a process approach in order to provide students with a learning process that is transferable across content areas as well as from the academic environment to real life. These models share several underlying concepts:

- Student constructs meaning from information.
- Student creates a quality product through a process approach.
- Student learns how to work independently (self-directed) and as a member of a group.
- Student uses information and information technology responsibly and ethically.

Instructional models for inquiry-based learning incorporate essential inquiry and lifelong learning skills: planning, locating and gathering, selecting and organizing, processing, representing and sharing, and evaluating. Process-based instructional models also enhance self-directed learning skills (i.e., metacognition) and collaborating skills. These skills are best developed progressively within a subject context, with topics and problems drawn from the curriculum.

Planning skills are essential for any research task, assignment, project, essay, or topic. At the initial stages of an inquiry, planning activities include framing appropriate questions, identifying likely resources and possible information-seeking strategies, and building a reasonable timeline. Throughout the inquiry process, students will amend their plans in response to unanticipated challenges and obstacles.

Locating and gathering skills are fundamental to information seeking tasks. These skills include an understanding of alphabetical and numerical order, use of different kinds of strategies for information seeking in computer databases and on the Internet, and use of indexes and reference sources. Generating information may include, in addition to the study of sources, methods such as survey, interview, experiment, and observation.

Selecting and organizing skills require critical and evaluative thinking. Selecting involves finding information that is relevant and pertinent to the focus of the inquiry. Applying criteria such as authoritativeness, completeness, timeliness, accuracy, and point of view helps the student to make informed and ethical decisions about the information found.

Processing information involves constructing meaning using such skills as integrating information from a variety of sources, making inferences, drawing conclusions, and building connections to prior knowledge. Through these skills, students develop an understanding of the information they have gathered, transforming the information gathered into their personal knowledge.

Representing and sharing involves creating quality products that communicate ideas clearly, that reflect established aims and criteria, and that demonstrate effective presentation skills, including awareness of audience.

Evaluating skills involves assessing both the process and the product of the inquiry. Students need to be able to think critically about their effort and what they have achieved. They should be able to relate their finished product to the original plan and determine if the product has achieved its purpose, distinguish the strengths and weaknesses of the learning project, and reflect on improvements and implications for future assignments.

Self-directed learning skills are critical in the development of lifelong learners. Students need to be guided throughout an inquiry to think about their thinking and learning processes (i.e., metacognition) and to use that self-knowledge to establish learning goals and to manage progress towards achieving them. Self-directed learners are able to use media sources for information and personal needs, seek answers to questions, consider alternative perspectives, and evaluate differing points of view. They recognize that information, information sources, and libraries are complex in organization and structure, and they are able to ask for help when needed.

Collaborating skills are developed when students work together in groups with diverse individuals and diverse resources and technology. Students learn how to defend opinions as well as how to criticize opinions constructively. They acknowledge diverse ideas and show respect for the others' backgrounds and learning styles. They work together to create projects that reflect differences among individuals and contribute to synthesizing individual tasks into a finished product.

The process approach to inquiry-based learning goes beyond the location of information to the use of information, beyond the answering of a specific question to the seeking of evidence to shape a topic. It considers the process of a search for information as well as the product of the search. It calls for an awareness of the complexity of learning from information: Learning from information is not a routine or standardized task, and it involves the affective as well as the cognitive domains.

In deciding to use a process approach to inquiry-based learning, school librarians and teachers face the same fundamental issue, no matter the size of their library and the nature of its collections and technology—how to influence, orient, and motivate the pursuit of learning using a process of discovery that encourages curiosity and the love of learning. Process-based models support a view of inquiry-based learning as an opportunity for students to experience discovery and personal growth. When implemented effectively, student learning through inquiry is characterized by exploration and risk–taking, by curiosity and motivation, by engagement in critical and creative thinking, and by connections with real life situations and real audiences.

Process-based models are theory-based and grounded in research from the fields of education and of library and information studies. From education comes learning theory and from LIS information seeking behaviour theory. For example, from education comes the knowledge that learners vary in the level of abstraction they can handle, depending on their cognitive development and their prior knowledge and experience. From education also comes the constructivist concept of learners actively building or constructing their knowledge and of learners experiencing changes in feelings as well as changes of thoughts as they use information. From LIS comes the knowledge that users of information progress through levels of question specificity, from vague notions of information need to clearly defined needs or questions, and that users are more successful in the search process if they have a realistic understanding of the information system and of the information problem.

Like other learning programs at school, inquiry-based learning activities should be designed to promote progression and continuity in students' learning. This means that skills must be introduced progressively through stages and levels. A school librarian should take a leadership role in ensuring there is a systematic approach to teaching an inquiry process that is guided by a school-based continuum of media and information skills and strategies.

Where there is no locally or nationally developed model for inquiry-based teaching and learning, a school librarian should work with the classroom teachers and school leaders to select a model. As the teachers and students apply the model they may wish to adapt the model to serve school goals and local needs. However, caution should be exercised in adapting any model. Without a deep understanding of the theoretical foundations of the model, adaptations may eliminate the power of the model.

> *Example*
> Secondary school students in Uppsala, Sweden, begin their inquiry-based projects by reading a dystopian novel. The novel is discussed in reading groups. The students focus their individual inquiries on subjects from the book such as surveillance, global warming, or diseases. They search for information, first broadly and then in depth, to formulate a very specific individual inquiry focus (e.g., going from everything on surveillance to a very concrete inquiry such as how

governments can monitor people on their smartphones). The final product for the project is an essay, written as an exam, using the material each student has collected and filed in a portfolio.

5.6 Technology integration

School library research has shown the importance of the library's role in providing technological infrastructure and tools and providing instruction in the use of information technology. Technology helps to extend the reach of the library and its resources into the classrooms and beyond. School librarians help students learn to use online search strategies important for using the resources of the Internet as well as databases and production tools. School librarians work in collaboration with technology specialists in the school, when such positions exist, to ensure that the roles of the two positions are clearly defined and that there are no gaps or redundancies in the technology services and programs provided for teachers and students in the school.

5.7 Professional development for teachers

The school library supports teachers through providing professional development for teachers, especially related to new materials and technologies, new curriculum, and new instructional strategies. The school librarian often provides informal professional development through working as a partner in learning with teacher colleagues in a variety of ways:

- providing resources for teachers which will widen their subject knowledge or improve their teaching methodologies;
- providing resources for different evaluation and assessment strategies;
- working as a partner in planning the tasks to be done in the classroom and/or library; and
- using the library as an access point to a broader set of resources through its interlibrary loans also personal and digital networks.

5.8 Instructional role of a school librarian

A qualified school librarian works in concert with teaching colleagues to provide the optimum learning experiences for students. Ideally, a school librarian co-teaches with other teachers, and each member of the teaching team contributes their different areas of expertise to the design and implementation of teaching and learning activities.

Following are four approaches to co-teaching in which school librarians and classroom teachers may work collaboratively as instructors: *supportive*, *parallel*, *complementary* and *team teaching*.

1) *Supportive teaching* – one instructor takes the lead instructional role and the other moves around among the learners to provide support on a one-to-one basis as required. This has been referred to as 'one teaches/one drifts.'
2) *Parallel teaching* – two or more instructors work with different groups of learners simultaneously in different parts of the classroom or library. This has been referred to as 'station teaching.'
3) *Complementary teaching* – one instructor does something to enhance the instruction provided by the other instructor(s). For example, one instructor might paraphrase the other's statements or model note-taking skills.

4) *Team teaching* – two or more instructors plan, teach, assess, and take responsibility for all students in the classroom or library, taking an equal share of responsibility, leadership, and accountability.

Each of these approaches to co-teaching is enhanced through collaborative planning by the co-instructors related to the content, delivery, and evaluation of instruction. Collaborative planning between a school librarian and classroom teacher(s) also enhances the quality of instruction when, as is the case in some situations, a school librarian is expected to be the sole instructor for students in the library or classroom. Collaboration is essential for providing media and information literacy instruction that is integrated into the curriculum and is connected with students' interests and needs.

Useful Resources

Asselin, M., & Doiron, R. (2013). *Linking literacy and libraries in global communities.* London: Ashgate.

Gordon, C., & Lu, Y-L. (2008). "I hate to read—Or do I?": Low achievers and their reading. *School Library Research, 11.* Retrieved from www.ala.org/aasl/slmr/volume11/gordon-lu

Hughes-Hassell, S., Barkley, H. A., & Koehler, E. (2009). Promoting equity in children's literacy instruction: Using a critical race theory framework to examine transitional books. *School Library Research, 12.* Retrieved from www.ala.org/aasl/slmr/volume12/hughes-hassell-barkley-koehler

Krashen, S. D. (2004). *The power of reading: Insights from the research* (2nd ed.). Westport, CT: Libraries Unlimited.

Kuhlthau, C.C. (2004). *Seeking meaning: A process approach to library and information service* (2nd ed.). Westport, CT: Libraries Unlimited.

Markless, S. (Ed.). (2009). *The innovative school librarian: Thinking outside the box.* London: Facet Publishing. [See Chapters 7, pp.127-142 Becoming integral to teaching and learning.]

Eduscol [Ministry of Education, France]. (2012). *Vademecum vers des centres de connaissances et du culture* [Short guide to knowledge centres and culture]. Retrieved from http://eduscol.education.fr/cid60332/-vers-des-centres-de-connaissances-et-de-culture-le-vade-mecum.html

Trelease, J. (2013). *The readaloud handbook* (7th ed.). New York: Penguin Books.

Villa, R. A., Thousand, J. S., & Nevin, A. I. (2008). *A guide to co-teaching: Practical tips for facilitating student learning* (2nd ed.). Thousand Oaks, CA: Corwin Press/Council for Exceptional Children.

Chapter 6
School Library Evaluation and Public Relations

"The school library is essential to every long-term strategy for literacy, education, information provision and also economic, social, and cultural development."

School Library Manifesto

6.1 Introduction

There is a great deal of research related to the positive impact on student achievement of well-resourced school libraries staffed with professional school librarians. For example, see LRS (2015) *School Libraries Impact Studies* in the USA (www.lrs.org/data-tools/school-libraries/impact-studies) and Williams, Wavell, C., and Morrison (2013) in the United Kingdom (www.scottishlibraries.org/storage/sectors/schools/SLIC_RGU_Impact_of_School_Libraries_2013.pdf). However, this research is not well known or understood beyond the school library community, and school libraries continue to face cutbacks in many parts of the world. The effect of cutbacks often has resulted in losses to the professional staffing of school libraries. Without qualified school librarians, the potential of the school library as a force for educational improvement and student achievement is lost.

Major findings from the last ten years of school library impact studies continue to confirm that the strongest impact on student achievement comes from school library programs with fulltime certified/qualified school librarians. Findings on the positive impact of the school library on student learning include helping to close the achievement gaps commonly seen for students who are poor, minority, and/or have disabilities. In addition to having fulltime certified/qualified school librarians, other school library factors that are correlated with improved student achievement include: collaboration, instruction, scheduling, access, technology, collections, budget, and professional development. Because well-resourced school libraries are now offering students and teachers access to resources and services online at any time, future research will be needed to evaluate how space, time, and use are impacted by digital possibilities.

Evaluation is an essential aspect of implementing school library programs and services. Evaluation can address decision-making or problem solving (accountability concerns); it also can influence people's thinking about a school library and develop support for the school library (transformation concerns). The evaluation process can help to determine the way forward and also can inspire the creation of new visions for a school library of the future.

In effect, a school library evaluation cannot be separated from an evaluation of the school's educational plan. Evaluation is also part of the planning process and needs to be an integral part of the school's quality assurance plan.

6.2 School library evaluation and evidence-based practice

School libraries and school librarians are rarely evaluated in a consistent and systematic way, but evaluation helps to ensure that the library's programs and services support the goals of the school. Evaluation can indicate the extent to which students and teachers perceive that they benefit from those programs and services: It can also help to shape those programs and services and enhance the understanding of and commitment to those programs and services for both library staff and library users.

Evidence-based practice focuses on data collection and analysis for the purpose of improvements in practice. Evaluations conducted as part of evidence-based practice are generally narrow in scope, conducted by school-level evaluators, and result in recommendations for practice. The data collected and analyzed for purposes related to evidence-based practice can come from a variety of sources, depending on the aspect of practice being queried such as the online circulation and cataloging system (OPAC) records and instructional patterns, by class, grade or subject (evidence in practice – data for decision-making), or various student learning products and surveys of students, teachers, and/or parents (evidence of practice – data supporting library impacts).

6.3 Approaches to school library evaluation

The evaluation of a school library includes consideration of its environment and context. A school library evaluation focused on the overall quality of the program is generally wide in scope, conducted by evaluators who are external experts, and results in a quality rating (see Appendix D: Sample School Library Evaluation Checklist and Appendix E: School Library Evaluation Checklist for Principals). Most school library evaluations include a self-study conducted by a school librarian. Other possible approaches to school-based school library evaluation, in addition to program quality, include: stakeholder perceptions, program content, and program impact. An ongoing approach to school library evaluation is evidence-based practice.

6.3.1 Program Quality

A school library evaluation focusing on overall program quality is normally a long-term project, often completed over several years and involving a variety of activities. Evaluations of program quality typically begin with a framework to guide activities such as a school accreditation process or a provincial or national standards document. A comprehensive program evaluation should be undertaken only with strong administrative support and with access to outside expertise such as a district consultant. However, value can be derived from undertaking a partial program evaluation, carefully planned to limit the resources needed. For example, a self-study might address the scope of library-based instructional activities over a single term or over one academic year in order to assess what percentage of students and teachers have been involved in these activities. A comparison to standards might be limited to one aspect of the library program or services such as facilities or collection.

6.3.2 Stakeholder Perceptions

Research studies offer many inspiring and comprehensive examples of the evaluation of stakeholder perceptions. While a major research study is beyond the resources of most schools or school districts, there are simple but effective alternatives. Two such examples are a) district satisfaction surveys and b) school-based surveys or feedback groups.

Most school districts or education authorities have some version of an annual satisfaction survey that is completed by students, teachers, and parents. It is very worthwhile to try to get a question or two added to the survey related to library programs and services. Even if efforts are unsuccessful at first, lobbying for such a question can be an important way to develop a better understanding of library programs and services within the district administrative group.

An approach to gathering student perceptions about the library might be to enlist the help of the principal to survey each class in the school, beginning with the first grade, asking the students questions such as "What makes our school library good?" and "What should we do more of to make it better?" Data from the surveys would then be analysed and shared with teachers and support staff and also with parents. An approach suited to secondary schools would be to organize meetings of student representatives, several from each class, to give feedback on the school library's services and resources. Over the course of several feedback sessions, students could be asked to identify what they would like more or less of in their school library and what other issues need to be addressed to make their school library a better place for them as learners. Both approaches could be easily adapted to evaluate a specific part of the library's suite of programs and services.

6.3.3 Program Content

A school library evaluation focusing on program content could be broad or narrow in scope and could be one-time or ongoing. A self-study might be designed to analyze the learning outcomes addressed through library-based instruction activities over a term or over several years. The learning outcomes addressed through library-based instruction activities might be compared to the learning outcomes in one or more curricula.

Another approach might be the use of focus groups of classroom teachers and/or department heads which might consider what learning outcomes should be addressed through library–based instructional activities. For best results (i.e., rich discussions and frank observations), focus groups are best organized and facilitated not by the school librarian but by a third party, that is, an outside evaluator such as a librarian colleague from another school or a district learning consultant.

6.3.4 Program Impact

Impact evaluation for a school library focuses on the concept of 'value-added' and can be designed to identify the contribution of school library inquiry activities to student learning. Here is where it is important to find out from the students what they have learned. For example, inquiry projects should result in students developing a deep understanding of a topic, knowing how the process of inquiry works, and appreciating the importance of their learning. For example, to discover to what extent inquiry projects had an impact on student learning, elementary students from Grades 1-6 in the *Library Power* project (Oberg, 1999) were interviewed at the end of their project and asked:

- Could you tell me about your project—how you used the books and computers? What worked well, what caused problems?
- How did you get started? What did you do in the middle? How did you finish? How did you feel at each of these points?
- What did you learn; what stands out in your memory? Did you share your project outside of school? How is your project like things people do outside of school?

A similar approach to be used with secondary students is the *School Library Impact Measure*, also called the *Student Learning Impact Measure* or *SLIM* (Todd, Kuhlthau & Heinstrom, 2005). At three points in the inquiry process, students are asked to complete reflection sheets with these questions:

- Take some time to think about your topic; write down what you know about it.

- How interested are you in this topic?
- How much do you know about this topic?
- Thinking back on your research project, what did you find easiest to do?
- Thinking back on your research project, what did you find most difficult to do?
- What did you learn in doing this research project? (This question is only asked at the end for the project.)

Other aspects of student learning that might be examined through interviews, reflection sheets, learning logs, or inquiry groups include the:

- ability to identify the source, the reliability, the validity, and the relevance of information;
- ability to create reliable and well informed products; or
- ability to responsibly manage one's digital identity.

Analysis of student responses to interview questions or reflection sheets will be a demanding and time-consuming exercise for school librarians and teachers, but these professionals will be able to see how students have developed their knowledge and understanding of curriculum content as well as information handling and process skills that are important for school, work, and beyond. Involving students in discussions of their inquiry learning process also helps students to be aware of and to be able to monitor and adapt their personal learning processes.

6.3.5 Evidence-based Practice

Evidence-based practice is a holistic and integrated approach to using data for decision-making. Evidence-based practice in school libraries integrates three kinds of data: a) evidence FOR practice (using findings from formal research to inform practice); b) evidence IN practice (using locally produced data for transforming practice); and c) evidence OF practice (using user-reported and user-generated data to show the results of what school librarians do) (Todd, 2007). School librarians gain access to evidence FOR practice through their professional education and from the many published summaries of school library research (e.g., Haycock, 1992; Kachel et al, 2013). School librarians use evidence generated IN their practice, such as circulation records and schedules of instructional activities, to make decisions, for example, related to purchases of resources for reading promotion activities and related to plans to ensure all students have opportunities to experience inquiry-based learning.

6.4 Impacts of school library evaluation

Evaluation is a critical aspect of an ongoing cycle of continuous improvement. Evaluation helps to align a library's programs and services with the goals of the school. Evaluation demonstrates to students and teachers, to library staff, and to the wider educational community the benefits derived from school library programs and services. Evaluation gives the evidence needed to improve those programs and services and helps both library staff and library users understand and value those programs and services. Successful evaluation leads to renewal of programs and services as well as development of new programs and services. Evaluation also is essential to guide initiatives related to public relations and advocacy.

6.5 School library public relations

The concept of public relations focuses on long-term interaction and strategic communication that build beneficial relationships between an organization and its publics—a school library and its stakeholders (see section 3.5.4 Community engagement).

Marketing and promotion focus on more immediate products and services developed to meet the wants and needs of a library's users. In contrast, advocacy is fundamentally about action for change or the advancement of an idea or issue. In the long term, supportive relationships need to be built with the school library's stakeholder groups and supporters: This is school library advocacy. Both promotion and marketing and also advocacy need to be planned and implemented in a systematic way. Promotion and marketing are a part of the school-based work of a school librarian; a school librarian also has a part to play in advocacy but usually advocacy is planned and carried out by a group such as a school library association. The primary focus of school library promotion and marketing is the users of the library: Here the concern is library use. The focus of school library advocacy is the decision-makers and the people who can influence the decision-makers: Here the concern is library funding and other kinds of support that make the work of a school librarian possible.

6.5.1 Promotion and Marketing

Promotion is one-way—communicating to users about what a library has to offer. Marketing is a two-way exchange—trying to match the library's services to the needs and preferences of potential users. The services and facilities provided by a school library must be actively promoted and marketed so that the target groups (both the school and the larger community) are aware of the library's role as a partner in learning and a provider of desirable services and resources.

A school library should have a written promotional and marketing plan worked out in cooperation with stakeholders. The plan should include: desired objectives; an action plan that indicates how the objectives will be achieved; and evaluation methods by which the success of promotion and marketing actions will be assessed. The promotional and marketing plan should be evaluated, reviewed, and revised annually; the plan as a whole should be discussed thoroughly by a school librarian and the school administration at least once every second year.

6.5.2 Advocacy

Advocacy is a planned, sustained effort to develop understanding and support incrementally, over time. Advocacy is related to but different from promotion and marketing. School library advocacy is about developing understanding and support from key decision-makers; it is about raising awareness and increasing knowledge; and it takes time and planning. School library advocacy efforts should focus on engaging decision-makers and those who influence decision-makers, rather than school library users.

Advocacy is about building relationships.

Advocacy is about influencing others. Research has established six universal principles related to influencing others (Cialdini, 2006). These principles of persuasion are essential to advocacy success: reciprocity, liking, authority, social proof, consistency/commitment, and scarcity.

Reciprocity and Liking are about building relationships. People often do things for others because others have done something for them and because they like the other person. Authority and Social Proof are about making decisions in times of uncertainty. People often do things because someone in authority recommends an action or because others like them are doing that. Consistency/Commitment and Scarcity are about moving people to action. People are more willing to do something if they perceive that the action is consistent with their values and if they perceive that action will prevent them from losing something that they value.

These universal principles should be kept in mind to guide the planning of an advocacy program. For example, school librarians often need to target other librarians in the national library association to bring them onside to support a school library policy issue. Following are some guiding questions that might be helpful in planning an advocacy program.

- Scarcity: What might other librarians lose if school libraries are not well supported?
- Consistency/Commitment: What values do they share with you?
- Authority: Whose opinions do they respect?
- Social Proof: What other national associations have supported school library policy?
- Reciprocity: How can you support other librarians in the association with their issues?
- Liking: What do you like about other librarians and how can you show that?

Advocacy is something that school librarians and their allies can do if they join together with others and move forward in a planned way. The IFLA *Online Learning Platform* (www.ifla.org/bsla) provides resources for those who want to advocate for libraries and want to know more about how to do that. This site includes materials specific to school library advocacy, including case studies about forming a school library network, about changing school library legislation, and about developing school libraries as a force for educational reform. Advocacy is essential for enhancing and maintaining school library development. Both advocacy and evaluation build understanding and support for the work of improving teaching and learning for all individuals in our schools.

Useful Resources

American Association of School Librarians. (2014). *Advocacy*. Retrieved from www.ala.org/aasl/advocacy

Cialdini, R. B. (2006). *Influence: The psychology of persuasion* (Rev. ed.). New York: Harper Business Books.

Department for Education and Office for Standards in Education, Children's Services and Skills [UK]. (2006). *Improving performance through school self-evaluation and improvement planning.* Retrieved from http://dera.ioe.ac.uk/5986/1/Improving_%20performance%20through%20school%20self-evaluation%20and%20improvement%20planning%20(PDF%20format).pdf

Department for Education and Skills and the School Libraries Working Group [UK]. (2004). *Self-evaluation model: School libraries resource materials.* Retrieved from www.informat.org/schoollibraries/index.html

FADBEN. (2012). *The FADBEN manifesto: Teaching information-documentation and information culture.* Retrieved from http://fadben.asso.fr/2012-FADBEN-Manifesto.html

Haycock, K. (1992). *What works: Research about teaching and learning through the school's library resource center.* Seattle, WA: Rockland Press.

Kachel, D. E., et al. (2013). *School library research summarized: A graduate class project.* Mansfield, PA: Mansfield University. Retrieved from http://sl-it.mansfield.edu/upload/MU-LibAdvoBklt2013.pdf

LRS (Library Research Service, Colorado State Library, Department of Education). (2015). *School libraries impact studies.* Retrieved from www.lrs.org/data-tools/school-libraries/impact-studies/

Mollard, M. (1996). *Les CDI à l'heure du management* [CDI on time management]. Paris: École nationale supérieure des sciences de l'information et des bibliothèques.

Oberg, D. (2009). Libraries in schools: Essential contexts for studying organizational change and culture. *Library Trends, 58*(1), 9-25.

Todd, R. (2007). Evidence based practice and school libraries: From advocacy to action. In S. Hughes-Hassell & V. H. Harada (Eds.), *School reform and the school library media specialist* (pp. 57-78). Westport, CT: Libraries Unlimited.

Todd, R. J., & Kuhlthau, C. C. (2005a). Student learning through Ohio school libraries, Part 1: How effective school libraries help students. *School Libraries Worldwide, 11*(1), 63-88.

Todd, R. J., & Kuhlthau, C. C. (2005b). Student learning through Ohio school libraries, Part 2: Faculty perceptions of effective school libraries. *School Libraries Worldwide, 11*(1), 89-110.

Todd, R., Kuhlthau, C., & Heinstrom, J. (2005). *SLIM Toolkit.* New Brunswick, NJ: Center for International Scholarship in School Libraries, Rutgers University. Retrieved from http://cissl.scils.rutgers.edu/index.html

Todd, R. J., Kuhlthau, C. C., & OELMA. (2004). *Student learning through Ohio school libraries: The Ohio research study.* Columbus, OH: Ohio Educational Library Media Association. Retrieved from www.oelma.org/studentlearning/default.asp

Williams, D., Wavell, C., & Morrison, K. (2013). *Impact of school libraries on learning: Critical review of published evidence to inform the Scottish education community.* Aberdeen, Scotland: Robert Gordon University, Institute for Management, Governance & Society (IMaGeS). Retrieved from www.scottishlibraries.org/storage/sectors/schools/SLIC_RGU_Impact_of_School_Libraries_2013.pdf.

GLOSSARY

The scope of this glossary is based on suggestions from reviewers and contributors to the guidelines document. For further information related to library-related terminology, readers may wish to consult ODLIS (Online Dictionary for Library and Information Science), written by Joan M. Reitz and published by ABC-CLIO at www.abc-clio.com/ODLIS/odlis_l.aspx Hardcover and paperback editions of the dictionary are available from Libraries Unlimited.

Advocacy: a planned, sustained effort to develop understanding and support incrementally, over time.

Bibliographic instruction: Teaching users how to use the library's texts and systems, often referred to as "BI" (See also Library instruction; Media and information literacy; User education.)

Cataloguing: the process of describing an information resource and creating entries for a catalogue. Usually includes bibliographic description, subject analysis, assignment of classification notation, and activities involved in physically preparing the item for the shelf.

Circulation: The process of borrowing and returning library materials. Also refers to the total number of items checked out over a period of time and to the total number of times a given item is checked out during a period of time, usually one year.

Citizenship: The legal and political status of being a member of a community (i.e., a citizen), along with the rights, duties, and privileges of being a citizen. In addition to involving the individual's basic rights and responsibilities, it also involves the quality of an individual's character and how he or she acts as a person within the community.

Civic engagement: The taking of individual and collective actions designed to identify and address issues of public concern; developing the knowledge, skills, values, and motivation necessary to act to make a difference in the quality of life of the community.

Code of ethics: A set of standards governing the conduct and judgment of librarians, library staff, and other information professionals in their work. Usually includes standards for equitable access, intellectual freedom, confidentiality, respect for intellectual property rights, excellence, accuracy, integrity, impartiality, courtesy, and respect for colleagues and for library users.

Collection: All materials that the library collects, organizes, and makes available. Usually refers to physical items but could also refer to digital resources, sometimes called "holdings." The documents in a collection may be physical or digital; in print or non-print formats; located locally or remotely; owned by the library, accessible through the library for a fee, or freely available from other institutions.

Culture of information: The body of knowledge necessary for enabling students to understand the nature of information and how it is created, to develop an enlightened understanding of the stakes and mechanisms of the information and communication industries, and to develop a critical approach to the endless technological innovations and the "documentarisation" of human beings when personal data are being used. Also includes developing ethical and responsible attitudes regarding the use of information. (See also Media and information literacy.)

Curation: The development, care, organization, and supervision of a museum, gallery, or other exhibit space and all the objects stored or displayed in it. Also, developing collections of digital objects, such as websites. The person in charge of such special collections (i.e., curator) requires specialized knowledge and experience related to selecting items of merit and to assisting users in locating and interpreting the items in the collections.

Database: A large, regularly updated file of related information, consisting of records of uniform format organized for ease and speed of search and retrieval and managed with the aid of database management system software. Databases frequently used in school libraries include catalogues, periodical indexes, abstracting services, and full-text reference resources, usually leased annually under licensing agreements that limit access to library members and library staff.

Indigenous: A term used to identify the universal population of indigenous peoples, although some may choose to define and identify themselves in their own languages or specific tribal identities. Some may use other labels or names such as Native, Native American, Aborigine, First Nation, etc.

Information literacy: The set of skills, attitudes, and knowledge necessary to access, evaluate, and use information effectively, responsibly, and purposefully. Usually includes the ability to know when information is needed to solve a problem or make a decision, to articulate that need, to locate and utilize information, to share it with others if necessary, and to apply it to the problem or decision. Also known as "information competence" and "information fluency." (See also Media and information literacy.)

Library instruction, an inquiry-based approach to: Teaching that emphasizes thinking about information and using information within a problem-solving perspective and that integrates the knowledge of tools, sources, and search strategies within the teaching of thinking and problem solving. This approach began to be emphasized in the 1990s.

Library instruction, a sources approach to: Teaching users about the nature and uses of the library's tools and sources, especially reference texts and indexes for finding information. An approach emphasized during the 1960s and 1970s.

Library instruction, a pathfinder approach to: Teaching users how to use search strategies, that is, to use logical patterns based on expert practice, to access library tools and sources. Recommended search strategies are often outlined in published guides called "pathfinders" or "guides to the literature." This approach began to be emphasized during the 1980s.

Library instruction, a process approach to: Teaching users how to develop a personal learning process through mediating the affective, cognitive, and physical aspects (feelings, thoughts, actions) of using information to develop knowledge or solve problems. This research-based approach, based on the Information Search Process (Kuhlthau, 1985), began to be emphasized in the 1990s.

Library program: (See School library program.)

Media literacy: (See Media and information literacy.)

Media and information literacy: The set of skills, attitudes, and knowledge necessary to understand and utilize the various kinds of mediums and formats in which information is communicated and to understand and utilize the information being communicate through those mediums and formats. Includes such concepts as "information and media are created by humans, for personal, social, political, and economic purposes, and are inherently biased."

Pathfinder: A recommended search strategy to access library tools and sources. Sometimes called "library guide" or "guide to the literature."

Program: (See School library program.)

School librarian: A teacher with education in librarianship who has responsibility for leading or initiating the activities, programs, and services of a school library. In addition to managing daily operations, a school librarian supports the curriculum through collection development, teaches media and information literacy skills appropriate to grade level, assists students with selecting reading materials appropriate to their reading level, and helps classroom teachers integrate library services and materials into instructional programs. A school librarian may be known by various professional designations (e.g., teacher-librarian, library media specialist, learning resources teacher).

School library: A physical and digital learning space within a public or private elementary or secondary school that serves the information needs of its students and the curriculum needs of its teachers and staff. A school library provides a collection of education materials appropriate to the grade levels of the school. A school library is managed by a school librarian who is dedicated to enhancing the cognitive, personal, social, and cultural growth of students and teachers through activities and services related to reading, inquiry, and research. The school library is known by various terms (e.g., school library media centre, centre for documentation and information, library resource centre, library learning commons).

School library program: A planned comprehensive offering of teaching and learning activities designed to develop students' media and information literacy skills, research and inquiry skills, engagement in reading, digital skills, and other literacy-related and curriculum-based competencies.

User education: Any means used to help users understand a library, its texts and systems, and its services, including signage, handouts, and guides to the literature as well as direct teaching. (See also Bibliographic instruction; Library instruction; Media and information literacy.)

BIBLIOGRAPHY

At the end of each chapter in this guidelines document are listed **Useful Resources** related to the topics addressed in that chapter. This bibliography includes resources consulted during the process of revising the guidelines and resources suggested by reviewers and contributors to the guidelines document; however, it excludes resources listed at the end of chapters.

Alexandersson, Mi., & Limberg, L. (2004). *Textflytt och sökslump: Informationssökning via skolbibliotek* [Moving text and searching by chance: Information retrieval through the school library]. Stockholm, Sweden: Myndigheten för Skolutveckling.

American Association of School Librarians. (2009). *Empowering learners: Guidelines for school library programs.* Chicago: American Library Association.

American Association of School Librarians. (2008). *Learning 4 life: A national plan for implementation of Standards for the 21st-Century Learner and Guidelines for the School Library Media Program.* Chicago: ALA. Retrieved from www.ala.org/aasl/learning4life.

American Association of School Librarians. (2009). *Standards for the 21st-century learner in action.* Chicago: AASL.

Asselin, M., & Doiron, R. (2013). *Linking literacy and libraries in global communities.* Farnham, England: Ashgate Publishing.

Barrett, H., et al. (2010). *Skolbibliotekets möjligheter: Från förskola till gymnasium* [The possibilities of the school library: From pre-school to senior high school]. Lund, Sweden: BTJ Förlag.

Capra, S., & Ryan, J. (Eds.). (2002). *Problems are the solution: Keys to lifelong learning.* Capalaba, Australia: Capra Ryan & Associates.

Chapron, F. (2012). *Les CDI des lycées et collèges: De l'imprimé au numérique* [CDI or school libraries in high schools and junior high schools: From print to digital] (nouvelle édition). Paris, France: Presses universitaires de France.

Coatney, S. (Ed.). (2010). *The many faces of school library leadership.* Santa Barbara, CA: Libraries Unlimited.

Connaway, L., & Powell, R. (2010). *Basic research methods for librarians.* Westport, CT: Libraries Unlimited.

Cook, D., & Farmer, L. (Eds.). (2011). *Using qualitative methods in action research.* Chicago, IL: American Library Association.

Court, J. (Ed.). (2011). *Read to succeed.* London [UK]: Facet Publishing.

Crowley, J. D. (2011). *Developing a vision: Strategic planning for the school librarian in the 21st century* (2nd ed.). Santa Barbara, CA: Libraries Unlimited.

Das, L., & Walhout, J. (2012). *Informatievaardigheden en de mediathecaris* [Information literacy and the school media specialist]. Rapport 30. Heerlen, Netherlands: Open Universiteit, Ruud de Moor Centrum.

Erikson, R., & Markuson, C. (2007). *Designing a school library media center for the future* (2nd ed.). Chicago: American Library Association.

Farmer, L. (2014). *Introduction to reference and information and services in today's school library.* Lanham, MD: Rowman & Littlefield.

Farmer, L. (2011). *Instructional design for librarians and information professionals.* New York: Neal-Schuman.

Farmer, L., & McPhee, M. (2010). *Technology management handbook for school library media centers.* New York: Neal-Schuman.

Hughes-Hassell, & Harada, V. H. (2007). *School reform and the school library media specialist.* Westport, CT: Libraries Unlimited.

Gordon, C. (2000). *Information literacy in action.* Melton, Woodbridge, UK: John Catt Educational.

Guldér, M., & Helinsky, Z. (2013). *Handbok för skolbibliotekarier: Modeller, verktyg och praktiska exempel* [Handbook for school libraries: Models, tools and practical examples]. Lund, Sweden: BTJ Förlag.

Hart, G. (2011). The "tricky business" of dual use school community libraries: A case study in rural South Africa, *Libri, 61*(3), 211-225.

Hart, G. (2012). Teacher-librarians leading change: Some stories from the margins. *School Libraries Worldwide, 18*(2), 51-60.

Hoel, T., Rafste, E. T., & Sætre, T. P. (2008). *Opplevelse, oppdagelse og opplysning: fagbok om skolebibliotek* [Adventure, discovery and enlightenment: A textbook about school libraries]. Oslo, Norway: Biblioteksentralen.

Kelsey, M. (2014). *Cataloging for school librarians.* Lanham, MD: Rowman & Littlefield.

Kiefer, B., & Tyson, C. (2009). *Charlotte Huck's children's literature: A brief guide.* New York: McGraw Hill.

Kuhlthau, C. C., Maniotes, L. K., & Caspari, A. K. (2012). *Guided inquiry design: A framework for inquiry in your school.* Santa Barbara, CA: Libraries Unlimited.

Kuhlthau, C. C., Maniotes, L. K., & Caspari, A. K. (2015). *Guided inquiry: Learning in the 21st century school* (2nd ed.). Westport, CT: Libraries Unlimited.

Lester, J., & Koehler, W. (2007). *Fundamentals of information studies* (2nd ed). New York: Neal-Schuman.

Limberg, L. (2003). *Skolbibliotekets pedagogiska roll: En kunskapsöversikt* [The pedagogical role of the school library: A systematic review]. Stockholm, Sweden: Statens skolverk.

Limberg, L., Hultgren, F., & Jarneving, B. (2002). *Informationssökning och lärande: En forskningsöversikt* [Information retrieval and learning: A research review]. Stockholm, Sweden: Skolverket.

Limberg, L., & Lundh, A. H. (Eds.). (2013). *Skolbibliotekets roller i förändrade landskap.* [The role of school libraries in changing landscapes]. Lund, Sweden: BTJ Förlag. Retrieved from www.kb.se/Dokument/Bibliotek/projekt/Slutrapport 2013/Skolbibliotekets roller slutrapport 2013.pdf

Liquete, V. (Ed.) (2014). *Cultures de l'information* [Cultures of information]. CNRS Editions: Paris, France.

Malmberg, S., & Graner, T. (2014). *Bibliotekarien som medpedagog eller Varför sitter det ingen i lånedisken?* [The librarian as co-pedagogue, or Why is nobody sitting at the library desk?]. Lund, Sweden: BTJ Förlag.

Markuson, C., & European Council of International Schools. (2006). *Effective libraries in international schools.* Saxmundham, UK: John Catt Educational.

Morris, B. J. (2010). *Administering the school library media center* (5th ed.). Santa Barbara, CA: Libraries Unlimited. Available on the World Wide Web as an e-book.

Niinikangas, L. (1995). An open learning environment – new winds in the Finnish school library. *Scandinavian Public Library Quarterly 4*, 3-10.

Pavey, S. (2014). *Mobile technology and the school library.* Swindon, UK: School Library Association UK. Series: SLA Guidelines Plus

Rosenfeld, E., & Loertscher, D. V. (Eds.). (2007). *Toward a 21st century school library media program.* Lanham, MD: Scarecrow Press.

Sardar, Z., & Van Loon, B. (2010). *Introducing media studies: A graphic guide.* London, England: Icon Books.

School Library Association [UK]. *Guideline series.* Retrieved from www.sla.org.uk/guidelines.php

Schultz-Jones, B. A., & Ledbetter, C. (2013). Evaluating students' perceptions of library and science inquiry: Validation of two new learning environment questionnaires. *Learning Environments Research, 16*(3), 329-348.

Shaper, S. (Ed). (2014). *The CILIP guidelines for secondary school libraries.* London, UK: Facet Publishing.

Schlamp, G.(Ed.). (2013). *Die schulbibliothek im zentrum: Erfahrungen, berichte, visionen* [The school library in the centre: Experiences, stories, visions]. Berlin, Germany: BibSpider.

Thomas, N. P., Crow, S. R., & Franklin, L. L. (2011). *Information literacy and information skills instruction: Applying research to practice in the 21st century school library* (3rd ed.). Santa Barbara, CA: Libraries Unlimited. Available on the World Wide Web as an e-book.

Tilke, A. (2011). *The International Baccalaureate Diploma Program and the school library: Inquiry-based education.* Santa Barbara, CA: Libraries Unlimited. Available on the World Wide Web as an e-book.

Tomlinson, C., & Lynch-Brown, C. (2009). *Essentials of young adult literature* (2nd ed.). Old Tappan, NJ: Pearson.

Wilson, C., Grizzle, A., Tuazon, R., Akyempong, K., & Cheung, C. K. (2012). *Education aux médias et à l'information: programme de formation pour les enseignants* [Media education and information: A training program for teachers]. Paris, France: UNESCO.

Woolls, B., Weeks, A. C. & Coatney, S. (2013). *School library media manager* (5th ed.). Westport, CT: Libraries Unlimited.

Zamuda, A., & Harada, V. H. (2008). *Librarians as learning specialists: Meeting the learning imperative for the 21st century.* Westport, CT: Libraries Unlimited.

Appendix A:

IFLA/UNESCO School Library Manifesto (1999)

[www.ifla.org/publications/iflaunesco-school-library-manifesto-1999]

The School Library in Teaching and Learning for All

The school library provides information and ideas that are fundamental to functioning successfully in today's information and knowledge-based society. The school library equips students with life-long learning skills and develops the imagination, enabling them to live as responsible citizens.

The Mission of the School Library

The school library offers learning services, books, and resources that enable all members of the school community to become critical thinkers and effective users of information in all formats and media. School libraries link to the wider library and information network in accord with the principles in the *UNESCO Public Library Manifesto.*

The library staff supports the use of books and other information sources, ranging from the fictional to the documentary, from print to electronic, both on-site and remote. The materials complement and enrich textbooks, teaching materials, and methodologies.

It has been demonstrated that, when librarians and teachers work together, students achieve higher levels of literacy, reading, learning, problem solving, and information and communication technology (ICT) skills.

School library services must be provided equally to all members of the school community, regardless of age, race, gender, religion, nationality, language, professional, or social status. Specific services and materials must be provided for those who are unable to use mainstream library services and materials.

Access to services and collections should be based on the United Nations Universal Declaration of Human Rights and Freedoms, and should not be subject to any form of ideological, political, or religious censorship, or to commercial pressures.

Funding legislation and networks

The school library is essential to every long-term strategy for literacy, education, information provision and also economic, social, and cultural development. As the responsibility of local, regional, and national authorities, the school library must be supported by specific legislation and policies. School libraries must have adequate and sustained funding for trained staff, materials, technologies, and facilities. School libraries must be free of charge.

The school library is an essential partner in the local, regional, and national library and information network.

Where the school library shares facilities and/or resources with another type of library, such as a public library, the unique aims of the school library must be acknowledged and maintained.

Goals of the school library

The school library is integral to the educational process.

The following are essential to the development of literacy, information literacy, teaching, learning, and culture and are core school library services:

- supporting and enhancing educational goals as outlined in the school's mission and curriculum;
- developing and sustaining in children the habit and enjoyment of reading and learning, and the use of libraries throughout their lives;
- offering opportunities for experiences in creating and using information for knowledge, understanding, imagination, and enjoyment;
- supporting all students in learning and practising skills for evaluating and using information, regardless of form, format, or medium, including sensitivity to the modes of communication within the community;
- providing access to local, regional, national, and global resources and opportunities that expose learners to diverse ideas, experiences, and opinions;
- organizing activities that encourage cultural and social awareness and sensitivity;
- working with students, teachers, administrators, and parents to achieve the mission of the school;
- proclaiming the concept that intellectual freedom and access to information are essential to effective and responsible citizenship and participation in a democracy; and
- promoting reading and the resources and services of the school library to the entire school community and beyond.

The school library fulfils these functions by developing policies and services, selecting and acquiring resources, providing physical and intellectual access to appropriate sources of information, providing instructional facilities, and employing trained staff.

Staff

The school librarian is the professionally qualified staff member responsible for planning and managing the school library, supported by as adequate staffing as possible, working together with all members of the school community, and liaising with the public library and others.

The role of school librarians will vary according to the budget and the curriculum and teaching methodology of the schools, within the national legal and financial framework. Within specific contexts, there are general areas of knowledge that are vital if school librarians are to develop and operate effective school library services. These include resource, library, and information management and teaching.

In an increasingly networked environment, school librarians must be competent in planning and teaching different information-handling skills to both teachers and students. Therefore they must continue their professional training and development.

Operation and Management

To ensure effective and accountable operations:

- The policy on school library services must be formulated to define goals, priorities, and services in relation to the school's curriculum.
- The school library must be organized and maintained according to professional standards.
- Services must be accessible to all members of the school community and operate within the context of the local community.
- Co-operation with teachers, senior school management, administrators, parents, other librarians and information professionals, and community groups must be encouraged.

Implementing the Manifesto

Governments, through their ministries responsible for education, are urged to develop strategies, policies, and plans, which implement the principles of this Manifesto. Plans should include the dissemination of the Manifesto to initial and continuing training programmes for librarians and teachers.

Appendix B:

Budget Plan for the School Library

School librarians need to understand the following, related to developing a budget plan for the school library:

- School budgeting process
- Timetable for the budget cycle
- Key staff associated with the budget process
- Identified needs of the library
- Budget accountability processes

The components of the budget plan include the following:

- Amount for new resources (e.g., books, periodicals, multimedia, and digital material)
- Amount for supplies and administrative materials
- Amount for promotional events and materials
- Amount for services (e.g., duplication, repairs)
- Costs of using ICT equipment, software and licensing costs, if these are not included in a general ICT budget for the school

As a general rule, the school library material budget should be at least 5% of the per student expenditure for the school system, exclusive of all salaries, special education expenses, transportation, and capital improvement funds.

Staff costs may be included in the library budget; however, at some schools, it may be more appropriate to have them included in the general staff budget. Regardless, estimating staff costs for the library is a task in which the school librarian should be involved. The amount of money available for staffing is closely related to important issues such as how many opening hours the school library can manage and what quality and range of services it can offer. Special projects and other developments such as new shelving or facility renovation may require a separate bid for funds.

Appendix C:

Instructional Models for Inquiry-Based Learning

Some well-developed models of the inquiry-based learning process include:

Michael Marland's Nine Questions (United Kingdom)
Marland, M. (1981). *Information skills in the secondary curriculum.* Schools Council Methuen.

Stripling and Pitts' REACTS Model (USA)
Stripling, B., & Pitts, J. (1988). *Brainstorms and blueprints: Teaching research as a thinking process.* Westport, CT: Libraries Unlimited.

The Information Process (Australia)
Australian School Library Association and Australian Library and Information Association. (2001). *Learning for the future: Developing information services in schools* (2nd ed.). Carlton South, Australia: Curriculum Corporation.

Focus on Inquiry (Canada)
Alberta Learning. (2003). *Focus on inquiry: A teacher's guide to inquiry-based learning.* Edmonton, AB: Alberta Learning, Learning Resources Branch.

Guided Inquiry (USA)
Kuhlthau, C. C., Maniotes, L. K., & Caspari, A. K. (2007). *Guided inquiry: Learning in the 21st century.* Westport, CT: Libraries Unlimited.

Kuhlthau, C. C., Maniotes, L. K., & Caspari, A. K. (2012). *Guided inquiry design: A framework for inquiry in your school.* Westport, CT: Libraries Unlimited.

Schmidt, R. (2013). *A guided inquiry approach to high school research.* Westport, CT: Libraries Unlimited.

Appendix D:

Sample School Library Evaluation Checklist (Canada)

From: *Achieving Information Literacy: Standards for School Library Programs in Canada* (pp. 74-77). Ottawa, Canada: The Canadian School Library Association and The Association for Teacher Librarianship in Canada, 2003.

1. Program focuses on teaching information literacy and promoting reading	YES	Some-what	NO
a. Inquiry-based learning connected to a continuum of information literacy skills			
b. Integration of information literacy program across the curriculum			
c. Collaboration between teachers, teacher-librarians, administrators, parents and community members			
d. Teacher-librarian involved in assessment and reporting of student achievement			
e. Equitable access for all students to library programs			
f. Reading and literacy program development, support and implementation			
2. Staffing model includes qualified, competent and highly motivated teacher-librarian(s), supported by technical and clerical staff	YES	Some-what	NO
a. Collaborative planning and teaching with classroom teachers where subject goals and information literacy goals are met through resource-based, inquiry projects.			
b. Teacher-librarian teaching technology and information literacy skills to staff and to students in inquiry projects and on as-need basis			
c. Collection development of a variety of resources based on provincial curriculum requirements and local interests			
d. Efficient management of human resources (clerical, technical staff, student pages, volunteers)			
e. Efficient management of equipment (loans, acquisition and maintenance)			
f. Efficient management of the facility (bookings, layout, furniture, maintenance)			
g. Clerical processes (circulation, acquisitions, budgets, ordering, tracking, cataloguing, shelving, reporting, data entry)			
h. Leadership (incorporation of new learning theories in resource based joint projects, teaching new technologies)			
i. Personal enthusiasm and commitment to student learning			
j. Professional development (e.g. web based activities and opportunities)			
3. A funding model which involves inclusive and long-range planning, connected to the school goals	YES	Some-what	NO
a. Program budget prepared yearly by teacher-librarian, based on curricular needs and interests of all staff and programs			
b. Budget with a base plus yearly amount per student for long range planning			
c. Budget to include on-going and new school initiatives			
d. Budget to include resources, supplies, repairs, equipment, service contracts, professional development and capital expenditures			
e. Budget that identifies and prioritizes needs of the school			
f. Budget that reflects input of stakeholders			
g. Funding for special programs - author visits, reading initiatives, etc.			

4. Library has a wide range of appropriate learning resources, which are carefully and expertly selected to meet the formal and informal needs of all learners.	YES	Some-what	NO
a. There is a selection policy that reflects the learning needs of the school			
b. There is balance in the variety of formats (e.g., print, serials, video, audio, electronic, online databases, internet, others)			
c. There is balance in the accessibility levels of materials			
d. Sufficient computer work stations and printers			
e. Sufficient viewing and listening equipment			
f. Sufficient number of items per student (quantitative)			
g. High correlation between resources and learning needs of community, i.e. curriculum and interests (qualitative)			
h. The collection is current (weeded and replenished) and in good repair			
i. Access to a central union database			
j. Access to digital library resources			
k. Access to website information			
l. Procedures for access, coordination and sharing of resources			
5. Library has technologies that are current, readily accessible and supportive of curriculum expectations	YES	Some-what	NO
a. Library program teaches effective and responsible use of technologies			
b. Contains sufficient workstations and software to assist students to seek, analyse, synthesize and communicate information in new and meaningful ways			
c. Access for all students and teachers throughout the school to current information resources and some databases 24/7			
d. Organization and management of basic library routines through automated systems.			
6. Library facilities are safe, flexible, spacious and well designed to accommodate a variety of learning activities	YES	Some-what	NO
a. Has workspace for individuals, small group learning and class instruction			
b. Is designed to adapt to new emerging technologies and applications			
c. Allows for flexibility in restructuring and reconfiguring library for new and traditional functions, efficiency, quality and growth			
d. Is comfortable - sound, lighting, temperature, wiring, furniture			
e. Is accessible before, during and after the instructional day			
f. Is visually attractive			
g. Is safe			

Appendix E:

School Library Evaluation Checklist for School Principals

A 12 Point Library Program Checklist for School Principals (USA)

From: Doug Johnson's Blue Skunk Blog
Retrieved from http://doug-johnson.squarespace.com/blue-skunk-blog/2012/1/10

The purpose of this tool is not to serve as a formal evaluation of either the librarian or library program, but to help the building administrator become aware of areas where you may need additional resources and assistance in order to make a major impact on your school's overall program.

Rapid changes in technology, learning research, and the library profession in the past 20 years have created a wide disparity in the effectiveness of school library programs. Is your school's library keeping current? The checklist below can be used to quickly evaluate your program.

1. Professional staff and duties

- Does your library have the services of a fully licensed school librarian?
- Is that person fully engaged in professional duties? Is there a written job description for all library personnel: clerical, technical, and professional?
- Does the librarian understand the changing roles of the librarian as described in current professional publications by state and national library organizations?
- Does the librarian offer regular staff development opportunities in information literacy, information technologies, and integration of these skills into the content area?
- Is the librarian an active member of a professional organization?
- Is the librarian considered a full member of the teaching faculty?

2. Professional support

- Is sufficient clerical help available to the librarian so that she/he can perform professional duties rather than clerical tasks?
- Is sufficient technical help available to the librarian so that she/he can perform professional duties rather than technical tasks?
- Is there a district library supervisor, leadership team, or department chair who is responsible for planning and leadership?
- Does the building principal, site leadership committee and staff development team encourage library personnel to attend workshops, professional meetings, and conferences that will update their skills and knowledge?
- Does the librarian participate in your district's Professional Learning Communities and in informal Personal Learning Networks?

3. Collection size and development

- Does the library's book and audiovisual collection meet the needs of the curriculum? Has a baseline print collection size been established? Is the collection well-weeded?
- Is a variety of media available that will address different learning styles?
- Have on-line resources been added to the collection when appropriate? Are there sufficient computers and Internet bandwidth for groups of students to take advantage of these resources?
- Has a recent assessment been done that balances print collection size and digital resources? Have some print materials been supplanted by on-line subscriptions? Has space formerly used to house print materials been effectively repurposed?
- Are new materials chosen from professional selection sources and tied to the curriculum through collection mapping?

4. Facilities

- Is the library located so it is readily accessible from all classrooms? Does it have an outside entrance so it can be used for community functions evenings and weekends?

- Does the library have an atmosphere conducive to learning with serviceable furnishings, instructional displays, and informational posters? Is the library carpeted with static-free carpet to reduce noise and protect electronic devices? Is the library climate-controlled so that materials and equipment will not be damaged by high heat and humidity, and so that it can be used for activities during the summer?
- Does the library contain general instructional areas, a story area (in elementary schools), a presentation area (in secondary schools), and spaces for individuals, small groups and entire classes to work?
- Does the library contain a computer lab or wireless laptops/netbooks for students and teachers working with a class or independently in the library and for the librarian to use to teach? Does the library contain and support multi-media workstations and digital video production facilities?
- Is the library fully networked with voice, video and data lines in adequate quantities? Does the library serve as the "hub" of these information networks with routers, file servers, video head ends, and technical staff housed there?
- Does the library maintain a useful, up-to-date web presence with linked resources for students, staff and families?

5. Curriculum and integration

- Is the librarian an active member of grade level and/or team planning groups?
- Is the librarian an active member of content curriculum writing committees?
- Is the librarian a part of grade-level or content area Professional Learning Communities?
- Are library resources examined as a part of the content areas' curriculum review cycle?
- Are library and information technology skills taught as part of content areas rather than in isolation? Are the information literacy skills of evaluating, processing and communicating information being taught as well as accessing skills?
- Is the safe and appropriate use of online resources a part of the information and technology literacy curriculum?

6. Resource-based teaching

- Does the librarian with assistance from building and district leadership promote teaching activities that go beyond the textbook and provide materials to help differentiate instruction?
- Do teachers and administrators view the librarian as an instructional design and authentic assessment resource? Does the library program support inquiry based and student centered learning activities throughout all curricular areas? Does the librarian collaborate with students and teachers to create a wide range of opportunities that enable the development and practice critical thinking skills and responsible digital citizenship?
- Does some flexible scheduling in the building permit the librarian to be a part of teaching teams with classroom teachers, rather than only covering teacher preparation time?
- Is a clear set of information literacy and technology benchmarks written for all grade levels available? Are these benchmarks assessed in a joint effort of the librarian and classroom teacher? Are the results of these assessments shared with stakeholders?

7. Information technology

- Does the library give its users access to recent information technologies such as:
- an on-line library catalog and circulation system for the building collection
- access to an on-line union catalog of district holdings as well as access to the catalogs of public, academic and special libraries from which interlibrary loans can be made
- full on-line access to the Internet
- a wide variety of online reference tools like full text periodical indexes, encyclopaedias, atlases, concordances, dictionaries, thesauruses, reader's advisors and almanacs
- a wide variety of computerized productivity programs appropriate to student ability level such as word processors, multi-media and presentation programs, spreadsheets, databases, desktop publishing program, graphic creation programs, still and motion digital image editing software
- access to collaborative learning/networking tools such as wikis, blogs and other online sharing programs and cloud computing resources such as online productivity tools and file storage?
- access to desktop conferencing equipment and software
- educational computer programs including practices, simulations and tutorials that support the curriculum
- Are the skills needed to use these resources being taught to and with teachers by the librarian?

8. Reference, networking & interlibrary loan

- Does your librarian have the expertise needed to provide effective and timely reference services to the building students and staff?
- Is your school a member of a regional multi-type system or library consortium?
- Does the librarian use interlibrary loan to fill student and staff requests that cannot be met by building collections?
- Does the librarian participate in cooperative planning and purchasing opportunities with other schools, both locally and regional?

9. Planning/yearly goals

- Does the library program have a district-wide set of long-range goals?
- Does the librarian set yearly goals based on the long-term goals that are tied directly to building and curriculum goals in collaboration with building leadership?
- Is a portion of the librarian's evaluation based on the achievement of the yearly goals?
- Is the library program represented on the building planning committees? On the district technology planning committee?

10. Budgeting

- Is the library program budget zero or objective based? Is the budget tied to program goals?
- Does the librarian write clear rationales for the materials, equipment, and supplies requested?
- Does the budget reflect both a maintenance and growth component for the program?
- Does the librarian keep clear and accurate records of expenditures?
- Does the librarian write grant applications when available?

11. Policies/communications

- Are board policies concerning selection and reconsideration polices current and enforced? Is the staff aware of the doctrines of intellectual freedom and library user privacy? Do these policies extend to digital resources?
- Does the district have a CIPA-compliant safe and acceptable use policy (or responsible use policy) for Internet and technology use?
- Does the librarian serve as an interpreter of copyright laws? Does the librarian help others determine the rights they wish to assign to their own intellectual property?
- Does the librarian have a formal means of communicating the goals and services of the program to the students, staff, administration, and community? Is the library's web presence professional, easy-to-navigate, current and useful? Does the librarian use social networking tools to communicate with stakeholders?

12. Evaluation

- Does the librarian determine and report ways that show the goals and objectives of the program are being met and are helping meet the building and district goals? Does the librarian create an annual library report for administrators, staff and parents that includes qualitative and quantitative measurements?
- Do all new initiatives involving the library and technology program have an evaluation component?
- Does the district regularly evaluate the library program using external teams of evaluators as part of any accreditation process?
- Does the librarian participate in formal studies conducted by academic researchers when requested?

THE IFLA/UNESCO

학교도서관 가이드라인

2002

이종권 옮김

제1장 사명과 정책

제2장 자원

제3장 인력관리

머리말

The IFLA/UNESCO 학교도서관 선언 : 우리 모두를 위한 교수 학습의 중심 학교도서관은 2000년에 발행된 것입니다. 이 선언문은 전 세계에 전파되었고, 많은 언어로 번역되었습니다. 또한 계속적으로 새로운 번역이 이루어지고 있고, 전 세계의 사서들은 이 선언문을 활용하여 그들이 속한 학교와 지역사회에서 학교도서관의 위상을 높여나가고 있습니다.

본 선언문은 : 각국 정부는 교육을 담당하는 부서를 통하여 본 선언문의 원칙을 실행할 수 있는 전략, 정책, 계획을 개발할 것을 권고합니다.

본 가이드라인은 전 세계의 국가적 지역적 모든 수준의 정책결정자들에게 정보를 제공하기 위해, 그리고 전 세계 도서관 공동체에 지원과 지침을 주기 위해 개발된 것입니다. 또한 각종 학교에서 본 선언서의 원칙을 실행하는데 도움이 될 수 있도록 기술하였습니다.

본 가이드라인의 작성에는 세계 여러 나라의 전문가들이 참여하였으며, 각기 상이한 지역상황에서 모든 형태의 학교들의 요구를 충족시킬 수 있도록 노력하였습니다. 본 가이드라인은 항상 해당 지역과의 맥락 속에서 읽고, 활용해야 할 것입니다.

IFLA총회에서 많은 워크숍을 열었고, 수많은 회의를 가졌으며, 도서관 전문가들 사이에 개별적으로 많은 토론과 이메일을 통한 의견교환이 있었습니다. 이 가이드라인은 그러한 토론과 협의의 결과물이기에 그분들의 노고에 감사드립니다. 또한 현존 학교도서관 분과위원회 회원님, 각국에서 IFLA/UNESCO에 보내온 가이드라인들, 그리고 특히 2001년에 출판된 IFLA공공도서관가이드라인 등도 많은 도움이 되었음을 밝혀둡니다.

학교도서관 분과위원회는 또 2002년에 『학교도서관 오늘과 내일』이라는 출판물을 발행하였습니다. 우리는 본 선언문과 비전 및 가이드라인이 세계 모든 곳에서 훌륭한 학교도서관의 기반을 함께 구축할 수 있기를 희망합니다.

Tove Pemmer Saetre

with Glenys Willars

2002

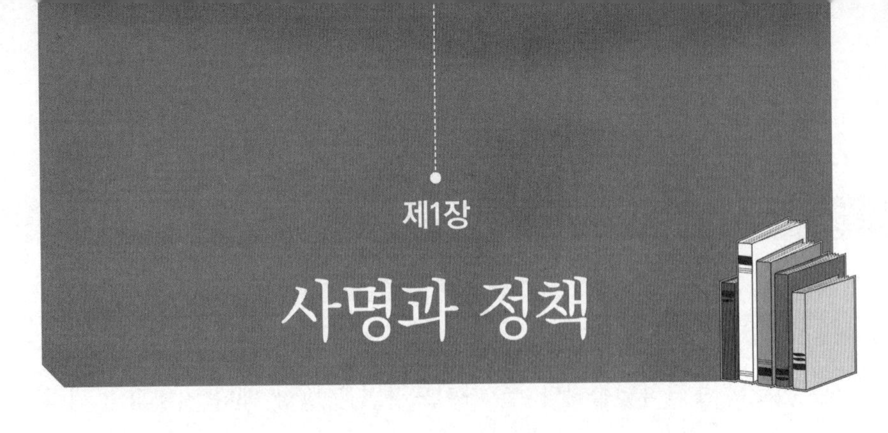

제1장
사명과 정책

학교도서관은 모두를 위한 교수학습의 중심이다.

1.1 사명

학교도서관은 나날이 발전하는 지식정보기반 사회를 성공적으로 이끌 수 있는 기초적인 정보와 아이디어를 제공한다. 학교도서관은 학생들에게 평생학습의 능력을 갖추게 하고, 상상력을 길러줌으로써 장차 책임 있는 시민으로 살아갈 수 있게 해준다.

1.2 정책

학교도서관은 명확하게 구성된 정책 틀 안에서 경영되어야 한다. 도서관 정책은 학교의 전체적인 정책 및 필요성을 감안하여 작성되어야 하며, 학교의 전통과 교풍, 목적 그리고 실제의 상황을 반영하여야 한다.

정책은 도서관의 잠재능력을 충분히 발휘할 수 있도록 언제, 어디서, 누가 일을 수행할 것인가를 상세히 정해야 한다. 도서관 정책은 정책에 제시되는 목적과 목표를 전체 학교사회가 참여하고 기여할 수 있도록 실행 가능성을 확보해야 한다. 따라서 실용적인 내용으로 많은 협의를 통해 작성되어야 하며 그 결과는 인쇄하여 널리 공유해야 한다. 정책의 실행과 개발을 위한 철학, 아이디어, 개념, 의도 등을 분명히 하고 학교사회의 공통된 이해를 통해 실행을 보증하며 이를 토대로 효과적이고 열정적으로 실천할 수 있는 정책을 수립해야 한다.

정책은 종합적이고 활용가능성이 있어야 한다. 정책은 사서교사 단독으로 작성해서는 안 되며, 교사들 및 학교경영자들과 공동으로 만들어야 한다. 정책 초안은 학교사회에 폭넓게 의견을 구하고, 철저한 공개토론을 거쳐야 한다. 정책문서와 부속 계획서들은 다음의 사항과 관련하여 도서관의 역할을 구체화해야 한다.

- 학교의 교육과정
- 학교에서의 학습방법
- 국가 및 지역 수준의 기준 충족 여부

• 학생들의 학습 및 개성의 개발 필요성
• 교사들의 수업 필요성
• 성취수준의 증진

효과적이고 성공적인 학교도서관 경영에 기여하는 요소들은 다음과 같다.

• 재정 및 예산
• 시설 설비
• 자원
• 조직
• 인사
• 도서관 이용
• 업무개선

이 모든 요소들은 실현 가능한 정책 틀의 형성과 실행계획 수립에 필수적인 것들이다. 본 가이드라인에서는 이 요소들을 다룰 것이다. 실행계획은 전략, 업무, 목표, 관찰 및 평가의 과정으로 구성된다. 정책과 계획들은 정기적인 검토를 통해 그 실효성을 유지해야 한다.

1.3 관찰 및 평가

학교도서관의 목적을 이루어가는 과정에서 각 전략들이 명시된 목적을 달성하는지를 확인하기 위해 각 서비스의 수행과정을 지속적으로 관찰해야 한다. 경향성을 파악하기 위해서는 통계적 연구도 수행해야 한다. 연례 평가에서는 모든 계획의 주요 부문에 걸쳐 다음 사항들을 확인하여야 한다.

- 도서관의 목적과 목표, 교육과정과 학교의 목적과 목표의 달성 여부
- 각 업무의 학교사회에 대한 필요성 충족 여부
- 변화하는 상황의 요구를 충족시킬 수 있는지 여부
- 자원이 적절하게 지원되는지 여부
- 각 업무들이 비용 효과적인지 여부

다음과 같은 수행지표는 도서관의 목적 달성여부를 점검, 평가하는 데 유용한 도구이다.

이용지표:

- 학교 구성원 1인당 대출 수(학생과 교직원 구분)
- 학교 구성원 1인당 총 도서관 방문 횟수(학생과 교직원 구분)

- 자료 당 대출 수(예: 자원 회전 정도)
- 개관시간 당 대출 수(학교 일과시간 및 방과 후)
- 구성원 1인당 참고질문 수(학생과 교직원 구분)
- 컴퓨터 및 온라인 정보원 이용

자원지표

- 학교 구성원 1인당 장서 수
- 학교 구성원 1인당 컴퓨터 터미널
- 학교구성원 1인당 온라인 컴퓨터 접근

인력지표

- 학교 구성원 수 대 상근 인력 비율
- 도서관 이용에 대한 상근 인력 비율

품질지표

- 이용자 만족도 조사
- 포커스 그룹
- 상담활동

비용지표

- 기능, 서비스, 활동에 따른 단위비용
- 기능별 인력비용(예: 대출 책 수)
- 학교구성원 당 총 도서관 비용
- 학교 총예산 대 도서관 총예산 비율
- 도서관 총 비용 대 미디어 비용

비교지표

- 비슷한 규모와 특성을 지닌 다른 학교의 비교가능한 도서관 서비스 통계 벤치마킹

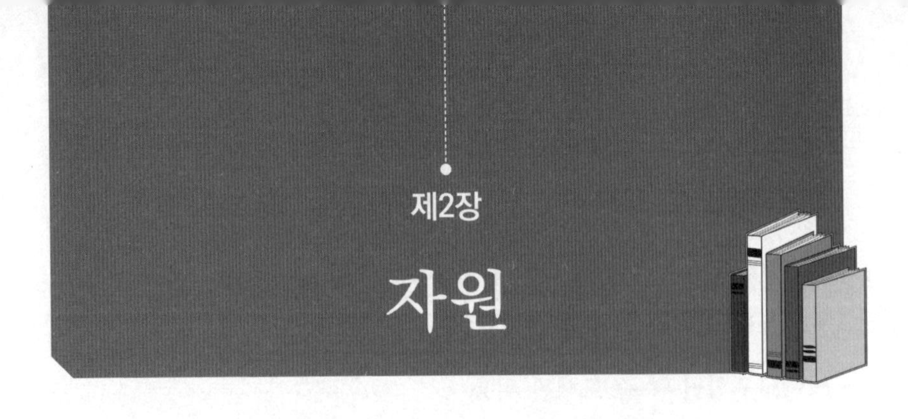

학교도서관은 숙련된 인력, 자료, 기술 및 시설, 무료접근을 보장하기 위한
적정한 자금을 지속적으로 확보하지 않으면 안 된다.

2.1 학교도서관의 예산 및 재정

도서관이 학교예산의 공정한 배분을 보장받기 위해서는 다음 사항이 매우 중요하다.:

- 학교 예산책정 과정에 대한 이해
- 예산 책정 순환과정의 시간스케줄 파악
- 예산 책정의 핵심인물 파악
- 도서관의 정체성 및 필요성에 대한 인식 확보

예산계획에는 다음 요소들이 반드시 포함되어야 한다. :

- 신규 구입 자료의 량(예: 도서, 연속간행물 및 비도서), 이용 촉진 자료의 량(예: 포스터)
- 문방 및 행정 소모품의 량
- 이용 홍보를 위한 이벤트의 개최정도
- 정보기술 장비이용 비용, 소프트웨어 및 라이선스 비용(이러한 비용이 학교의 일반 예산에 포함되어 있지 않은 경우)

일반적으로 학교도서관 자료예산은 인건비, 특수교육비, 교통비, 자본 증액기금을 제외한 학교시스템의 학생 1인당 경비의 최소한 5%는 되어야 한다.

인건비는 도서관예산에 포함될 수도 있지만, 학교의 일반 인건비 예산에 포함되는 것이 더 적절하다. 그러나 도서관 인력비의 산정에 반드시 사서가 참여해야 한다는 것을 강조할 필요가 있다. 인력비용의 예산은 도서관의 개관시간 및 서비스의 수준과 같은 중요한 문제와 밀접하게 연관된다. 특별 프로젝트나 새로운 배가시스템 같은 개발업무에는 별도의 예산을 책정해야 한다.

예산은 연간 사용계획을 주의 깊게 수립하고 정책의 틀에 맞추어 집행해야 한다. 연간 운영보고서는 도서관의 예산이 어떻게 사용되었고,

집행금액은 해당 업무를 적절히 수행하는데 충분했는지, 정책목표를 달성 했는지를 밝히는 데 초점을 맞추어야 한다.

사서교사는 학교도서관 예산의 중요성을 분명하게 인식하고, 경영진에게 이를 잘 설득함으로써 도서관이 전체 학교사회에 봉사할 수 있도록 해야 한다. 도서관의 예산 증가의 이유는 다음과 같은 관점에서 그 정당성을 확보할 수 있다.

- 학교도서관의 인력과 장서 규모는 교육성취를 측정하는 가장 적절한 지표라는 점.
- 표준 평가에서 우수한 성적을 받는 학생들은 다른 경제적인 요인과는 상관없이 도서관의 인력과 장서, 정기간행물 및 비디오 자료가 풍부한 학교에서 배출된다는 점.

2.2 위치와 공간

학교도서관의 교육적 역할은 시설, 가구, 설비에 충분히 반영되어야 한다. 학교도서관의 기능 및 이용문제는 학교의 건물 신축이나 기존 건물의 재설계시 종합 검토되어야 할 매우 중요한 요인이다.

학교도서관 시설에 대한 국제적인 산정표준은 없지만, 기본 계획 수립에 있어 일정한 공식을 적용하는 것은 매우 유용하며, 그렇게 함으로써 새로 설계된 도서관이 학교의 요구를 가장 효과적으로 충족시킬 수 있다. 다음은 학교도서관 설계과정에 고려해야 할 사항들이다.

- 학교의 중앙에 위치하는지, 가능하면 1층
- 접근성, 모든 수업 장소로부터 가까운지
- 소음, 최소한 도서관의 한 부분에서는 외부소음이 없을 것.
- 적절하고도 충분한 조명, 창문을 통한 자연조명 및 인공조명
- 연중 내내 장서보존은 물론 및 작업하기 좋은 적정 실내 온도(예: 에어컨, 히터),
- 장애 이용자의 특수한 요구를 충족할 수 있는 설계
- 자료(책, 비소설, 소설, 하드커버, 페이퍼백, 신문 및 잡지, 비인쇄자료 소장)를 위한 공간, 학습연구 공간, 독서 공간, 컴퓨터 워크스테이션, 상영 공간, 직원의 작업 공간 등 적정 규모의 공간 확보
- 다양한 활동을 위한 공간 유동성 및 교과과정이나 기술 변화 등 미래 변화의 수용성

다음은 지역은 다르더라도 새 도서관을 설계할 때 고려할 사항들이다.

- 정보데스크, 목록, 온라인워크스테이션, 학습연구 테이블, 컴퓨터 워크스테이션, 참고자료 및 기본 장서를 이용할 수 있는 학습 및 연구 공간
- 문해력 향상, 평생교육, 여가독서 등 자유 독서를 위한 도서 및 연속간행물 이용 공간
- 적정 교육기자재와 상영시설을 갖춘 소규모 집단, 중규모 집단, 학급 단위로 공식적으로 수업할 수 있는 '수업 공간'
- 매체 시설을 갖춘, 개별단위, 팀 단위, 학급단위의 작업 및 회의를 위한 그룹 프로젝트 및 제작 공간
- 대출데스크, 사무실, 자료처리 공간, 시청각 기자재 보존 공간, 각종 공급물품 및 재료 보관을 위한 공간

2.3 가구 및 설비

학교도서관의 디자인은 도서관이 학교에 대하여 좋은 서비스를 수행하는 데 중요한 역할을 한다. 심미적 디자인은 학교 구성원들에게 환영하는 느낌을 줄 뿐 아니라 도서관에서 시간을 보내고 싶은 욕구를 갖게 해준다.

설비가 잘 갖추어진 학교도서관의 특징은 다음과 같다.

- 안전성
- 적정 조명
- 튼튼하고, 오래가며, 기능적인 가구 설비 및 이용자의 요구 및 활동을 충족할 수 있는 특수한 공간
- 규제를 최소화 하면서 학교 구성원들의 특수한 요구를 수용할 수 있는 디자인
- 도서관 프로그램, 학교 교육 프로그램, 시청각 및 데이터 기술의 변화를 수용할 수 있는 디자인
- 가구배치의 이용자 배려 및 안전성, 설비, 공급 재료를 적절히 이용할 수 있는 디자인
- 조직된 다양한 자료 자원에 적절하고 신속히 접근할 수 있는 정리정돈 관리
- 이용자에게 심미적 느낌을 주는 휴식과 학습을 제공하는 디자인, 분명하고 매력적인 안내 표지

2.4 전자 및 시청각기자재

학교도서관은 오늘의 정보기반 사회로 접근하는 중요한 관문으로서의 기능을 수행한다. 그러기에 학교도서관은 모든 필요한 전자자료, 컴

퓨터, 시청각자료에 대한 접근을 제공해야 한다. 이러한 기자재는 다음과 같다.

- 인터넷 컴퓨터 워크스테이션
- 연령대 및 학생 급별에 맞는 전산 목록
- 녹음장비
- CD-ROM 장비
- 스캐닝 기자재
- 비디오 플레이어
- 컴퓨터 장비, 특히 시각장애인 또는 기타 신체장애자를 위한 컴퓨터장비

컴퓨터용 가구는 어린이에게 알맞도록, 어린이들의 각기 다른 체형으로 조절 할 수 있도록 설계된 것이라야 한다.

2.5 자료자원

학교도서관은 수준 높은 도서관의 수용성과 고품질의 광범한 자료자원을 필수적으로 갖추어야 한다. 따라서 장서관리정책은 매우 중요하다. 장서관리정책은 장서의 목적, 범위, 내용, 외부 자료원에의 접근 등

에 관하여 규정한다.

2.6 장서관리정책

학교도서관은 교육, 정보, 인성개발과 관련하여 이용자의 요구를 충족할 수 있도록 광범한 자료자원의 접근이 가능하게 해야 한다. 장서는 이용자들이 계속 최신자료를 선택할 수 있도록 끊임없이 개발해야 한다.

학교도서관의 직원은 실용적 장서관리정책 개발을 위해 학교경영자 및 교사들과 협력하여야 한다. 장서관리정책은 교과과정, 학교 구성원들의 관심과 요구에 기초하면서 학교 밖 사회의 다양성을 반영해야 한다. 정책에 포함할 요소들은 다음과 같다.

- IFLA/UNESCO 학교도서관 선언문-사명
- 지적자유에 관한 입장
- 정보의 자유
- 장서관리정책의 목적, 학교 및 교과과정과의 관계
- 장단기 목표들

2.7 자료수집

학생 1인당 책 수가 10권은 되어야 좋은 장서라고 할 수 있다. 아무리 작은 학교라도 최소한 최신자료 2500권은 되어야만 각 연령대, 능력, 배경에 적합한 균형 잡힌 장서를 보장할 수 있다. 장서의 60%는 교과과정과 관련되는 비소설(non-fiction) 책으로 구성해야 한다.

또한, 학교도서관은 소설, 음악, 컴퓨터게임, 비디오카세트, 레이저디스크, 잡지, 포스터 등 여가목적의 자료도 구비해야 한다. 이러한 자료들은 학생들과 협력하여 건전한 윤리기준을 벗어나지 않는 범위에서 학생들의 관심과 문화를 반영해야 한다.

2.8 전자정보자원

전자정보원도 교과과정 및 이용자의 관심과 요구를 반영하여 접근서비스를 제공해야 한다. 전자정보원은 인터넷, 특수 참고자료, 전문(full text)데이터베이스, 교육용 컴퓨터 소프트웨어를 포함한다. CD-ROM과 DVD도 이용 가능해야 한다.

국제적, 국가적 서지표준에 따라 자원을 분류, 목록하는 도서관 목록시스템을 선택하는 일도 매우 중요하다. 이는 광범한 네트워크에 포괄되어 있는 자료검색을 쉽게 해준다. 세계의 많은 곳에서 지역사회에 속해 있는 학교도서관들은 동일한 목록시스템으로 연결함으로서 편익을 얻고 있다. 이러한 협력을 통해 자료처리과정의 품질과 효율을 증대시킬 수 있다.

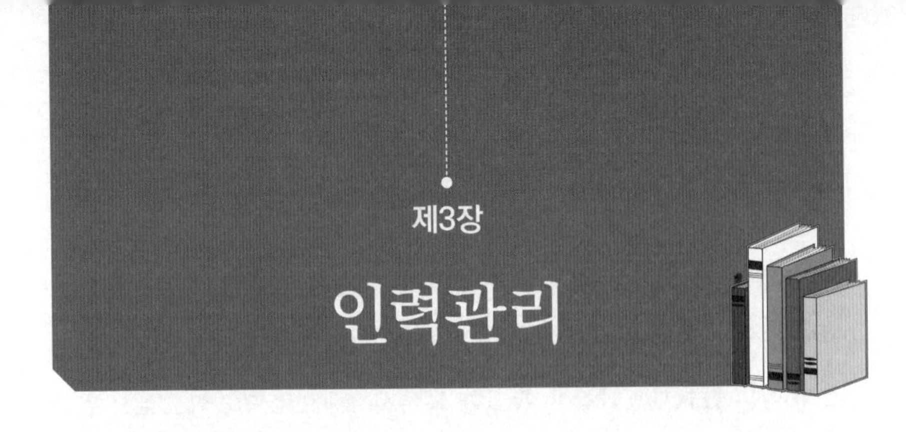

제3장 인력관리

사서교사는 학교도서관의 계획 및 경영책임자로서 인사관리에서 전문 능력과 자질을 갖춘 적임자를 배치함으로서 전문성을 보장해야 한다. 사서교사는 학교의 모든 구성원들과 협력하여 일하고, 공공도서관 및 기타 기관과도 유대관계를 가지고 업무를 수행해야 한다.

3.1 도서관의 인사

도서관의 풍요와 서비스의 질적 수준은 도서관 내·외부에서 활동하는 인력자원에 달려있다. 그렇기 때문에 잘 교육받고 동기가 부여된 직원을 선발하고, 학교의 규모 및 도서관서비스의 요구에 대응하는 충분한 인력을 확보하는 것은 매우 중요하다. 여기서 "인력"이라는 말은 잘 교육받은 사서교사 및 사서보조원을 의미한다. 또한 교사, 기술자, 학부모, 기타 자원봉사자와 같은 지원인력도 포함된다. 사서교사는 전문적인 교육과 자질을 갖춘 자, 나아가 교육이론 및 학습방법론에 대한 교육을 받은 자라야 한다.

학교도서관 인사관리의 가장 중요한 목표는 모든 직원들이 도서관 서비스 정책을 분명하게 이해하고, 의무와 책임을 명확히 하며, 직업의 전문성을 고려한 경쟁력 있는 급여와 합리적인 고용조건을 확보하는 것이다.

자원봉사자는 급여를 받는 직원의 업무를 대신 해주어서는 안 되며, 학교도서관활동에서 자원봉사자의 몫으로 정해진 공식적 협정의 틀에 의거 지원업무를 수행해야 한다. 학교도서관 서비스 개발과 관련한 상담업무는 지역적 또는 국가적 수준에서 외부 전문가를 활용할 수 있다.

3.2 사서교사의 역할

사서교사의 주요 역할은 학교평가를 포함한 학교의 사명과 목적에 기여하는 것으로서 학교도서관을 통해 그러한 목적활동을 개발, 실행하는 것이다. 사서교사는 학교의 경영자, 행정 관리자, 교사들과 협력하여 계획의 개발 및 교과과정의 수행에 참여해야 한다. 사서교사는 정보 및 정보문제의 해결, 인쇄자료와 전자자료의 모든 정보자원 이용에 대한 전문적 지식과 기술을 갖추어야 한다. 그들의 지식과 전문적 기술이 학교사회의 특수한 서비스 요구를 충족시키는 것이다. 또한 사서교사는 독서캠페인을 주관하고 어린이의 문해력, 미디어, 문화에 대한 활용능력을 길러주어야 한다.

도서관이 통합교과적인 활동을 수행할 경우에는 학교 경영자의 지원이 필수적이다. 사서교사는 교장, 교감에게 직접 보고할 수 있어야 한다. 사서교사가 다른 전문 직원과 동등하게 전문인으로 인정받고, 학교의 도서관 부서장으로서 팀 활동이나 회의에 필수 참여요원으로 인정을 받는 것은 매우 중요하다.

사서교사는 여가환경과 매력적인 학습 환경을 창출해야 하며, 모든 사람들이 편견이나 두려움 없이 도서관에 올 수 있는 환영하는 분위기를 조성해야 한다. 학교도서관에서 일하는 모든 직원은 어린이, 청소년, 어른들과 친근한 소통을 유지해야 한다.

3.3 사서보조원의 역할

사서보조원은 사서교사에게 보고하고 사서교사가 기능을 잘 할 수 있도록 지원한다. 사서보조원은 행정적, 기술적인 지식과 능력을 갖추어야 한다. 사서보조원은 사전에 도서관에 관한 기본적 훈련을 받아야 한다. 그렇지 않으면 도서관에서 기본훈련을 시켜야 한다. 사서보조원의 의무는 일상적으로 반복적인 일들, 서가정리, 대출, 반납, 도서관자료의 운반 등이 포함된다.

3.4 교사와 사서교사의 협력

도서관서비스의 능력을 극대화하기 위해서는 교사와 사서교사의 협력이 필수적이다.

사서교사와 교사는 다음 사항을 달성하기 위해 함께 일해야 한다.

- 교과과정을 통한 학생들의 학습개발, 교육 및 평가
- 학생들의 정보 활용 기술, 정보 지식 개발 및 평가
- 수업 계획서 개발
- 도서관을 포함한 연장 학습에서 수행되는 특별 프로젝트의 준비 및 시행
- 독서프로그램 및 문화 이벤트의 준비 및 시행
- 교과과정상 정보기술의 통합교과적 지도
- 도서관의 중요성에 대한 학부모 인식 제고

3.5 학교도서관 직원의 자질과 기술

학교도서관은 학습자, 교사, 행정직, 상담자, 학부모 등 모든 학교사회 구성원들에게 서비스를 제공한다. 이 모든 그룹에는 특수한 의사소통 및 협력기술이 필요하다. 주요 이용자는 학생들과 교사들이지만 행정직과 상담자와 같은 다른 부류의 전문직도 포함되는 것이다.

학교도서관 직원에게 기대되는 기초적 자질과 기술은 다음과 같다.

- 어린이 및 성인들에게 능동적이고 열린 마음으로 의사소통하는 능력
- 이용자들의 필요를 이해하는 능력
- 학교 안과 밖에서 개인 및 집단에게 협력하는 능력
- 문화의 다양성에 대한 지식과 이해 능력
- 학습방법 및 교육학 이론에 대한 지식
- 정보기술 및 정보이용 방법에 대한 지식
- 도서관 장서의 구성과 접근방법에 대한 지식
- 어린이문학, 미디어, 문화에 대한 지식
- 경영관리 및 마케팅에 관한 지식과 기술
- 정보기술 분야에 대한 지식과 기술

3.6 사서교사의 책무

사서교사는 다음 사항을 수행할 의무가 있다.

- 학교공동체의 정보자원 필요성 분석
- 서비스 개발을 위한 정책 형성 및 실행
- 도서관 자원을 위한 수서정책 및 수서시스템 개발
- 도서관 자료의 분류 목록
- 도서관 이용 교육
- 정보지식 및 정보기술 교육
- 도서관 자원 및 정보기술 이용에 대한 학생 및 교사 지원
- 최적 자료 이용을 위한 참고 정보 질문 해결
- 독서 프로그램 및 문화 이벤트의 발전적 수행
- 교과과정 수행과 관련된 기획활동 참여
- 학습활동의 준비, 실행, 평가 참여
- 학교 전체 평가시스템의 일부로서 도서관 서비스 평가 방법 개선
- 다른 외부조직과의 파트너십 구축
- 예산의 편성 및 집행
- 전략계획의 수립
- 도서관 직원의 관리 및 교육훈련

3.7 윤리기준

학교도서관 직원은 학교공동체의 전 구성원을 대하는데 있어 높은 윤리기준을 지킬 책임이 있다. 모든 이용자에게 그들의 능력과 배경에 상관없이 동등하게 대해야 한다. 서비스는 개별 이용자의 필요에 맞추어 적절히 조정되어야 한다. 학교도서관 직원은 개방적이고 안전한 학습 환경으로서의 학교도서관의 역할을 확립하기 위해 전통적 의미의 교육자에서 탈피하여 조력자로서의 기능을 강화해야 한다. 도서관 서비스를 제공함에 있어 사서들의 편견과 태도에 치우치지 말고, 이용자의 관점에서 서비스 노력을 기울이는 것이 가장 중요하다.

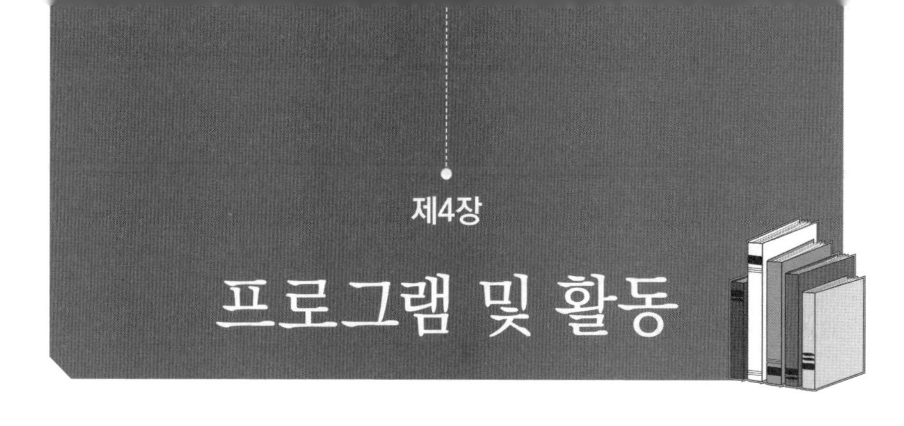

제4장 프로그램 및 활동

학교도서관은 교육과정 수행에 절대적으로 필요하다.

4.1 각종 프로그램

국가 차원의 교육과정 및 교육개발 프로그램에 있어 학교도서관은 교육의 원대한 목적을 달성하기 위한 필수불가결한 수단으로서 다음과 같은 관점에서 고려해야 한다.

- 학교를 통한 점진적인 정보 리터러시 개발 및 적응
- 모든 교육수준의 학생들에게 정보자원 활용능력 제고
- 모든 학생들이 민주주의와 인권의식을 체험할 수 있는 정보와 지식의 자유로운 소통

지역 차원에서도 학교도서관의 목적 달성을 위해 특별 프로그램들을 설계하여 운영하는 것이 바람직하다. 이러한 프로그램들은 각기 그 도서관이 처한 지역과의 맥락 속에서 여러 가지 목적으로 수행할 수 있다. 예를 들면 다음과 같다.

- 학교도서관을 위한 국가적(지역적) 표준 및 가이드인 개발 및 공표
- '최선의 실천사례'를 보여주는 모델 도서관 제시
- 국가 및 지역차원의 학교도서관운영위원회 구성
- 국가 및 지역차원의 학교도서관과 공공도서관 간 공식적 협력의 틀 구축
- 전문적 사서교사 교육훈련 프로그램 개발 및 제공
- 독서운동과 같은 학교도서관 프로젝트의 예산지원
- 학교도서관 활동의 발전에 관한 연구프로젝트의 발의 및 예산지원

4.2 공공도서관과의 자원공유 및 협력

지역사회에서 어린이 청소년을 위한 도서관서비스를 증진하기 위해서는 학교도서관과 공공도서관이 협력하는 것이 매우 바람직하다. 협력을 위한 공식 문건에는 다음 사항을 포함해야 한다.

- 협력을 위해 조치할 일반적 공통사항
- 협력 부문들에 대한 세부적 정의와 명세
- 경제적 수혜관계 및 공동부담 비용의 명확화
- 협력기간 동안의 시간 스케줄

협력 부문의 예는 다음과 같다.

- 직원의 교육훈련
- 협력적 장서개발
- 협력적 프로그램 개발
- 전자 및 네트워크 서비스 조정 협력
- 학습도구의 개발 및 이용자 교육 협력
- 학급단위 공공도서관 견학
- 독서 및 리터러시 증진 공동 노력
- 어린이 청소년에 대한 도서관 서비스 공동 마케팅

4.3 학교 급별에 따른 활동

학교도서관은 광범한 활동을 통해서 학교의 사명과 비전을 달성하는데 중심적 역할을 수행해야 한다. 학교사회의 모든 잠재 이용자에게 서비스를 할 뿐 아니라 다양한 대상 집단의 특수한 요구를 충족시켜야 한다.

프로그램 및 각종 활동은 다음과 같은 학교구성원들과 면밀히 협조하여 설계해야 한다.

- 교장/교감
- 부장교사
- 일반교사
- 지원인력
- 학생

이용자 만족의 정도는 학교도서관이 개인 및 집단의 요구를 파악하고 학교사회의 변화를 지속적으로 반영하여 서비스를 개발, 제공하는 능력에 달려 있다.

학교장과 학교도서관

학교의 교육 경영 리더로서 그리고 교육과정 수행의 기본적 틀과 환경을 제공하는 핵심으로서 학교장은 학교도서관의 중요성을 인식하고 도서관을 활용하도록 용기를 북돋아 주어야 한다.

학교장은 학교발전계획 수립, 특히 정보 리터러시 및 독서증진프로그램과 관련한 학교발전계획을 수립할 경우 학교도서관과 긴밀하게 협의해야 한다. 또한 그러한 계획의 효과적인 이행을 위해 교장은 교사 및 학생들이 도서관과 서비스에 접근할 수 있도록 수업시간 및 소요자원을 탄력적으로 운영할 수 있게 보장해야 한다.

학교장은 교사와 사서의 협력을 보장해야 한다. 학교장은 사서교사가 수업, 교과과정계획, 지속적 인력개발, 프로그램 평가 및 학생들의 학습평가에 참여할 수 있게 보장해야 한다.

학교의 평가에 있어서 학교장은 도서관을 반드시 포함하고(제1장 참조), 좋은 학교도서관 서비스가 학교의 교육목적 달성에 크게 기여한다는 점을 부각시켜야 한다.

부장교사 및 사서교사

각 부장교사는 각 부서에서 전문적 활동을 수행하는 핵심요원으로서 해당 주제 분야에서 필요로 하는 정보자원과 도서관서비스를 활용할 수 있도록 도서관과 협력하여야 한다. 부장교사는 학교장과 마찬가지로 도서관 발전계획에 참여하고, 도서관을 중요한 학습 환경 내지 학습 자원센터로 인식, 직접적인 관심을 기울여야 한다.

교사와 도서관

교사와 사서 간의 협조에 대해서는 이미 3.4에서 언급하였다. 여기서는 보완사항에 초점을 맞추어 논의한다.

교사의 교육철학은 교수방법에 있어 자신의 이념적 기반을 고수한다. 전통적 관점의 교육방법은 가장 중요한 학습자원을 교사와 교과서에 두는 것이며, 이는 학습과정으로서의 학교도서관의 역할과 가치를 폄하시킨다. 이러한 관점의 교육은 교실 문을 걸어 잠그고 학생들의 학습활동을 강력히 통제한다. 이 경우 중요한 정보지원기관인 학교도서관은 더 이상 교사들의 안중에 없는 것이다. 그러나 대부분의 교사들이 '교육자료 은행 개념'으로서 학생들이 주어진 지식을 수동적으로 채워 넣게 하는 경우라 해도 학교도서관은 교과과정을 지원하는 역할을 해내고 있는 것이다. 교사들의 생각 속에 도서관을 학습 파트너로 자리 잡게 하는 효과적 전략은 교사들을 위해 좋은 도서관 서비스를 제공하는 것이다. 이를 위한 중점 개선사항들은 다음과 같다.

- 교사들에게 주제지식을 넓혀 주거나 교수방법을 개선할 수 있는 자료의 제공 능력
- 여러 가지 평가전략 수립을 위한 자료의 제공 능력
- 교실에서 이루어지는 업무들을 도와주는 파트너 능력
- 여러 이질적인 교실 상황에서 더욱 많은, 더욱 민감한 학생들에게 특별한 서비스를 창출, 제공함으로써 교사들을 지원할 수 있는 능력
- 상호대차 및 전자네트워크를 통한 국제사회의 관문으로서의 도서관의 능력

진보적인, 열린 교육이념을 가진 교사들은 도서관을 열성적으로 이용한다. 위에서 언급한 기능 및 가능성에 더하여, 교사들은 도서관을 가르치는 장소로 인정하고, 실제로 도서관에서 수업을 진행함으로서 전통적인 방법에서 탈피한다. 교사들은 배우는 학생들에게 활력을 넣어주고, 독립적인 학습능력을 길러주기 위해 다음과 같은 영역에서 학교도서관과 협력할 수 있다.

- 학생들의 '탐구정신'개발, 정보 리터러시 및 활발하고 창의적인 정보 이용자 육성
- 프로젝트 및 과제 수행

- 개인 또는 집단을 위해 모든 수준의 학생들에게 독서 동기 부여

학생과 도서관

학생들은 학교도서관의 주된 이용 집단이다. 다른 구성원들과의 협력은 학생들에게 도움이 될 때만이 중요한 것이다.

학생들은 여러 가지 목적으로 도서관을 이용할 수 있다. 비 위협적인 열린 학습 환경으로서의 학교도서관은 학생들이 개별적으로 또는 집단적으로 많은 종류의 과제들을 수행할 수 있는 경험의 장이 되어야 한다.

도서관에서의 학생 활동은 다음과 같은 사항을 포함한다.

- 숙제 해결
- 프로젝트 작업 및 문제 해결 과제 수행
- 정보 추구 및 정보 활용
- 선생님과 동료학생들에게 발표할 자료 및 작품 제작

인터넷 이용

새롭게 등장한 전자 정보원은 도서관 이용자에게 또 하나의 도전이다. 전자정보원의 이용은 매우 혼란스럽다. 사서교사는 전자정보원이 교수학습과정에 활용될 수 있는 하나의 도구이지만, 그것은 목적 달성을 위한 수단일 뿐 목적 자체는 아니라는 점을 안내해야 한다.

도서관 이용자가 인터넷에 접속하면 모든 정보문제가 해결된다고 생각한다면 그것은 오산이다. 그 반대의 생각도 또한 같다. 사서는 이용자가 인터넷을 이용할 수 있게 하면서 정보탐색에서 야기되는 혼란과 좌절을 최소화 하도록 도와주어야 한다. 여기서 중요한 것은 인터넷으로부터 최단시간 안에 관련된 양질의 정보를 선택하는 일이다. 학생들은 스스로 정보의 소재를 파악하고, 종합하고, 모든 주제 분야로부터 새로운 정보와 지식을 통합할 수 있는 능력을 점진적으로 개발해 나아야 한다. 따라서 정보 리터러시 프로그램을 마련하여 효과적으로 실행하는 것은 학교도서관의 가장 중요한 일에 속한다(앞서 언급한 '교사와 도서관' 부분 참조).

학교도서관의 문화적 기능

도서관은 다양한 저널, 소설 등 출판물 및 시청각 자원을 보유하므로 심미적인 문화 활동을 촉진하는 장이다.

도서관에서는 각종 전시회, 작가 초청, 국제 이해의 날 등 여러 가지 특별 이벤트를 개최할 수 있다. 공간이 충분하다면 학생들은 학부모 및 동료들을 위해 각종 공연을 할 수 있고, 사서들은 저학년 어린이를 위한 북 토크나 스토리텔링을 실행할 수 있다. 사서들은 독서 흥미의 유발과 문학 감상능력 개발을 위한 독서증진 프로그램을 운영할 수 있다. 독서 증진 활동들은 문화적인 측면과 학습적인 측면을 함께 가지고 있다. 독서의 수준과 학습의 결과는 직접적인 연관이 있다. 사서들은 이용자에게 독서 자료를 제공할 때 항상 실용성과 융통성을 고려하여야 하며, 독자들의 개인적 권리를 인정하고 독자들이 선택할 수 있도록 도와주어야 한다. 학생들은 그들의 요구와 수준에 적합한 소설, 비소설을 읽음으로서 사회화 과정을 촉진하고 자아 정체성을 개발해 나가는 것이다.

학부모와의 협력

학부형들의 학교 활동 참여의 전통은 나라에 따라 다양하다. 도서관은 학부모들에게 학교활동 참여의 기회를 제공할 수 있다. 학부모들은 자원봉사자로서 실제적인 일을 돕고, 도서관 직원을 보조할 수 있다. 또한 가정에서 자녀들의 독서활동에 동기를 제공하는 독서 증진 프로그램에 참여할 수 있다. 또한 문학 토론 그룹에 자녀들과 함께 참여하여 학습 과정을 도와줌으로써 독서활동의 목적 달성에 기여할 수 있다.

또 다른 학부모 참여방법은 '도서관의 친구' 모임을 구성하는 것이다. 이러한 모임은 도서관 활동에 대한 추가적 재정지원이라고 할 수 있으며, 도서관이 쓸 수 있는 자원 한계를 초과하는 특별 이벤트의 수행에 도움을 줄 수 있다.

제5장

지속적 발전책

5.1 개관

학교도서관이 제공하는 서비스와 시설은 지속적으로 개선되어야 하며, 그렇게 함으로써 여러 이용자 그룹들이 도서관을 학습 파트너로서 핵심 역할을 하는 곳으로, 그리고 모든 종류의 정보자원에 접근하는 관문으로서의 역할을 하는 곳으로 항상 인식할 수 있다. 이용자 그룹에 대해서는 앞선 여러 장에서 언급한 바 있다. 그들은 교장 및 학교 경영진, 부장교사, 교사, 학생, 기관장 및 학부모 등이다. 중요한 것은 학교의 성격, 여러 이질적 대상그룹의 특성에 따라 개선의 방법을 적절히 조정하는 것이다.

5.2 정책 개발

도서관은 목표와 전략을 명시한 성문화된 마케팅 및 발전정책이 있어야 한다. 발전정책은 학교의 경영진과 교사들의 협력을 얻어 수립해야 한다.

정책에는 다음 사항을 포함해야 한다.

- 목표와 전략
- 목표 달성을 위한 활동계획
- 평가 방법

필요한 활동들은 목적 및 지역 환경에 따라 다르다. 발전정책을 홍보하는 방법으로서 핵심적 문제들을 제시하면 다음과 같다.

- 서비스를 개선할 수 있는 학교도서관의 웹사이트 개설 및 운영, 관련 있는 다른 웹사이트 및 포털사이트의 링크
- 각종 전시회 개최
- 개관시간, 서비스, 장서에 관한 정보를 담은 홍보 출판물 발행
- 정보자원의 목록, 교과과정 및 연계 교과과정 토픽에 관한 안내문 작성, 배포

- 신입생과 그 학부모 회의에 도서관에 관한 정보 제공
- 학부모 기타 주민에 의한 '도서관의 친구들'모임 운영
- 독서 설명회, 독서와 리터러시 캠페인 전개
- 도서관 내부 및 외부의 효과적인 시각 표지물 제공
- 지역의 다른 기관들과의 연계 형성(예: 공공도서관, 박물관, 지역의 역사학·협회)

각종 활동 계획은 매년 평가와 검토를 거쳐 개정해야 하며, 전체적인 정책문서는 적어도 2년에 1회 전반적으로 검토해야 한다.

5.3 이용자 교육

교사와 학생들에게 도서관 이용방법을 가르치기 위한 프로그램 및 과정들은 가장 효과적인 도서관 마케팅의 수단이다. 따라서 이러한 프로그램들을 잘 설계하고 프로그램의 균형과 범위를 적절히 갖추는 것은 매우 중요하다.

이러한 프로그램은 도서관의 핵심 역할을 수행하기 때문에 제4장에 나와 있는 사항들을 적절히 고려하는 것이 좋다. 그러나 모든 이용자 교

육에 있어 마케팅은 매우 필수적이므로 본장에서 좀 더 다루고자 한다.

교사를 위한 도서관 이용안내 과정에서는 사서가 수행 할 수 있는, 교수 학습 활동에 도움을 주는 도서관의 역할을 분명하게 제시해야 한다. 교사를 위한 과정에서는 특히 각 교사들이 가르치는 주제 분야와 관계되는 정보를 직접 탐색해보는 훈련을 중점적으로 시행해야 한다. 교사들이 이미 관련 자료를 추구하는 경험이 있다하더라도, 학교도서관이 교실 수업을 보충할 수 있고, 전반적인 교육과정을 통합적으로 지원할 수 있다는 것을 깊이 인식할 수 있게 해주어야 한다.

학교의 다른 프로그램과 마찬가지로, 학생들을 위한 여러 가지 과정 요인들은 논리적 순차성을 가지고 전달되어야만 학습의 지속성과 발전을 도모할 수 있다. 이는 도서관의 능력과 자원들이 각 단계와 수준에 따라 점진적으로 제시되어야 한다는 것을 뜻한다. 학교도서관 사서교사는 이용자 교육에 대해 주된 책임을 져야 하지만, 교과과정과 관련되는 여러 가지 이질적 요소들과 긴밀하게 연계하기 위해서는 교사들과 협조하지 않으면 안 된다. 교사는 사서교사와 협조하여 도서관 프로그램의 안내자 및 조력자로서 도서관 프로그램에 참여하여 학생들을 지도해야 한다.

이용자교육에서 고려할 2가지 주요 요소는 다음과 같다.

- 도서관에 관한 지식 ; 목적, 이용 가능 서비스의 종류, 모든 종류의 자료 조직 방법
- 정보 탐색 기술 및 공식 비공식 학습 프로젝트 수행에 있어서 도서관을 이용하게 하는 이용동기의 유발

5.4 학습 및 정보 리터러시 프로그램 모델

철학

정보는 학생들이 독립적 학습자여야 한다는 것을 일깨워 준다. 학생들은 정보의 필요성을 인식하고, 능동적으로 아이디어의 세계로 진입한다. 학생들은 스스로 문제 해결능력에 자신감을 가지고 관련 정보가 무엇인지를 알아낸다. 그들은 정보에 접근하고 소통하기 위한 기술적 도구를 운용할 수 있어야 한다. 그들은 여러 가지 복합적 해답이 존재하는 상황과 해답이 아예 없는 상황을 잘 판단할 수 있어야 한다. 학생들은 그들의 공부에 있어 높은 수준을 유지하면서 질 높은 학습결과를 창출해야 한다. 정보는 학생들에게 유연하고, 변화 적응적이며, 개별 또는 집단적으로 제 기능을 다할 수 있게 해주는 것이다.

정보 리터러시 가이드라인은 모든 학생들에게 학습 환경으로부터 실생활에 이르기까지 전 부분에 걸쳐 상호 유기적인 배움의 과정을 안내해 준다. 정보 리터러시 가이드라인의 세부 사항은 다음과 같다.

- 학생은 정보로부터 의미를 구축할 수 있어야 한다.
- 학생은 양질의 학습 결과물을 만들어내야 한다.
- 학생은 독립적으로 학습해야 한다.
- 학생은 학습조의 일원으로서 조별활동에 효과적으로 참여해야 한다.
- 학생은 책임감과 윤리의식을 가지고 정보 및 정보기술을 이용해야 한다.

이러한 '철학'을 활성화할 수 있는 학습기술에는 다음과 같은 것들이 있다.

- 자기 주도적 학습 능력
- 협력 능력
- 기획 능력
- 정보 소재파악 및 수집 능력
- 선택 및 평가 능력
- 조직 및 기록 능력

- 의사소통 및 실천 능력
- 평가 능력

자기 주도적 학습능력

자기 주도적 학습능력은 평생 학습자로서의 능력 발전에 매우 중요하다. 자발적 학습자는 정보의 목적을 분명하게 설정할 수 있어야 하고, 목적 달성을 위한 진행과정을 관리할 수 있어야 한다.

학습자는 개인적인 정보 욕구, 의문에 대한 해답, 대안적 방안 모색, 여러 다른 시각에서의 평가 등을 위해 미디어 자원을 활용할 수 있어야 한다. 학습자는 도서관에 도움을 요청할 수 있어야 하고, 도서관의 조직과 구조를 알고 있어야 한다. 사서는 학생들의 학습활동에서 가르치는 역할보다는 학습 동료로서 도와주는 역할을 해야 한다.

협력 능력

학교도서관은 각기 다른 특성을 지닌 개인들과 다양한 정보자원 및 정보기술이 얽혀있는 그물망이다. 학생들이 그룹별 활동을 할 경우, 서로 의견을 교환하고 이를 건설적으로 평가할 수 있는 기법을 배운다. 그들은 다양한 의견을 인정하고, 다른 사람의 학습 배경 및 스타일을 존중하는 태도를 보여야 한다. 나아가 참여 학생들의 다양한 의견이 반영되고, 개인별 분담 작업들이 종합되어 결과도출에 기여할 수 있는 창의적인 프로젝트를 수행해야 한다. 사서는 학습그룹의 상담자로서 문제해결 활동에 필요한 도서관 자원의 이용을 지원해 주어야 한다.

기획 능력

기획은 연구, 과제수행, 프로젝트, 글쓰기, 주제선정의 전제가 되는 핵심능력이다. 학습과정의 초기 단계에서 브레인스토밍, 적정질문 형성 및 키워드 도출과 같은 활동들은 규칙에 준하면서도 동시에 창조적이라야 한다.

기획을 담당하는 학생은 목표를 개발하고, 해결책을 도출하며, 목적달성을 위한 연구방법을 설계할 수 있는 능력이 있어야 한다. 사서는 학생들이 희망하는 정도까지 기획과정에 개입하여야 한다. 사서는 학생들에게 이용 가능한 자원을 알려주고, 작업과정의 초기단계 부터 해당 과제를 실행할 수 있도록 도와주어야 한다.

정보 소재파악 및 수집능력

정보의 소재 파악 및 수집 능력은 학생들이 독립적 학습자로서 도서관의 정보를 검색, 활용하는 데 기본적으로 요구되는 능력이다. 이러한 능력은 도서관자료의 알파벳 및 숫자 정열방식을 이해하고, 여러 가지 상이한 데이터베이스 및 인터넷 정보검색 도구를 활용할 줄 아는 기술 능력이다. 이러한 정보 소재 파악능력은 지속적으로 강화되어야한다. 이러한 능력은 전 과정에 관련되는 것이며, 각 해당 주제의 맥락에서 개발될 필요가 있다. 이를 위해서는 색인의 이용, 광범한 참고자료 및 정보기술 이용에 대한 훈련이 필요하다. 이러한 기술을 갖춘 학생은 조사, 인터뷰, 실험, 관찰, 정보원의 연구와 같은 여러 방법들을 통합적으로 활용하여 공부할 수 있다. 사서는 개인 및 그룹 이용자들이 자기들의 특수한 요구에 맞는 정보 소재를 파악하고 수집할 수 있도록 이용자 훈련과정을 설계 운영해야 한다. 그러한 과정은 교사들과 협력하여 수행해야 한다. 이러한 정보 활용 능력개발 교육은 도서관 이용교육에 가장 핵심적인 사항이라 하겠다.

선택 및 평가 능력

학생들은 자료의 중요성을 판단 평가하는 기술을 개발할 필요가 있다. 이러한 판단 평가기술은 위에 언급한 여러 기술과 더불어 도서관 이용 시 최적 결과를 얻을 수 있는 가장 핵심적 기술이다.

이를 위한 훈련프로그램에는 다음과 같은 연습과정이 포함되어야 한다.

- 적절한 질문의 구성
- 유사한 자료의 식별
- 다양한 전략 활용
- 합리적 시간 계획
- 윤리에 맞는 결정

사서는 학생들에게 최신의 개정 정보를 탐색하는 방법, 편견이나 부정확성을 알아내는 방법을 중점적으로 안내해야 한다. 가설과 결론이 광범한 지식에 근거하여 도출되었는지 확인하기 위해서는 광범위한 자원에 걸쳐 상담, 비교, 평가를 해보아야 한다. 유능한 학생은 정보원의 권위, 완전성, 형식 및 관련성, 관점, 신뢰성, 적시성에 관한 평가 기준을 인지하고 있다.

조직 및 기록 능력

도서관의 기능은 전통적으로 정보의 선택과 수집에 한정되는 것으로 여겨왔다. 선택 및 수집의 후속 과정인 정보조직과 활용은 선행과정과 동일하게 인식되지 못하였다. 그러나 학교도서관에서는 이 부분이 시작 단계인 정보의 선택과 수집 못지않게 매우 중요하다. 사서는 학생들이 프로젝트와 과제를 수행할 때 정보의 조직과 활용능력을 개발할 수 있도록 도와주어야 한다. 따라서 사서는 과제발표를 조직하는 전문가가 되어야 하며, 학생들에게 제목의 설정, 장절의 배치, 참고자료 등을 조직하고 기술(記述)하는 방법을 가르쳐주어야 한다. 또한 학교도서관 사서는 학생들이 요약, 인용, 서지사항 작성 능력을 기를 수 있도록 지원해야 한다. 학생들이 정보를 잘 기록, 보존, 활용할 수 있도록 해주어야 한다.

의사소통 및 실천 능력

정보를 해석하고 활용하는 두 가지 기술은 프로젝트와 과제를 수행할 때 직면하는 가장 어려운 학습기술이다. 학생들이 스스로 제시하는 정보에 대하여 제대로 이해하고 있는지 아닌지 여부는 그들의 정보해석 및 활용능력을 통해 드러나는 것이다. 수집된 정보를 학습자의 지식으로 소화하는 일은 매우 도전적인 활동인 것이다.

학생들은 다음과 같은 맥락 선상에서 정보를 활용할 수 있어야 한다.

- 다양한 정보원으로부터 정보 통합
- 추론하기
- 결론의 도출
- 의미의 구성
- 기존 지식과의 연결

또한 학생들은 다음과 같은 사항을 수행할 수 있어야 한다.

- 명확한 의사소통
- 설정된 연구목적과 방법기준의 반영
- 효과적인 표현 및 발표

여기서 사서의 역할은 학생들의 이러한 활동을 지원하고 훈련시키며, 도서관에서 학생들의 요구에 적합한 학습 환경을 조성해주는 것이다.

평가능력

학습 프로젝트의 최종 단계는 학습과정과 결과에 대한 평가이다. 학생들이 자신의 노력과 성취를 비판적으로 생각할 수 있게 하는 것은 매우 중요하다. 따라서 학생들은 다음 사항을 실행할 수 있어야 한다.

- 원래의 계획과 완성된 결과를 관련지어 프로젝트의 목적 달성여부를 판단하기
- 학습 프로젝트의 강점과 약점 구분하기
- 개선점 및 향후 과제에 대한 시사점 제시하기

사서는 교사들과 함께 평가과정에 참여해야하는데 그 이유는 다음 두 가지다. 하나는 도서관이 이용자의 요구를 충족했는지를 알아내기 위해서이다. 또 하나는 학습의 과정과 결과에 비추어 사서교사가 능동적인 학습 파트너로 기여했는지를 판단하기 위해서이다.

여러 나라에서, 지역 교육당국과 학교도서관은 이용자 교육을 위해 성공적인 계획들을 수립 제시해왔다. 이 가운데 몇몇은 인터넷으로도 이용가능하다.

2002

THE IFLA/UNESCO

SCHOOL LIBRARY GUIDELINES

Table of Contents

INTRODUCTION

The *IFLA/UNESCO School Library Manifesto: the school library in teaching and learning for all* was published in 2000. It has been extremely well received all over the world and translated into many languages. New translations continue to be made and librarians all over the world are using the manifesto to raise the profile of school libraries in their own schools, own regions and own countries.

The manifesto states:

> *Governments, through their ministries responsible for education, are urged to develop strategies, policies and plans that implement the principles of this Manifesto.*

These new guidelines have been produced to inform decision makers at national and local levels around the world, and to give support and guidance to the library community. They have been written to help schools to implement the principles expressed in the manifesto.

The drafting of the guidelines involved many people from many countries, with very different local situations, to try and satisfy the needs of all types of school. The guidelines will need to be read and used within a local context.

Workshops have been organised during IFLA conferences; meetings have taken place, and discussions held between library experts in person and using email. The resulting guidelines are the product of much debate and consultation, for which the editors are very indebted and grateful. They also acknowledge the contributions of members of the standing committee of the section of school libraries and resource centres, and the guidelines from many countries that have informed the IFLA/UNESCO guidelines, especially *The Public Library Guidelines* published by IFLA in 2001.

The section has also published *The School Library Today and Tomorrow*, during 2002. We hope that the manifesto, visions and guidelines together will form a foundation for excellent school libraries everywhere.

Tove Pemmer Sætre
with Glenys Willars
2002

CHAPTER 1. MISSION AND POLICY

"The school library in teaching and learning for all"

1.1. Mission

The school library provides information and ideas that are fundamental to functioning successfully in our increasingly information- and knowledge-based present day society. The school library equips students with lifelong learning skills and develops their imagination, thereby enabling them to live as responsible citizens.

1.2. Policy

The school library should be managed within a clearly structured policy framework. The library policy should be devised bearing in mind the overarching policies and needs of the school and should reflect its ethos, aims and objectives as well as its reality.

The policy will specify when, where, for whom and by whom the full potential of the library will be realised. The library policy will become feasible if the whole school community supports and contributes to the aims and objectives set out in the policy. Therefore it should be written with as much involvement as viable, with as much consultation as practicable, and it should be as widely shared as possible in its printed form. In this way, the philosophy, the ideas, the concept and the intentions for practice and development will become clear and will be commonly understood and endorsed, and will thus be ready to be put into practice effectually and enthusiastically.

The policy must be comprehensive and workable. It should not be drafted by the school librarian alone, but jointly with the teaching staff and senior managers. The draft should be consulted widely throughout the school and supported by exhaustive open discussion. The document and subsequent plans will specify the role of the library in relation to the following aspects:

- the school curriculum
- learning methods in the school
- satisfying national and local standards and criteria
- students' learning and personal development needs
- staff's teaching needs
- raising levels of achievement.

The components which contribute to effective successful well-managed school libraries are the following:

- finance and budgeting
- accommodation
- resources

- organisation
- staffing
- library use
- promotion

All these components are essential in a realistic policy framework and action plan. They will be considered throughout this document. The action plan should be made up of strategies, tasks, targets, monitoring and evaluation routines. The policy and plan should be an active document subject to regular review.

1.3. Monitoring and Evaluation

In the process of attaining the goals of the school library, the management must continually monitor the performance in the services to ensure that the strategies are achieving the specified objectives. Statistical studies should be carried out periodically in order to identify trends. An annual evaluation should cover all the main areas of the plan document to ascertain the following points:

- whether they are achieving the objectives and declared goals of the library, the curriculum and the school
- whether they are meeting the needs of the school community
- whether they are able to meet changing needs
- whether they are adequately resourced
- and whether they are cost effective.

The following key performance indicators may prove useful tools for monitoring and evaluating the achievement of the library goals:

Usage indicators:

- loans per member of school community (specified per student and per staff member)
- total library visits per member of the school community (specified per student and per staff member)
- loans per item (i.e. turnover resources)
- loans per opening hour (during school hours and after school)
- reference enquiries per member of school community (specified per students and per staff member)
- use of computers and on-line information sources.

Resource indicators:

- total book stock per member of school community
- provision of terminals/personal computers per member of school community
- provision of on-line access computers per member of school community

Human resource indicators:

- ratio of full-time equivalent staff to members of school community
- ratio of full-time equivalent staff to library use

Qualitative indicators:

- user satisfaction surveys
- focus groups
- consultation activities

Cost indicators:

- unit costs for functions, services and activities
- staff costs per functions (e.g. book loans)
- total library costs per member of the school society
- total library costs expressed in percentage of total school budget
- media costs expressed in percentage of total library costs

Comparative indicators:

- Benchmark statistical data against other relevant and comparable library services at other schools of similar size and characteristics.

CHAPTER 2. RESOURCES

"The school library must have adequate and sustained funding for trained staff, materials, technologies and facilities, and its access shall be free of charge"

2.1. Funding and Budgeting for the School Library

In order to ensure that the library receives its fair share of the school's financial resources, the following points are important:

- understand the school budgeting process
- be aware of the timetable for the budget cycle
- know who the key staff are
- make sure that the needs of the library are identified.

The components of the budget plan will need to include the following:

- an amount for new resources (e.g. books, periodicals and non-printed material); an amount for promotional materials (e.g. posters)
- an amount for stationery and administrative materials
- an amount for promotional events
- the costs of using ICT equipment, software and licensing costs, if these are not included in a general ICT budget for the school..

As a general rule, the school library material budget should be at least 5% of the per student expenditure for the school system, exclusive of all salaries, special education expenses, transportation and capital improvement funds.

Staff costs may be included in the library budget but, at some schools, it may be more appropriate to have them included in the general staff budget. It is however important to emphasise that estimating staff costs for the library is a task which the school librarian should be involved in. The amount of money available for staffing is closely related to important issues such as how many opening hours the school library can manage and what standard and range of services it can offer. Special projects and other developments such as new shelving may require a separate bid for funds.

Spending of the budget should be carefully planned for the whole year and be related to the policy framework. Annual reports should throw light on how the library budget has been used and clarify whether the amount of money spent on the library has been enough to cover its tasks and attain the policy targets.

The school librarian must be clear about the importance of an adequate budget for the library, and may need to convey this to the senior management as the library serves the whole school community. It may be worth justifying an increase in financial support along the following lines:

- the size of school library's staff and collection is the best school predictor of academic achievement
- students who score higher on standardised tests tend to come from schools with more school library staff and more books, periodicals, and video material regardless of other factors such as economic ones.

2.2. Location and Space

The strong educational role of the school library must be reflected in the facilities, furniture and equipment. It is of vital importance that the function and use of the school library is incorporated when planning new school buildings and reorganising existing ones.

There is no one universal measurement for school library facilities but it is useful and helpful to have some kind of formula on which to base planning estimates so that any new or newly designed library meets the needs of the school in the most effective way. The following considerations need to be included in the planning process:

- central location, on the ground floor if possible
- accessibility and proximity, being close to all teaching areas
- noise factors, with at least some parts of the library free from external noise
- appropriate and sufficient light, both through windows and artificial light.
- appropriate room temperature (e.g. air-conditioning, heating) to ensure good working conditions all year round as well as the preservation of the collections
- appropriate design to meet the special needs of disabled library users
- adequate size to give space for the collection of books, fiction, non-fiction, hardback and paperback, newspapers and magazines, non-print resources and storage, study spaces, reading areas, computer workstations, display areas, staff work areas and a library desk
- flexibility to allow multiplicity of activities and future changes in curriculum and technology

The following list of different areas may also be worth considering when planning a new library:

- study and research area space for information desk, catalogues, on-line stations, study and research tables, reference materials and basic collections
- informal reading area space for books and periodicals that encourage literacy, lifelong learning, and reading for pleasure
- instructional area space with seats catering for small group, large groups and whole classroom formal instruction, 'teaching wall' with appropriate instructional technology and display space
- production and group project area space for functional work and meetings of individuals, teams and classes, as well as facilities for media production
- administrative area space for circulation desk, office area, space for processing of library media materials, audiovisual equipment storage, and storage space for supplies and materials

2.3. Furniture and Equipment

The design of the school library plays a central role in how well the library serves the school. The aesthetic appearance contributes to the feeling of welcome as well as the desire for the school community to spend time in the library.

An appropriately equipped school library should have the following characteristics:

- safety
- good lighting
- designed to accommodate furniture that is sturdy, durable and functional as well as meeting the specific space, activity and user requirements of the library
- designed to accommodate the special requirements of the school population in the least restrictive manner
- designed to accommodate changes in library programmes, the school's instructional programme as well as emerging audio, video and data technology
- designed to enable proper use, care and security of furnishing, equipment, supplies and materials
- arranged and managed to provide equitable and timely access to an organised and diverse collection of resources
- arranged and managed so that it is aesthetically appealing to the user and conducive to leisure and learning, with clear attractive guiding and signposting

2.4. Electronic and AV Equipment

The school library serves an important function as a gateway to our information-based present day society. For this reason, it must provide access to all necessary electronic, computer and audiovisual equipment. This equipment will include the following:

- computer work stations with Internet access
- public access catalogues adjusted to the different ages and levels of students
- tape recorders
- CD-ROM players
- scanning equipment
- video players
- computer equipment, specially adjusted to the visually or otherwise physically handicapped

Computer furniture should be designed for children and easy to adjust in order to fit their different sizes.

2.5. Material Resources

A high standard of library accommodation and a wide range of high quality resources are essential. For this reason, a collection management policy is vital. This policy defines the purpose, scope and contents of the collection as well as access to external resources.

2.6. Collection Management Policy

The school library should provide access to a wide range of resources that meet the needs of the users regarding education, information and personal development. It is imperative that collections continue to be developed on an ongoing basis to ensure that the users have constant choice of new materials.

The school library staff must cooperate with administrators and teachers in order to develop a common collection management policy. Such a policy statement must be based upon curriculum, particular needs and interests of the school community, and reflect the diversity of society outside the school. The following elements should be included in the policy statement:

- IFLA/UNESCO School Library Manifesto - the mission
- statements of intellectual freedom
- freedom of information
- purpose of the collection management policy and its relation to school and curriculum
- long and short term objectives

2.7. Materials Collection

A reasonable collection of book resources should comprise ten books per student. The smallest school should have at least 2500 relevant and updated items to ensure a wide balanced book stock for all ages, abilities and backgrounds. At least 60% of the stock should consist of curriculum-related non-fiction resources.

In addition, a school library should acquire materials for leisure purposes such as popular novels, music, computer games, videocassettes, video laser disks, magazines and posters. These kinds of materials may be selected in cooperation with the students to ensure it reflects their interests and culture, without crossing reasonable limits of ethical standards.

2.8. Electronic Resources

The range of services must include access to electronic information resources which reflect the curriculum as well as the users' interests and culture. The electronic resources should include access to Internet, special reference and full-text databases, as well as instruction-related computer software packages. These may be available in CD-ROM and DVD.

It is vital to choose a library catalogue system which is applicable for classifying and cataloguing the resources according to accepted international or national bibliographic standards. This facilitates their inclusion in wider networks. In many places around the world, school libraries within a local community benefit from being linked together in a union catalogue. Such a collaboration may increase the efficiency and quality of book processing and make it easy to combine resources for maximum effect.

CHAPTER 3. STAFFING

"The school librarian is the professionally qualified staff member responsible for planning and managing the school library, supported by staffing who is as adequate as possible, working together with all members of the school community, and liasing with the public library and others."

3.1. The Library Staff

The richness and quality of the library provision depend upon staffing resources available within and beyond the school library. For this reason, it is of paramount importance to have a well-trained and highly motivated staff, made up of a sufficient number of members according to the size of the school and its special needs for library services. The term 'staff' means, in this context, qualified librarians and library assistants. In addition, there may be supporting staff, such as teachers, technicians, parents and other kinds of volunteers. School librarians should be professionally trained and qualified, with additional training in educational theory and learning methodology.

One of the main objectives for staff management in school libraries should be that all staff members have a clear understanding of library service policy, well defined duties and responsibilities, and properly regulated conditions of employment and competitive salaries which reflect the professionalism of the job.

Volunteers should not work as substitutes for paid staff, but may work as support based upon a contract that gives a formal framework for their involvement in the school library activities. Consultants at local or national level can be used as external advisers in matters concerning the development of the school library service.

3.2.The Role of the School Librarian

The librarian's main role is to contribute to the mission and goals of the school including the evaluation procedures and to develop and implement those of the school library. In cooperation with the senior school management, administrators and teachers, the librarian is involved in the development of plans and the implementation of the curriculum. The librarian has the knowledge and skills regarding the provision of information and solution of information problems as well as the expertise in the use of all sources, both printed and electronic. Their knowledge, skills and expertise meet the demands of a specific school society. In addition, the librarian should lead reading campaigns and the promotion of child literature, media and culture.

The support of the school management is essential if the library is to carry out interdisciplinary activities. The librarian must report directly to the headteacher or deputy head. It is extremely important for the librarian to be accepted as an equal member of the professional staff and be entitled to participate in the teamwork and all meetings as the head of the library department.

The librarian should create an environment for leisure and learning which is attractive, welcoming and accessible for everyone without fear or prejudice. Everyone who works in the school library should have a good rapport with children, young people and adults.

3.3. The Role of the Library Assistant

The library assistant reports to the librarian and supports them in their functions. This position requires clerical and technological knowledge and skills. The assistant should have prior basic library training. Otherwise, the library should provide it. Some of the duties of the job include routine functions, shelving, lending, returning and processing library material.

3.4. Cooperation between Teachers and School Librarian

Cooperation between teachers and the school librarian is essential in maximising the potential of the library services.

Teachers and librarians work together in order to achieve the following:

- develop, instruct and evaluate pupils' learning across the curriculum
- develop and evaluate pupils' information skills and information knowledge
- develop lesson plans
- prepare and carry out special project work to be done in an extended learning environment, including the library
- prepare and carry out reading programmes and cultural events
- integrate information technology in the curriculum
- make clear to parents the importance of the school library

3.5. Skills of the School Library Staff

The school library is a service addressed to all members of the school community: learners, teachers, administrators, counsellors as well as parents. All these groups require special communication and cooperation skills. The main users are the learners and the teachers, but also other categories of professionals such as administrators and counsellors should be included.

The fundamental qualities and skills expected from the school library staff can be defined as follows:

- the ability to communicate positively and open-mindedly with children and adults
- the ability to understand the needs of users
- the ability to cooperate with individuals and groups inside and outside the school community
- knowledge and understanding of cultural diversity
- knowledge of learning methodology and educational theory

- knowledge of information skills and of how to use information
- knowledge of the materials which compose the library collection and how to access it
- knowledge of child literature, media and culture
- knowledge and skills in the fields of management and marketing
- knowledge and skills in the field of information technology

3.6. Duties of the School Librarian

The school librarian is expected to do the following:

- analyse the resource and information needs of the school community
- formulate and implement policies for service development
- develop acquisition policies and systems for library resources
- catalogue and classify library materials
- instruct in library use
- instruct in information knowledge and information skills
- assist students and teachers in the use of library resources and information technology
- answer reference and information enquiries using appropriate materials
- promote reading programmes and cultural events
- participate in planning activities connected to the implementation of the curriculum
- participate in the preparation, implementation and evaluation of learning activities
- promote the evaluation of library services as an ordinary part of the general school evaluation system
- build partnership with external organisations
- prepare and implement budgets
- design strategic planning
- manage and train library staff

3.7. Ethical Standards

The school library staff have the responsibility to observe high ethical standards in their dealing with all members of the school community. All users should be dealt with on an equal basis regardless of their abilities and background. Services should be adjusted to match the needs of the individual user. In order to strengthen the role of the school library as an open and safe learning environment, the staff should emphasise their function as advisors rather than as instructors in the traditional sense. This implies, first and foremost, that they must try to adopt the user's perspective rather than let themselves be biased by their own attitudes and prejudices in providing library service.

CHAPTER 4. PROGRAMMES AND ACTIVITIES

"The school library is integral to the educational process"

4.1. Programmes

In national curriculum and education development programmes at national level, school libraries should be considered as vital means for fulfilling ambitious goals regarding the following:

- information literacy for all, gradually developed and adopted through the school system
- availability of information resources for students at all educational levels
- open dissemination of information and knowledge for all student groups to exercise democratic and human rights

At national as well as local levels, it is advisable to have programmes designed specifically for the purposes of school library development. These kinds of programmes may involve different aims and actions related to the context they are in. Here are some examples of actions:

- develop and publish national (and local) standards and guidelines for school libraries
- provide model libraries to demonstrate 'best practice'
- establish school library committees at national and local level
- design a formal framework for cooperation between school libraries and public libraries at national and local level
- initiate and offer professional school librarian training programmes
- provide funding for school library projects such as reading campaigns
- initiate and fund research projects related to school library activities and development

4.2. Cooperation and Resource Sharing with Public Libraries

In order to improve library services for children and young persons in a given community, it may be a good idea for school libraries and public libraries to cooperate. A written cooperation agreement should include the following points:

- common measures for the cooperation
- specification and definition of cooperation areas
- clarification of economic implications and how to share costs
- scheduled time for cooperation period

Examples of cooperation areas are the following:

- sharing staff training
- cooperative collection development
- cooperative programming

- coordination of electronic services and networks
- cooperation in the development of learning tools and user education
- class visits to the public library
- joint reading and literacy promotion
- joint marketing of library services to children and young persons

4.3. Activities at School Level

The school library should cover a wide range of activities and should be a main role player in achieving the mission and vision of the school. It should aim to serve all potential users within the school community and meet the particular needs of different target groups.

The programmes and the activities must thus be designed in close cooperation with the following:

- principal/headteacher
- heads of departments
- teachers
- support staff
- students.

The users' satisfaction depends on the ability of the school library to identify the needs of individuals and groups, and on its capability to develop services which reflect changing needs in the school community.

<u>The Principal and the School Library</u>

As the instructional leader of the school and the key person in providing a framework and climate for implementing the curriculum, the principal should acknowledge the importance of an effective school library service and encourage the use of it.

The principal should work closely with the library in the design of school development plans, especially within the fields of information literacy and reading promotion programmes. When the plans are to be put into effect, the principal should ensure flexible scheduling of time and resources to allow teachers' and students' access to the library and its services.

The principal should also ensure cooperation between teaching staff and library staff. He or she must ensure that the school librarians are involved in instruction, curriculum planning, continuing staff development, programme evaluation and assessment of student learning.

In the evaluation of the whole school, the principal should integrate library evaluation (see Chapter 1) and highlight the vital contribution a strong school library service makes in the achievement of the established educational standards.

Heads of Department and the School Library

As the main person in charge of professional activities each departmental head should cooperate with the library in order to ensure that its range of information resources and services cover the special needs of the subject areas of the department. Like the principal, the head of department should involve the library in development planning and direct attention to the library as a vital part of the learning environment and as a learning resource centre.

Teachers and the Library

Cooperation between teacher and librarian has already been addressed in Section 3.4. Some complementary aspects are worth highlighting at this point.

The teachers' educational philosophy constitutes the ideological basis for their choice of teaching methods. Some of the methods that are based on a traditional view upon the teacher and the textbook as the most important learning resources do not favour the role of the school library in learning processes. If this view is combined with a strong wish to keep the door of the classroom closed and to have strict control over the students' learning activities, the library may be even more shut out of the mind of the teacher as an important support for information. Even if most teachers favour such a 'banking education ideology' and therefore look upon the students as passive stores to be filled up by transferring their selected knowledge to them, it is still important for the library to find its role as a supporting service linked to the curriculum. A useful strategy to establish a partnership in learning within the frames of the ideology just described could be to promote the services of the library especially for the teachers. This promotion should highlight the following:

- ability to provide resources for teachers which will widen their subject knowledge or improve their teaching methodologies
- ability to provide resources for different evaluation and assessment strategies
- ability to be a working partner in planning the tasks to be done in the classroom
- ability to help teachers to cope with heterogeneous classroom situations by organising specialised services to those who need more support and those who need more stimulation
- the library as a gateway to the global village through its interlibrary loans and electronic network

Teachers who have a more progressive and open educational ideology are likely to be keener library users. In addition to all the functions and possibilities mentioned above, they may include the library as a teaching place, and in so doing, move away from traditional teaching methods. In order to activate students in the learning process and develop their independent learning skills, teachers may cooperate with the library in fields such as the following:

- information literacy by developing the students' 'spirit of inquiry' and educating them to be critical and creative users of information
- project work and assignments
- do reading motivation with students at all levels, for individuals or for groups

Students and the Library

The students are the main target group of the school library. Cooperation with other members of the school community is important only because it is in the interest of the students.

Students can use the library for many different purposes. It should be experienced as an open free non-threatening learning environment where they can work on all sorts of assignments, as both individuals and groups.

The students activities in the library are likely to include the following:

- traditional homework
- project work and problem solving tasks
- information seeking and information use
- production of portfolios and material to be presented to teacher and classmates

Use of Internet

The new electronic resources are a special challenge for all library users. Using them can be very confusing. The librarian can provide the support to show that these resources are just tools in the learning and teaching process; they are means to an end and not an end in itself.

Library users become very frustrated when they look for information and think that, if they can access the Internet, then their information problems are resolved. The opposite is usually the case. The librarian can help users with Internet and can also help minimise the frustrations resulting from information searches. What is important here is to select relevant and quality information from the Internet in the shortest time possible. The students themselves should gradually develop the ability to locate, synthesise, and integrate information and new knowledge from all subject areas in the resource collection. Initiating and carrying into effect information literacy programmes are therefore amongst the most important tasks of the library (see Section 'Teachers and the Library' above for further consideration).

The Cultural Function of the School Library

The library can be used informally as an aesthetic, cultural and stimulating environment containing a variety of journals, novels, publications and audiovisual resources.

Special events can be organised in the library such as exhibitions, author visits and international literacy days. If there is enough space, students can do literature inspired performances for parents and other students, and the librarian can organise book talks and story telling for the younger students. The librarian should also stimulate interest in reading and organise reading promotion programmes in order to develop the appreciation of literature. Activities addressed to encourage reading involve cultural as well as learning aspects. There is a direct link between reading level and learning results. Librarians should always be pragmatic and flexible in their approach when providing reading material to users and supporting the individual preferences of the readers by acknowledging their individual rights. By reading fiction and non-fiction literature which fits their needs and levels, students may be stimulated in their socialisation process and identity development.

Cooperation with Parents

The tradition of involving parents and carers in school activities varies across countries. The library can provide an opportunity for the parents' involvement in the school. As volunteers, they can help with practical tasks and support the library staff. They may also participate in reading promotion programmes by being motivators at home in the reading activities of their children. They can also take part in literature discussion groups together with their children and thus contribute, in a way of master learning, to the outcome of reading activities.

Another way to involve the parents is to form a 'friends of the library' group. This kind of group may provide extra funding for library activities and can assist the library in organising special cultural events which require more resources than the library has at its disposal.

CHAPTER 5. PROMOTION OF THE LIBRARY AND LEARNING

5.1. Promotion

The services and facilities provided by the school library must be actively promoted so that the target groups are always aware of its essential role as a partner in learning and as a gateway to all kinds of information resources. The target groups have already been mentioned on several occasions in previous chapters. They are the principal and the other members of the school management group, heads of departments, teachers, students, governors and parents. It is important to adjust the type of promotion to the nature of the school and to the different target groups.

5.2. Marketing Policy

The school library should have a written marketing and promotion policy specifying objectives and strategies. It should be worked out in cooperation with the school management and teaching staff.

The policy document should include the following elements:

- objectives and strategies
- action plan which ensures that the objectives are attained
- evaluation methods

The actions that are needed will differ depending on aims and local circumstances. Some essential issues are provided on the following list as a way of illustration:

- starting and running school library websites which promote services and have linkages to and from related websites and portals
- organising displays and exhibitions
- writing publications containing information about opening hours, services and collections
- preparing and distributing resource lists and pamphlets linked to the curriculum, also for cross-curriculum topics
- giving information about the library at meetings for new students and their parents
- organising 'friends of the library' groups for parents and others
- organising book fairs and reading and literacy campaigns
- providing effective interior and exterior signposting
- initiating liaison with other organisations in the area (e.g. public libraries, museum services and local history associations).

The action plan should be evaluated, reviewed and revised annually and the whole policy document should be discussed throughout at least once every second year.

5.3. User Education

Library-based courses and programmes aimed at teaching students and teachers how to use the library are perhaps the most effective marketing tool. For this reason, it is extremely important that these courses are well designed and have width and balance.

Because these programmes play a key role in the library, it would also be appropriate to consider them in Chapter 4. The marketing aspect of all kinds of user education is, however, so essential that it may be even more suitable to deal with this topic in this chapter.

Courses specially designed for teachers should give them clear guidance on the role of the library in learning and teaching and on the support available from the library staff. These courses should especially emphasise the practical training in information seeking connected to the subject areas taught by the teachers. Through their own experiences in finding relevant resources, the teachers are likely to develop a deeper understanding of how the library can complement classroom work and be integrated within curriculum topics.

Like other learning programmes at school, the various components of the student courses should be delivered in logical sequences to promote progression and continuity in the student's learning. This means that skills and resources must be introduced progressively through stages and levels. The school librarian should have the main responsibility for user education programmes, but should cooperate with the teachers in order to link their different components as closely to the curriculum as possible. The teacher should always be present while students are having their library training programmes and act as an adviser in cooperation with the librarian.

In user education, there are three main teaching areas to be considered:

- knowledge about the library; what is its purpose, what kinds of services are available, how it is organised and what kinds of resources it has
- skills in information seeking and information using motivations for using the library in formal and informal learning projects.

5.4. Model for a Study Skills and Information Literacy Programme

Philosophy

Information literate students should be competent independent learners. They should be aware of their information needs and actively engage in the world of ideas. They should display confidence in their ability to solve problems and know what is relevant information. They should be able to manage technology tools to access information and to communicate. They should be able to operate comfortably in situations where there are multiple answers, as well as those with no answers. They should hold high standards in their work and create quality products. Information literate students should be flexible, able to adapt to change and able to function both individually and in groups.

Information literacy guidelines provide all students with a learning process that is transferable across content areas as well as from the academic environment to real life. These guidelines specify the following:

- the student should construct meaning from information
- the student should create a quality product
- the student should learn independently
- the student should participate effectively as a member of a work group
- the student should use information and information technology responsibly and ethically.

Learning skills which may contribute to make this 'philosophy' alive are included in the following list:

- self-directed learning skills
- cooperating skills
- planning skills
- locating and gathering skills
- selecting and appraising skills
- organising and recording skills
- communicating and realising skills
- evaluating.

Self-Directed Learning Skills

Self-directed learning skills are critical in the development of lifelong learners. Independent learners should be able to establish clear information goals and manage progress towards achieving them.

They should be able to use media sources for information and personal needs, seek answers to questions, consider alternative perspectives and evaluate differing points of view. They should be able to ask for help and recognise the organisation and structure of the library. The librarian plays a role as a learning partner, advising, not instructing, the students on their learning activities.

Cooperating Skills

The school library is a place where individual differences mesh with the diversity of resources and technology. When students are working in a group, they learn how to defend opinions as well as how to criticise opinions constructively. They acknowledge diverse ideas and show respect for the others' background and learning styles. Furthermore they help to create projects that reflect differences among individuals and contribute to synthesise individual tasks into a finished product. The librarian can act as a group counsellor and support them as much as necessary when they use the library as a resource in problem solving activities.

Planning Skills

Planning skills are an essential prerequisite for any research task, assignment, project, essay or topic. At the initial stages of a learning process, activities like brainstorming, appropriate question framing and keyword identification require creativity as well as regular practice.

A student with planning skills should be able to develop goals, spell out the problems to be solved and design working methods to be used for that purpose. The librarian should be involved in the planning process to the extent the students wish. The librarian is expected to advise them on available resources and on the viability of any given assignment from the very beginning of the working process.

Locating and Gathering Skills

Locating and gathering are fundamental skills to be acquired by the students in order to be able to tackle information seeking at the library as independent learners. These skills include an understanding of alphabetical and numerical order, use of different kinds of tools for information seeking in computer databases and on the Internet. Reinforcement is required for these locating skills. They need to be related to the whole curriculum and developed progressively within a subject context. Exercises in these skills should involve the use of indexes, a wide variety of reference sources and the full range of information technology. A competent student who masters these skills is able to integrate them when working with different methods of generating information such as survey, interview, experiment, observation and study of sources. The librarian should design courses in locating and gathering skills which can be adjusted to meet the special needs of individuals and groups. The design should be carried out in cooperation with the teachers. In many ways, training in these skills represents the most essential part of user education at the library.

Selecting and Appraising Skills

Students need to develop critical and evaluative thinking skills. Together with the skills mentioned above, these skills are vital in order to obtain optimal results out of library use.

Programmes designed to promote these skills should include exercise in the following:

- framing appropriate questions
- identifying likely resources
- using a variety of strategies
- building a reasonable timeline
- making ethical decisions.

The librarian should especially focus on student guidance in how to find relevant updated authoritative information and in how to detect any bias or inaccuracy. A wide range of resources need to be consulted, compared and appraised to ensure that hypotheses and conclusions are formed upon the widest possible knowledge base. The competent student should be able to identify criteria regarding authoritativeness, completeness, format and relevance, point of view, reliability and timeliness.

Organising and Recording Skills

Traditional conceptions about the function of a library are often limited to gathering and selecting information. The subsequent organisation and use of this information has not been acknowledged in the same way. However, in a school library, this part of the process is just as important as the starting point. The librarian should also support the students in the development of these skills when they are working with projects and assignments. For this reason, the librarian should be an expert in the structural conventions of a project report and should give the students advice on how to write headings, chapters and references. In addition, skills such as summarising, quoting and writing complete accurate bibliographies should be developed in the library and supported by the librarian. Competent students should be able to take notes, store information and make it ready for use.

Communicating and Realising Skills

Interpreting information and making use of it when working on projects and assignments are two of the most difficult learning skills. Through these skills, the students show whether they have a true understanding of the information they are providing or not. Transforming the information gathered into one's personal knowledge is indeed a challenging activity.

The competent student should be able to process information along the following lines:

- integrate information from a variety of sources
- make inferences
- draw conclusions
- construct meaning
- build connections to prior knowledge.

Furthermore, the competent student should be able to do the following:

- communicate clearly
- reflect established aims and criteria
- demonstrate effective presentation skills.

The librarian's role here is to advise and train students on these activities and provide a learning environment in the library which matches the student's support needs.

Evaluating Skills

The final stage of a learning project consists of evaluating process and result. It is of vital importance that the students are able to do critical thinking about their effort and what they have achieved. Therefore the competent student should be able to accomplish the following:

- relate the finished product to the original plan and determine if the product has achieved its purpose
- determine the strengths and weaknesses of the learning project
- reflect on improvement and implications for future assignments

The librarian should be involved in the evaluation process together with the teachers for two reasons. One is to be informed about how the library managed to meet user needs. The second reason is to be able to function as an active learning partner who may contribute to throw light on the relationship between the learning process and the finished product.

Many countries, local authorities and school libraries have worked out very successful plans for user education. Some of them are available on the Internet.

REFERENCES

A selective reference list

American Association of School Librarians, *Information power: guidelines for school library media programs*. ACET, 1988.

Australian School Library Association at www.asla.org.au/policy.htm
Policy statements on:
- Information literacy
- Electronic information literacy
- Resource based learning and the curriculum
- Resource provision
- Teacher librarian qualifications
- School library resource centre funding
- School library bill of rights

Canadian School Library Association, A Position Statement on Effective School Library Programs in Canada. www.cla.ca/divisions/csla/pub_3.htm

Convention of Scottish Local Authorities, *Standards for school library services in Scotland.* COSLA, 1999. ISBN 1872794467

Hannesdóttir, Sigrún Klara (ed), *School librarians: Guidelines for Competency Requirements.* IFLA, 1995. ISBN 9070916576

Haycock, Ken & Blanche Woolls. *School librarianship: International perspectives & issues.* Hi Willow Research & Publishing/ IASL, 1997. ISBN 1 89086 122 7

IFLA/UNESCO The school library manifesto: the school library in teaching and learning for all. IFLA, 2000
www.ifla.org/VII/s11/pubs/manifest.htm
www.ifla.org/VII/s8?unesco/eng.htm

Library Association of Ireland, *Policy Statement on School Library Services*, 1996. www.libraryassociation.ie/policy/schools.htm

Library Services for Education, *Central to excellence: guidelines for effective school libraries*. Leicestershire County Council, 2002. ISBN 0850224403

LISC Guidelines –second edition forthcoming. www.liscni.co.uk

The Primary school library guidelines. Library Association, 2000. ISBN 0953740404

School libraries: guidelines for good practice. Library Association of Ireland, 1994. ISBN 0946037248

School Library Standards and Evaluation: list of American websites at www.sldirectory.com/libsf/resf/evaluate.html

Scottish Library Association *et al*, *Taking a closer look at the school library resource centre: self-evaluation using performance indicators*.1999. www.slainte.org.uk/Slicpubs/schoolpis.pdf

South Africa, Department of Education. *A National Policy Framework for School Library Standards*, July 1997. http://education.pwv.gov.za/teli2/policydocuments/library1.htm

Stripling, Barbara K. *Learning and libraries in an information age: Principles & practice*. Libraries Unlimited, 1999. ISBN 1 56308 666 2

Tilke, Anthony (ed), *Library Association guidelines for secondary school libraries*. Library Association, 1998. ISBN 1856042782

National Library Associations are good sources of further information.

〉〉〉 옮긴이 〉〉〉

이 종 권

성균관대학교 대학원 문헌정보학과 석·박사과정 졸업(문학박사)
건국대학교 강의 및 겸임교수, 한성대, 상명대 강사 역임
현 서울 문정인문학도서관 관장, 성균관대, 대림대 강사
e-메일 : 450345@hanmail.net

주요저서
IFLA 학교도서관 가이드라인 2002
(번역, 한국학교도서관 활용수업사례집, 한국학교도서관협의회, 2009)
문헌정보학이란 무엇인가(문현, 2014)
공공도서관 서비스 경영론(공저, 문현, 2015)
인문과학 정보원(공편, 문현, 2015)
신나는 스토리텔링(공역, 국립어린이청소년도서관, 2015)
청소년 서비스 101(공역, 국립어린이청소년도서관, 2015)
도서관 경영론(이종권·이종엽, 글로벌콘텐츠, 2016) 외 다수

정 영 주

한밭대학교 산업디자인과 졸업
성균관대학교 한국사서교육원 졸업
국가평생교육진흥원 문헌정보학전공(2급정사서)
국립공주대학교 교육대학원 문헌정보교육 석사과정 재학
서울 세륜중학교 도서관 사서
e-메일 : yjjung86@naver.com

주요저서
학교도서관 프로그램 사례집: 서울 세륜중학교를 중심으로(강의자료, 2016)